DECOLONIAL ECOLOGIES

Decolonial Ecologies

The Reinvention of Natural History in Latin American Art

Joanna Page

https://www.openbookpublishers.com

©2023 Joanna Page

This work is licensed under a Creative Commons Attribution-NonCommercial-NoDerivatives 4.0 International (CC BY-NC-ND 4.0). This license allows you to copy and distribute the material in any medium or format in unadapted form only, for noncommercial purposes only, and only so long as attribution is given to the creator (but not in any way that suggests that they endorse you or your use of the work). Attribution should include the following information:

Joanna Page, *Decolonial Ecologies: The Reinvention of Natural History in Latin American Art*. Cambridge, UK: Open Book Publishers, 2023, https://doi.org/10.11647/OBP.0339

Copyright and permissions for the reuse of many of the images included in this publication may differ from the above. Copyright and permissions information for images is provided separately in the List of Illustrations.

Further details about CC BY-NC-ND licenses are available at: https://creativecommons.org/licenses/by-nc-nd/4.0/

All external links were active at the time of publication unless otherwise stated and have been archived via the Internet Archive Wayback Machine at https://archive.org/web

Every effort has been made to identify and contact copyright holders and any omission or error will be corrected if notification is made to the publisher.

ISBN Paperback: 978-1-80064-973-6
ISBN Hardback: 978-1-80064-974-3
ISBN Digital (PDF): 978-1-80064-975-0
ISBN Digital ebook (EPUB): 978-1-80064-976-7
ISBN XML: 978-1-80064-978-1
ISBN HTML: 978-1-80064-979-8
DOI: 10.11647/OBP.0339

Cover image by Rodrigo Arteaga, 'D'Histoire naturelle' from *Botánica sistemática* (2015). Book intervened with plants and earth. Carmen Araujo Arte, Caracas, Venezuela. Photograph by the artist. Background image: Mona Eendra. Flowers beside Yellow Wall, February 15, 2017, https://unsplash.com/photos/vC8wj_Kphak

Cover design by Jeevanjot Kaur Nagpal

Para Clara Kriger, con afecto y amistad

Contents

List of Illustrations	ix
Acknowledgments	xvii
Introduction	1
1. Bestiaries and the Art of Cryptozoology	25
2. New Cabinets of Curiosities	63
3. Floras, Herbaria, and Botanical Illustration	93
4. Retracing Voyages of Science and Conquest	137
5. Albums, Atlases, and their Afterlives	163
6. Taxidermy and Natural History Dioramas	201
Conclusion	237
Bibliography	249
Index	267

List of Illustrations

Fig. 1.1 Édgar Cano, 'Cronotopo' from *Animalia*, written by Rafael Toriz and illustrated by Édgar Cano (Mexico City: Vanilla Planifolia, 2015), 15. — 30

Fig. 1.2 Édgar Cano, 'La jirafa' from *Animalia*, written by Rafael Toriz and illustrated by Édgar Cano (Mexico City: Vanilla Planifolia, 2015), 17. — 32

Fig. 1.3 Édgar Cano, 'Ahuizotl' from *Animalia*, written by Rafael Toriz and illustrated by Édgar Cano (Mexico City: Vanilla Planifolia, 2015), 76. — 34

Fig. 1.4 Édgar Cano, 'Merovingio' from *Animalia*, written by Rafael Toriz and illustrated by Édgar Cano (Mexico City: Vanilla Planifolia, 2015), 91. — 39

Fig. 1.5 Claudio Andrés Salvador Francisco Romo Torres, 'El perezoso' (detail) from *Bestiario: Animales reales fantásticos*, written by Juan Nicolás Padrón and illustrated by Claudio Andrés Salvador Francisco Romo Torres (Santiago: LOM Ediciones, 2008), 48. — 41

Fig. 1.6 Claudio Andrés Salvador Francisco Romo Torres, 'Sinsimito' from *Bestiario mexicano*, trans. Federico Taibi (Modena: Logosedizione, 2018), 9. — 43

Fig. 1.7 Claudio Andrés Salvador Francisco Romo Torres, 'Waay Pop' from *Bestiario mexicano*, trans. Federico Taibi (Modena: Logosedizione, 2018), 37. — 45

Fig. 1.8 Claudio Andrés Salvador Francisco Romo Torres, 'Waay Pop' from *Bestiario mexicano*, trans. Federico Taibi (Modena: Logosedizione, 2018), 38. — 45

Fig. 1.9 Walmor Corrêa, *Curupira* from *Unheimlich: Imaginário popular brasileiro* (2005). Acrylic and graphic on canvas, 195 x 130 cm. — 51

Fig. 1.10 Walmor Corrêa, *Pinguisch* from *Natureza perversa* (2003). Acrylic and graphite on canvas, 80 x 80 cm (photograph by Fabio del Re). — 53

Fig. 1.11   Walmor Corrêa, *Teiniaguá, vista dorsal* from *Salamanca do*   58
            Jarau (2013). Acrylic and graphite on canvas, 90 × 110 cm
            (photograph by Hugo Curti).
Fig. 2.1   Installation view of Pablo La Padula, *Zoología fantástica* (2018).   65
            Centro de Arte y Naturaleza, Museo de la Universidad
            Nacional de Tres de Febrero, Buenos Aires, Argentina
            (photograph courtesy of the Museo de la Universidad de Tres
            de Febrero).
Fig. 2.2   Francesco Calzolari's cabinet, as shown in the frontispiece to   67
            Benedetto Ceruti, *Musaeum Franc. Calceolari iun. Veronensis*
            (1622).
Fig. 2.3   Installation view of Pablo La Padula, *Zoología fantástica*   68
            (2018). Centro de Arte y Naturaleza, Museo de la
            Universidad Nacional de Tres de Febrero, Buenos Aires,
            Argentina (photograph by Gabriela Schevach, courtesy of
            REV magazine).
Fig. 2.4   Installation view of Pablo La Padula, *Zoología fantástica* (2018).   68
            Centro de Arte y Naturaleza, Museo de la Universidad
            Nacional de Tres de Febrero, Buenos Aires, Argentina
            (photograph by the artist).
Fig. 2.5   Installation view of Pablo La Padula, *Teatro científico* (2020).   74
            Fundación Federico Jorge Klemm, Buenos Aires, Argentina
            (photograph by the artist).
Fig. 2.6   Installation view of Cristian Villavicencio, *Selecciones* (2019).   78
            Arte Actual Flacso, Quito, Ecuador (photograph by the
            artist).
Fig. 2.7   Installation view of Cristian Villavicencio, *Selecciones*.   78
            Exhibited as part of *Tecnologías de la experiencia* in the 15th
            Bienal de Cuenca, Ecuador (2021) (photograph by Ricardo
            Bohórquez).
Fig. 2.8   Still from video produced by Cristian Villavicencio   80
            for *Dimensiones paralelas* (2017). Fundación BilbaoArte
            Fundazioa, Bilbao, Spain.
Fig. 2.9   Installation view of Cristian Villavicencio, *Especímenes*, two-   80
            channel video projection from *Dimensiones paralelas* (2017).
            Fundación BilbaoArte Fundazioa, Bilbao, Spain (photograph
            by the artist).
Fig. 2.10   Cristian Villavicencio, *Megatherium*, shown without the   82
            glass dome with which it was exhibited, from *Dimensiones*
            paralelas (2017). Fundación BilbaoArte Fundazioa, Bilbao
            (photograph by the artist).

Fig. 2.11 Cristian Villavicencio, *Jardín* from *Dimensiones paralelas* (2017). Fundación BilbaoArte Fundazioa, Bilbao, Spain (photograph by the artist). 83

Fig. 2.12 Cristian Villavicencio and Agata Mergler, *Haptic Cameras—4 simultaneous cameras* (2016) (photograph by Cristian Villavicencio). 85

Fig. 2.13 Installation view of Cristian Villavicencio, *Tecnologías de la experiencia* (2021). *Tecnologías de la experiencia* (video, back wall); *Silbato*, 50.0 cm x 40.0 cm x 50.0 cm (back left); *Espejo sonoro*, 160 cm x 40 cm x 40 cm (back right); *Resonar/excavar* (foreground). 15th Cuenca Bienal, Cuenca, Ecuador (photograph by Ricardo Bohórquez). 88

Fig. 3.1 Alberto Baraya, *Taxones Tabatinga* (2014) from the *Herbario de plantas artificiales*. Found object "Made in China," photography and drawing on cardboard, 56.0 x 82.0 cm (photograph by the artist). 98

Fig. 3.2 Alberto Baraya, *Borrachero doble* (Double Devil's Trumpet, 2014) from the *Herbario de plantas artificiales*. Found object "Made in China," photography and drawing on cardboard, 112.0 x 82.0 cm (photograph by the artist). 100

Fig. 3.3 Juan Francisco Mancera, *Giganton. Datura* from the *Drawings of the Royal Botanical Expedition to the New Kingdom of Granada*. Image from the digitalization project of the drawings of the Royal Botanical Expedition to the New Kingdom of Granada (1783–1816) directed by José Celestino Mutis: www.rjb.csic.es/icones/mutis. Real Jardín Botánico-CSIC. Reproduced by kind permission of the Real Jardín Botánico. 101

Fig. 3.4 Alberto Baraya, *Cacao, beso de cacao* (2018) from the Tumaco Expedition, *Herbario de plantas artificiales*. Found object, drawing and photography on cardboard (photograph by the artist). 103

Fig. 3.5 Eulalia de Valdenebro, photograph of cactus from *Del páramo al desierto, 19–21* (2009). 50 x 70 cm. 107

Fig. 3.6 Eulalia de Valdenebro, photograph of climbing plant from *Del páramo al desierto, 19–21* (2009). 50 x 70 cm. 107

Fig. 3.7 Eulalia de Valdenebro, sketch from *Del páramo al desierto, 19–21* (2009). 30 x 25 cm (photograph by the artist). 109

Fig. 3.8 Eulalia de Valdenebro, *Heterogéneas/Criminales* (2012). Watercolour on paper for heterogeneous seeds, digital reproduction from original in watercolour for homogeneous seeds (GMO), 120 x 60 cm (photograph by the artist). 110

Fig. 3.9 Eulalia de Valdenebro, *Frailejonmetría comparada esc 1:1* (2020). Watercolour on paper, 240 x 160 cm. 113

Fig. 3.10 Eulalia de Valdenebro, *Mapa de relaciones táctiles esc 1:1* (2020). Ink prints on paper. 160 x 160 cm. 114

Fig. 3.11 Installation view of María Fernanda Cardoso, *On the Marriages of Plants* (2018) from *Human non Human*. Powerhouse Museum, Sydney, Australia (photograph by Carlos Velásquez). 118

Fig. 3.12 Installation view of María Fernanda Cardoso, *On the Marriages of Plants* (2018) from *Human non Human*. Powerhouse Museum, Sydney, Australia (photograph by Carlos Velásquez). 118

Fig. 3.13 Installation view of María Fernanda Cardoso, *On the Marriages of Plants* (2018) from *Human non Human*. Powerhouse Museum, Sydney, Australia (photograph by Carlos Velásquez). 121

Fig. 4.1 Alberto Baraya, *Orquídea Vanda y 4 antropometrías artificiales* (2013) from the *Herbario de plantas artificiales*. Found object, photograph and drawing on cardboard, 60 x 45 x 5 cm (photograph by the artist). 139

Fig. 4.2 Hermann Burmeister, *El Rio Paraná entre el Diamante y el Rio Carcaranal*, from *Vues pittoresques de la République Argentine: XIV planches avec 36 figures, dessinées la plupart d'après nature et accompagnées de descriptions* (1881), Plate III, Figure 5. Reproduced by kind permission of Cambridge University Library. 148

Fig. 4.3 Hermann Burmeister, *La Punta Gorda en el Rio Paraná y el pueblo Diamante*, from *Vues pittoresques de la République Argentine: XIV planches avec 36 figures, dessinées la plupart d'après nature et accompagnées de descriptions* (1881), Plate III, Figure 6. Reproduced by kind permission of Cambridge University Library. 149

Fig. 4.4 Facundo de Zuviría, black and white photograph from *Paraná Ra'anga: Imagen del Paraná* (2010–2013). 16.6 x 24 cm. 151

Fig. 4.5 Facundo de Zuviría, black and white photograph from *Paraná Ra'anga: Imagen del Paraná* (2010–2013). 16.6 x 24 cm. 151

Fig. 4.6 Still from Laura Glusman, *Ambá. Una especie de paraíso* (2010). Video available at https://www.youtube.com/watch?v=YHXY9A-KPgY 152

Fig. 5.1	Rodrigo Arteaga, *Atlas de la historia física y política de Chile* (2015–2016). Intervened cut-out illustrations, wooden structure, 140 x 120 x 8 cm. Sobering Galerie, Paris (photograph by the artist).	169
Fig. 5.2	Rodrigo Arteaga, from *Botánica sistemática* (2015). Book intervened with plants and earth. Carmen Araujo Arte, Caracas (photograph by the artist).	170
Fig. 5.3	Still from video of performance by Tiago Sant'Ana, *Refino #3* (2017) (image provided by the artist).	174
Fig. 5.4	Still from video of performance by Tiago Sant'Ana, *Refino #4* (2017) (image provided by the artist).	174
Fig. 5.5	Claudia Coca, four drawings from *Joyas remotas* (2020) from the *Tempestades* series (2015–2023). Charcoal and pastel on linen, 50 x 35 cm (photograph by the artist).	178
Fig. 5.6	Alexander von Humboldt, *The Chimborazo seen from the Plateau of Tapia*. Plate from *Vues des Cordillères et monumens des peuples indigènes de l'Amérique* (1810). Wellcome Collection. Attribution 4.0 International (CC BY 4.0).	183
Fig. 5.7	Oscar Santillán, *Lost Star* (2012–2013). 18 x 13 x 3 cm (photograph by Jhoeko). Courtesy of Jhoeko, Nest (The Hague) and the artist.	185
Fig. 5.8	Herbarium created by Fabiano Kueva. Installation view of *Archivo Alexander von Humboldt, 250 Jahre Jung: Celebrating Alexander von Humboldt's Birthday*, Humboldt Forum, Berlin, 13–14 September 2019 (photograph by David von Becker).	189
Fig. 5.9	Still from Fabiano Kueva, *Humboldt 2.0* (2011–2012). Video (image provided by the artist).	191
Fig. 5.10	Still from Fabiano Kueva, *Ensayo geopoético* (2011–2019). Video (image provided by the artist).	194
Fig. 5.11	Still from Fabiano Kueva, *Ensayo geopoético* (2011–2019). Video (image provided by the artist).	195
Fig. 5.12	Still from Fabiano Kueva, *Humboldt 2.0* (2011–2012). Video (image provided by the artist).	196
Fig. 5.13	Friedrich Georg Weitsch, *Alexander von Humboldt und Aimé Bonpland am Fuß des Vulkans Chimborazo* (1806). Public Domain, via Wikimedia Commons, https://commons.wikimedia.org/wiki/File:Humboldt-Bonpland_Chimborazo.jpg	197

Fig. 5.14　Cabinet created by Fabiano Kueva. Installation view of *Archivo Alexander von Humboldt, 250 Jahre Jung: Celebrating Alexander von Humboldt's Birthday*, Humboldt Forum, Berlin, 13–14 September 2019 (photograph by David von Becker).　199

Fig. 6.1　Daniel Malva, *Mandrillus Sphinx*, photograph from *Natural History Museum* (2013). 80 x 53.3 cm.　206

Fig. 6.2　Daniel Malva, *Elephas maximus: fetus*, photograph from *Natural History Museum* (2009). 30 x 20 cm.　207

Fig. 6.3　Daniel Malva, series of photographs of hearts, from *Natural History Museum* (from left to right): Caiman Latirostris, Equus Caballus, Homo Sapiens, Chrysocyon Brachyurus, Canis Lupus-Familiaris, Panthera Leo. 30 x 20 cm. As exhibited in a solo show entitled *OJardim*, Galeria Mezanino, São Paulo, Brazil, 2017 (photograph by the artist).　208

Fig. 6.4　Still from video produced by Adriana Bustos, *Paisajes del alma* (2011). Video available at https://vimeo.com/688169765　210

Fig. 6.5　Installation view of Rodrigo Arteaga, *Moorland from This Path, One Time, Long Ago* (2018). Potteries Museum & Art Gallery PMAG, Stoke-on-Trent, United Kingdom (photograph by the artist).　214

Fig. 6.6　Installation view of Rodrigo Arteaga, *The Victorian House* from *This Path, One Time, Long Ago* (2018). Potteries Museum & Art Gallery PMAG, Stoke-on-Trent, United Kingdom (photograph by the artist).　216

Fig. 6.7　Installation view of Rodrigo Arteaga, *Natural Selection* (2017). AirSpace Gallery, Stoke-on-Trent, United Kingdom (photograph by the artist).　217

Fig. 6.8　Installation view of Pablo La Padula, *Sala de Escape* from *Museo liberado* (2021). Museo Nacional de Historia Natural, Montevideo, Uruguay (photograph by Elena Téliz and Maite Silva, Espacio de Arte Contemporáneo).　220

Fig. 6.9　Installation view of Pablo La Padula, *Sala de Captura* from *Museo liberado* (2021). Museo Nacional de Historia Natural, Montevideo, Uruguay (photograph by Elena Téliz and Maite Silva, Espacio de Arte Contemporáneo).　221

Fig. 6.10　Installation view of Pablo La Padula, *Sala de Captura* from *Museo liberado* (2021). Museo Nacional de Historia Natural, Montevideo, Uruguay (photograph by Elena Téliz and Maite Silva, Espacio de Arte Contemporáneo).　221

Fig. 6.11　Walmor Corrêa, forged pilot's licence, *Sporophila Beltoni* (2018). Instituto Ling, Porto Alegre, Brazil (photograph by artist).　227

Fig. 6.12 Walmor Corrêa, diorama from *Para onde vão os pássaros quando morrem?* (2012). Plastic, taxidermy, paint, resin, paper and glass, 60 x 20 cm (photograph by Letícia Remião). 231

Fig. 6.13 Walmor Corrêa, scene from *Você que faz versos* (2010). Instituto Goethe de Porto Alegre, Porto Alegre, Brazil (photograph by Letícia Remião). 233

Fig. 6.14 Installation view of Grupo Etcétera, *Diorama, Museo del Neo Extractivismo* (2021). Centro Cultural Kirchner, Buenos Aires, Argentina (photograph by the author). 235

Acknowledgments

This book was originally conceived several years ago, finding its moment when another had to be delayed due to pandemic-related travel bans. As an in-between project, it was intended to be modest in scale and scope. Perhaps inevitably, it grew, as I discovered a corpus that was much richer and more diverse than I had initially expected and found new and fascinating interlocutors in the many artists I met in person or online. My first and most important thanks goes to them, for taking the time to share their ideas with me with such openness and enthusiasm. Their artistic and ethical commitment has been a continual source of inspiration.

A large part of this book was written during two terms of research leave from my post at the University of Cambridge, and I would like to thank colleagues there who took on some of my teaching, examining, and other responsibilities during this time, including Pedro Mendes Loureiro, Emily Price, Geoffrey Maguire, Rory O'Bryen, Geoffrey Kantaris, and Carlos Fonseca. Oliver Wilson-Nunn provided invaluable assistance in the preparation of the images for publication.

I would like to thank Cambridge University Library for its outstanding support for researchers, from tracking down elusive texts to finding inventive ways of providing access to its collections, even during the deepest pandemic. I also gratefully acknowledge the support of the British Academy in funding pre-pandemic fieldwork.

A final word of thanks to Alessandra Tosi and everyone else at Open Book Publishers. It is an honour to publish with a press that is so radically committed to ensuring open access for readers and authors, and to creating an infrastructure that allows other publishers to do the same.

Introduction

A white gallery wall is marked out at intervals to a length of twenty-five feet. Stretching out above, black capital letters stamp out the phrase "el cocodrilo de Humboldt no es el cocodrilo de Hegel" (Humboldt's crocodile is not Hegel's). Near the end on the left, a crocodile's eye appears on a monitor; at the right, another shows its tail. José Alejandro Restrepo's installation comments on a disagreement between two towering European figures whose influential writings on Latin America have significantly shaped the region's place in world history. For Hegel, whose theory of world history excluded both America and Africa as lands without a past, America's animals showed "the same inferiority" as its human inhabitants. Although its lions, tigers and crocodiles were similar to their Old World equivalents, they were "in every respect smaller, weaker, and less powerful."[1] This quotation from Hegel is reproduced on the gallery wall, alongside another from Humboldt that criticizes Hegel's "ignorance" and asserts that the "poor weak crocodiles" he has dismissed measure no fewer than twenty-five feet in length.[2] Both Hegel's sneering description of the continent's feeble crocodiles and Humboldt's impassioned exaggeration of their size fade into irrelevance as the real crocodile, manifestly absent, fixes the viewer in a stare and closes its eye in a wink.

Restrepo's *El cocodrilo de Humboldt no es el cocodrilo de Hegel* (1994) draws ironic attention to the frequent mistakes and misrepresentations present in European narratives about Latin America as well as to their enduring power. Hegel was expounding on the views of the French naturalist Georges-Louis Leclerc, Comte de Buffon, whose descriptions of the inferiority of nature in the New World gave rise to theories of

---

1 Hegel, *Lectures on the Philosophy of World History*, 163.
2 Postscript to a letter to Varnhagen von Ense (1837). Von Humboldt, *Letters of Alexander Von Humboldt*, 34.

degeneracy that were to be widely adopted for decades to come. Other texts and images produced by Europeans and their descendents since 1492 have depicted Latin America as a lost paradise, a source of unimaginable riches, and a land of barbarism or exoticism. As a scientist of the Enlightenment, Humboldt dedicated much energy to correcting misconceptions through patient empirical observation and measurement; however, his work continued to be deeply influenced by the assumptions of previous travellers to the continent and by Romantic conceptions of peoples, landscapes, and the unity of nature.

Restrepo's installation demonstrates how readily the natural world is caught up in—and obscured by—broader cultural and political debates, and never more so than in colonial and postcolonial contexts. Bruno Bosteels reminds us that Hegel's scholarship cannot be separated from imperial politics: that both his dialectic method and his world-historical system must be understood as "provincial self-legitimations of Europe's colonial ambitions."[3] Even the universal science envisioned by Humboldt, who is often read as progressive in his more enlightened attitudes toward indigenous people and his criticism of slavery, is based on practices of appropriation and accumulation that were made possible by colonialism and in turn paved the way for the increasing dominance of Western scientific models, the erasure of alternative approaches to the natural world, and the wholesale commodification and exploitation of nature under global capitalism.

This book is about images, ideas, and practices relating to Latin America that have emerged through the work of natural historians since the European colonization of the region, and how these have been recovered, contested, reworked, or replaced in recent art projects by Latin American artists. Many of these artists return to historical methods of collecting, organizing, and displaying nature, including the medieval bestiary, baroque cabinets of curiosities, the albums and atlases created by European travellers to the New World, taxidermy and natural history dioramas, as well as the floras and herbaria composed by eighteenth- and nineteenth-century naturalists. They do so in order to engage critically and creatively with these genres and archives, developing perspectives that may be described as decolonial and post-anthropocentric.

---

3   Bosteels, "Hegel in America," 72.

The artworks they produce forge a critique of modern Western science's abstraction and rationalization of nature. They hark back to pre-Enlightenment encounters between different kinds of knowledge and practice that were more fluid and holistic, or engage with indigenous philosophies that typically emphasize relations of interdependence and reciprocity between humans and the rest of the natural world. They expose a historical complicity between the natural sciences, colonialism, and capitalism, seeking to reconnect science with those forms of popular, indigenous, and spiritual knowledge and experience that it has systematically excluded since the eighteenth century. Their return to earlier scientific and artistic forms of representation also introduces folds in time, looping back to former genres and their contexts and rehabilitating "older" styles and imaginaries in ways that challenge an understanding of the cumulative advance of knowledge. I will argue that the folds these artworks create also become part of a broader critique of the modern, humanist, linear conceptions of temporality that often remain central to contemporary thought about environmental change and the Anthropocene. My readings of these artistic projects will also focus on how they combat the apocalyptic visions of environmental change that often dominate Western media, drawing on recent findings in biology, ecology, and environmental history to promote a renewed understanding of the resilience of the natural world and of alternative, more collaborative, ways in which humans might co-inhabit it.

Natural History and Empire

Since Columbus famously spied mermaids near the coast of Hispaniola on 8 January 1493, European descriptions of the flora and fauna of the New World have been spiced with marvels and misconceptions of all kinds. Reports on colonial expeditions portrayed American nature as fabulously prodigious; amid their many errors, however, these accounts significantly expanded what was known in Europe about the animals, plants, and minerals of the Americas. Colonial administrations made use of this knowledge in extensive mining, engineering, and agricultural operations that would extract American riches for European benefit. The many atlases, albums, bestiaries, floras, chronicles, encyclopaedias, and expedition reports compiled by colonial scientists can also be read as sites of encounter at which European and indigenous cosmologies and systems of knowledge came into contact, leading in some cases to fruitful exchanges and in others to epistemic violence.

It was to its colonies that Spain turned for resources to stem the political and economic decline that had begun in the seventeenth century; its mining operations there in particular became the principal source of finance to cover the costs of its wars in Europe, although botany was also of high economic importance.[4] In the quest to exploit America's natural resources, natural history took on a powerful role as a key instrument in fulfilling the Crown's ambitions.[5] This new alliance between European expansion, scientific exploration, and commercial exploitation was cemented in the great scientific expeditions to Latin America, many of which took place in the second half of the eighteenth century.

These expeditions aimed to produce an exhaustive survey of the colonies' natural resources and to map coastlines and borders with a view to their consolidation and defence. European expeditions to the New World in the eighteenth and nineteenth centuries were typically long in duration (many spanning a decade or more). They brought together a great number of experts and artisans with different specialisms: Europeans collaborated with *criollos* (people of Spanish descent born in the colonies) and indigenous people with expertise in mining, hydrology, or botany, whose contribution to the vast expansion of knowledge about the natural world that took place in these centuries is only now being more fully recognized.[6] Many scholars have described these expeditions as a second conquest of the region, with the difference that "no se trata de descubrir, conquistar y poblar, sino de observar, describir y explotar" (it was not about discovering, conquering, and populating, but about observing, describing, and exploiting).[7] Further surveys were commissioned by the newly independent republics of Latin America in the nineteenth century. As well as fostering a sense of national identity through the study of natural history, these expeditions

---

4   Nieto Olarte, *Remedios para el imperio*, 36; Bleichmar, *Visible Empire*, 187–88.
5   Lafuente, "Enlightenment in an Imperial Context," 159.
6   See, for example, Thurner and Cañizares-Esguerra, *The Invention of Humboldt: On the Geopolitics of Knowledge*, which was published as this book entered production.
7   Minguet, "La obra de Humboldt," 387.

also had the aim of extending state power over indigenous communities and more rural regions further from the nation's principal cities.

Artists often worked intensively alongside naturalists in these expeditions. This was particularly the case in Spanish America: over twelve thousand images were produced for the natural history expeditions conducted by Spain in the eighteenth century.[8] Given the challenges involved in collecting, preserving, and transporting plants and animals across the Atlantic, illustrations were essential to the circulation of knowledge and the growth of natural history and the more modern disciplines to which it gave rise. Many of these illustrations were not published at the time, reaching only a few specialist eyes.[9] But they were nevertheless instrumental in shaping how botanical and zoological knowledge were to be constructed, giving prominence to visual epistemology as "a way of knowing based on observation and representation."[10] The important role of artists in producing knowledge has been recognized in a raft of fascinating studies, such as Mauricio Nieto Olarte's *Remedios para el imperio: Historia natural y la apropiación del nuevo mundo* (2006), Daniela Bleichmar's *Visible Empire: Botanical Expeditions and Visual Culture in the Hispanic Enlightenment* (2012), José Ramón Marcaida López's *Arte y ciencia en el barroco español: Historia natural, coleccionismo y cultural visual* (2014), and several texts co-authored by Marcaida López and Juan Pimentel.[11] I draw on these studies in Chapter Three in particular, which traces how contemporary artists contest the extractive, dissociative vision of the natural world that emerges in botanical art produced for the great Spanish American expeditions of the eighteenth and nineteenth centuries.

It is perhaps surprising that many recent art projects have found a source of inspiration rather than a target of critique in the texts and images created by Spanish and Portuguese missionaries and explorers in the early colonial period. Walmor Corrêa's close engagement with the letters and chronicles of Padre José de Anchieta (1534–1597), for example, or the naming of the protagonists of Claudio Romo's *El álbum*

---

8 Bleichmar, *Visible Empire*, 10.
9 Bleichmar, 10.
10 Bleichmar, *Visual Voyages*, 123.
11 See, for example, Marcaida López and Pimentel, "Dead Natures or Still Lives?"; Marcaida and Pimentel, "Green Treasures and Paper Floras."

de la flora imprudente (2007) and *Herbolaria memorabile* (2021) after Fray Bernardino de Sahagún (*1499–1590*), are homages to these figures, seeing in them approaches and values that might even serve us in our own era. Anchieta, a Jesuit missionary, was a committed naturalist and a dedicated scholar of Tupi, even composing poetry and theatre in the language as well as publishing its first grammar. Corrêa's work conveys Anchieta's fascination with indigenous and popular legends and the natural wonders he related in copious letters to his superiors. The Franciscan friar Sahagún, a pioneering ethnographer, compiled the extraordinary *Historia general de las cosas de la Nueva España* (*General History of the Things of New Spain*, 1540–1590). Sahagún's manuscript is unparalleled in the early colonial period, both for the scope and depth of its engagement with indigenous cultures and the collaborative nature of its composition: he spent decades interviewing town elders and many sections were written or compiled by Nahua students. Romo's fictional Sahagún thus revives an approach to studying the New World that was much more pluralistic than many of the treatises that were to follow.

Natural History and the Enlightenment

In this way, many of these early voyages become emblematic of a more genuine form of cultural exchange and an interest in diverse systems of thought and knowledge that were to disappear in later periods, and specifically in the Enlightenment. It was the Enlightenment's quest to develop a universal scientific language—which could account for natural phenomena from a supposedly objective, neutral, distanced position and resolve the inconsistencies and uncertainties that arose from the use of local, everyday languages—that would have the greatest impact on indigenous knowledge in Latin America. This search for what the Colombian philosopher Santiago Castro-Gómez calls the "*punto cero de observación*" (zero-point of observation) would involve the active substitution of multiple forms of knowledge often practised in indigenous communities with "una sola forma única y verdadera de conocer el mundo: la suministrada por la racionalidad científico-técnica de la modernidad" (One single and reliable form of knowing the world: that which is supplied by the techno-scientific rationality of modernity).[12]

---

12   Castro-Gómez, *La hybris del punto cero*, 14, 16.

Modern science did not only serve the economic needs of Europe through the commercialization of crops in the colonies; at the hands of *criollo* elites it also, Castro-Gómez argues, became an instrument of social control via epistemicide, the suppression of indigenous forms of knowledge.¹³

To understand the role of Enlightenment philosophies and practices in Latin America requires us to pluralize and globalize European accounts of modernity. In company with other Latin American decolonial thinkers such as Aníbal Quijano and Walter Mignolo, Castro-Gómez affirms that the Enlightenment was not born in Europe and then disseminated around the globe: it developed at multiple sites as a result of the encounter between Europe and its colonies.¹⁴ While the role played by indigenous knowledge in the construction of European natural history was significant, it has been systematically unacknowledged: in global histories of science, the names of renowned European scientists have almost entirely supplanted those of indigenous experts who served as their guides and interlocutors. Yet the colonization of the New World produced fundamental changes in scientific practices in the metropolis. It was the newness of many phenomena found in the colonies that gave impetus to the decline in authority of classical texts on natural history in Europe and the rise of experimental techniques that are associated with Enlightenment science. The differences that early travellers found between Old World and New World animals challenged dominant (theological) ideas about the creation of the world. As Marcaida López points out, the lack of texts on New World nature led to an increased emphasis on observation, experimentation, description, and classification, which opened up new pathways for the study of the natural world that did not rely, as had been the tradition, on knowledge gained from books.¹⁵

---

13 Castro-Gómez, 18.
14 Castro-Gómez, 22, 50.
15 Marcaida López, *Arte y ciencia en el barroco español*, 57–58; see also Gascoigne, "Crossing the Pillars of Hercules," 226. Antonio Barrera-Osorio writes: "The Scientific Revolution did not start with Nicolaus Copernicus and his heliocentric ideas, or with the publication of books by artisans and painters. I argue that it started in the 1520s, in Spain, when merchants, artisans, and royal officials confronted new entities coming from the New World and had to devise their own methods to collect information about those lands: there were no avocados in Pliny's pages." *Experiencing Nature: The Spanish American Empire and the Early Scientific Revolution*, 2.

In the Enlightenment's search for an objective language with which to describe the natural world, vision acquired primacy. Indeed, as Foucault contends, sight became "natural history's condition of possibility."[16] Techniques of microscopy and illustration were used in the Enlightenment to render lines and forms more visible for the purposes of classification and characterization. The isolation of forms from their surroundings not only made them clearer and more available to study; it strengthened the illusion of objectivity and the perception that nature was a thing apart from ourselves. Senses other than sight were generally eliminated from descriptions from the eighteenth century onwards as they were too variable and too subjective.[17] A critique of the abstractive, universalizing vision of modern science has also been extensively developed by European and Anglophone scholars such as Donna Haraway, Mary Louise Pratt, and Isabelle Stengers. As Haraway contends, "there is no unmediated photograph or passive camera obscura in scientific accounts of bodies and machines; there are only highly specific visual possibilities, each with a wonderfully detailed, active, partial way of organizing worlds." Our pictures of the world should not, she proposes, be "allegories of infinite mobility and interchangeability," but of "elaborate specificity and difference."[18] For Haraway, a feminist science—which would also, in many ways, be a decolonized science—would recognize that "Vision is *always* a question of the power to see—and perhaps of the violence implicit in our visualizing practices."[19]

Latin American artists have more recently challenged the primacy of the visual in natural history by creating installations that engage with other senses, expanding our possible forms of interaction with the natural world. The importance of the taxonomies developed by natural historians of the Enlightenment lies not only in "what they make it possible to see," but also what they "screen off," which for Foucault was the anatomy of organisms and the functions of their systems.[20] What they also masked, we might add, is the organism's relations within a complex, dynamic ecosystem, into which we are also fully integrated.

---

16 Foucault, *The Order of Things*, 133.
17 Foucault, 132.
18 Haraway, *Simians, Cyborgs, and Women*, 191.
19 Haraway, 192.
20 Foucault, *The Order of Things*, 137.

This relational understanding of the natural world is the focus of many of the artworks discussed in this volume.

Decolonizing Natural History

Within the Latin American context, decolonial critiques of science have often taken the form of exposing the inequalities obscured by the "internationalization" of science (in the work of Oscar Varsavsky and Pablo Kreimer, for example), questioning the state's uncritical "transplantation" of ideas from the Global North (Diego Hurtado) or uncovering the unrecognized contributions made by indigenous knowledge-producers to global science (Jorge Cañizares-Esguerra).[21] Elements of all of these forms of critique are evident in the artworks discussed in this volume. Their principal aims in returning to previous methods of classifying and displaying nature, however, are to question the notion of a universal science and to diversify and pluralize epistemologies beyond the narrow strictures that have characterized modern Western science since the Enlightenment. If natural history since the eighteenth century has often sought to neutralize the position of the observer, to standardize names and to universalize systems of measurement, the artists featured in this book place value instead on the contingent, the local, and the plural, along with the apocryphal and that which exceeds the limits of rational knowledge. Returning to technologies of knowledge that were often designed to yield greater objectivity and universalism, they adapt these for different purposes: to re-entwine natural history with human history, to historicize a timeless and universal nature, and to reconnect modern science with those forms of knowledge it has marginalized since the eighteenth century.

One of the ways in which artists have sought to challenge and expand the limits of modern scientific rationality is to return to premodern accounts of the natural world. These take us back to the pluri-perspectivism of mediaeval and early modern science. The plants and animals depicted in these more recent works often hail, in a similar manner, from an enchanted realm of hyperbolic affects and affinities.

---

21 See, for example, Varsavsky, *Ciencia, política y cientificismo*, 27; Kreimer, *Ciencia y periferia*, 69, 201, 215; Hurtado, *La ciencia argentina*, 21; Cañizares-Esguerra, *Nature, Empire, and Nation*.

Classical and mediaeval marvels and monsters are resurrected as an alternative to the rationalization and standardization of farmed animals and monoculture crops. In this context, re-enchanting nature becomes a critical act, a defence of diversity and exceptionality, reversing "the shift from sensory impact to a rationalizing nomenclature," which was also, Barbara Stafford observes, "a move from the extraordinary to the ordinary."[22] In his use of the marvellous, for example, Claudio Romo proposes "una relación más emotiva con el entorno y no sólo como una bodega de recursos" (a more emotional relation with the environment and not only as a storehouse of resources).[23] Cryptozoology in his work becomes a technique to restore magic and wonder to a world that many perceive to have lost its mystique.[24] The appeal to wonder and marvels in the work of Romo, Corrêa and others becomes part of a critique of the limitations of Enlightenment rationality. As Lorraine Daston and Katherine Park argue, wonder in the mediaeval and early modern ages was "a cognitive passion, as much about knowing as about feeling," registering "a breached boundary, a classification subverted."[25] Only since the Enlightenment has wonder become "disreputable" and "redolent of the popular, the amateurish, and the childish."[26] Just as importantly, as I will show, these artists' inclusion of fables and the fantastic is a recommitment to represent animal life, not as a thing apart from us, but as deeply entwined with human culture.

The practice of natural history in the Western world has been thoroughly intertextual, involving a close engagement with previous texts as much as direct observation; indeed, the Enlightenment's increasing emphasis on empirical evidence did not immediately replace reference to classical thinkers. Works by Romo, Corrêa, and Rafael Toriz (see Chapter One) are consciously intertextual in a way that reveals much about the evolution of modern zoology and the continued influence, through to the eighteenth century, of philosophers from the ancient world. The visions of nature forged in classical philosophy did not only mould the incipient disciplines of botany and zoology, but also

---

22 Stafford, *Artful Science*, 266.
23 Farías, "'El álbum de la flora imprudente,'" 23.
24 Dendle, "Cryptozoology in the Medieval and Modern Worlds," 201.
25 Daston and Park, *Wonders and the Order of Nature, 1150–1750*, 14.
26 Daston and Park, 15.

significantly shaped visions of the New World. Like many Renaissance thinkers and natural historians, early Spanish chroniclers such as José de Acosta and Gonzalo Fernández de Oviedo y Valdés drew heavily on classical writers (Herodotus, Pliny and Aristotle) in their writings on America. Karl Enenkel finds that the flourishing of early modern zoology was paradoxically accompanied by a heightened interest in monsters; early modern zoologists were still strongly influenced in this respect by thinkers from antiquity (such as Pliny) and the Middle Ages (including Albertus Magnus). In this period, the literary tradition continued to be "the most important source of biological knowledge" and the authority of such writers "frequently outshone the evidence of empirical observation."[27]

This is nowhere more evident than in European accounts of the New World, which were often composed by scholars who had never travelled to Latin America on the basis of the journals and letters of those who had actually been there. For the writers of these descriptions and reports, "the relation between books and Nature, between words and natural phenomena or living beings, was so close that to talk or write about them was, in effect, to talk and write about what others had talked and written about."[28] Corrêa, Romo, Fabiano Kueva, Tiago Sant'Ana and other artists emphasize this iterative, citational dynamic as a way of recognizing the foundational role played by such texts in creating lasting visions of Latin America, as well as pointing out the errors they perpetuated. But intertextual techniques of this kind also become an important means of historicizing ideas of nature. If the "chief use" of history, for Hume, was "only to discover the constant and universal principles of human nature,"[29] for more recent artists, uncovering and adding to the palimpsestic nature of knowledge about the New World becomes a way of drawing attention to how knowledge is constructed, by whom, and for whom.

The folding-in of different times and temporalities that we may observe in recent reworkings of mediaeval bestiaries or cabinets of curiosities is also characteristic of artistic projects that re-enact the journeys of European explorers and scientists. These repetitions and

---

27 Enenkel, "The Species and Beyond," 113–14, 58–59.
28 Pimentel, "Baroque Natures," 101.
29 Hume, *An Enquiry Concerning Human Understanding*, 60.

recreations contest representations of nature as timeless; they also demonstrate how human relationships with the natural world have changed considerably from time to time and place to place. They allow us to see, as Raymond Williams famously observed, that "the idea of nature contains, though often unnoticed, an extraordinary amount of human history."[30] In the artworks I study in this book, this act of historicizing natural history encompasses both a critique of the past (and its legacies for the present) and a gesture toward the possibility of an alternative future. The critique is directed toward the reckless exploitation of natural resources in Latin America, both by imperial powers and independent republics, which has carried in its train not only environmental disaster but the violent dispossession of millions of the region's human inhabitants to make room for vast plantations and mines. The more utopian gesture lies in the recovery of different, more collaborative, ways in which humans have created relationships with the rest of the natural world, allowing us to envision alternative futures.

Decolonial Perspectives on Environmental Change

I argue that the artworks presented in this book offer decolonial perspectives on environmental change and environmental futures. Perhaps most obviously, the relationships they trace between colonialism, capitalist acquisition, and the commodification of nature help us understand that today's environmental crisis is not the result of over-population or industrialization, but is more deeply rooted in the constitution of the modern colonial-capitalist world system, in which cheap labour and natural resources extracted from certain regions of the world have funded unsustainable development in others. Understanding the historical relationship between empire and environmental change is a crucial first step toward grasping the enormous geopolitical transition that might be needed to address global warming or ecological destruction effectively.

A vital contribution made by many Latin American thinkers to Anthropocene debates stems from their insistence that today's ecological crises have little to do with ecology. Enrique Leff, a Mexican economist and environmentalist, argues that the global environmental crisis

---

30 Williams, *Culture and Materialism*, 73.

has been generated by the economic and judicial order of modernity, which is based on an instrumental rationality, and which continues to govern the processes of globalization.³¹ Some European scholars are in agreement. Ulrich Beck argues that "climate politics is precisely *not* about *climate* but about transforming the basic concepts and institutions of first, industrial, nation-state modernity."³² Instead, many current responses look for technological and economic solutions in ways that will simply perpetuate the current global order. Dominant responses to anthropogenic environmental change in the West often oscillate between scenarios in which humans would dramatically increase their intervention into the natural world—for example, through the technocratic management of CO_2 and geoengineering projects designed to remove greenhouse gases from the atmosphere—or, at the other end of the spectrum, entirely remove themselves from areas set aside for conservation. Both approaches simply reinforce the division between nature and culture that has led to environmental decline in the first place, setting humans above or apart from natural processes that they would seek either to govern more completely or to allow to revert to some Edenic state before human intervention.

Beck and other sociologists and geographers over the past decade have called for a repoliticization of the Anthropocene, arguing that ecological change should be framed within political, social, and ethical questions as well as technological and economic ones. Erik Swyngedouw calls attention to the "post-political" nature of "the consensual scripting of climate change imaginaries, arguments and policies."³³ This consensus leaves no room for political debate: it "forestalls the articulation of divergent, conflicting, and alternative trajectories of future environmental possibilities and assemblages."³⁴ In this context, "Disagreement is allowed, but only with respect to the choice of technologies, the mix of organizational fixes, the detail of the managerial adjustments, and the urgency of their timing and implementation, not with respect to the socio-political framing of present and future natures."³⁵ Political ecology in Latin America, which draws on traditional indigenous knowledge and

---

31 Leff, *Discursos sustentables*, 162.
32 Beck, "Climate for Change, or How to Create a Green Modernity?," 256.
33 Swyngedouw, "Depoliticized Environments," 266.
34 Swyngedouw, 267.
35 Swyngedouw, 267.

practices (among other sources), presents itself precisely as a challenge to the current consensus and a source of alternative approaches to sustainability that acknowledge the deep interconnections between ecology, ontology, culture, and politics.

Perhaps the most paralysing of Anthropocene discourses is the belief that human intervention in nature is necessarily damaging. For Beck, the gloomy stories told by environmentalists reinforce a sense that "nature is something separate from, and something victimized by, human beings. This paradigm defines ecological problems as inevitable consequences of human violations of nature."[36] Calls to protect nature from human impact often reinforce a sense of its passivity, as if its delicate balance could only be restored through the large-scale reduction of human activity. Conservation biology, invasion biology, and restoration ecology, which have collectively been dubbed "Edenic sciences," posit a pure and original state of nature beyond human interference to which we should return in our quest to prevent even greater losses of biodiversity in the future.[37]

One way that the artists discussed in this book reframe Anthropocene debates is by putting humans—sometimes literally—back into the picture. Pristine nature is largely an invention of European Romanticism; its existence has been robustly discredited by ecological studies in recent decades, including those that have focused on the ecological changes wrought in Amazon forests by indigenous people over millennia before the arrival of Europeans (see Chapter Three). Although the environmental impact of colonial societies in the Americas was often considerably higher (see Chapter Four), to underestimate the importance of precolonial change is to minimize the capacity of indigenous societies to transform their environments; this perceived incapacity was an argument frequently made to justify colonialism. It is also to ignore the very different models of cohabitation with other species within a shared environment that traditional indigenous communities have developed. Studying the extent of precolonial environmental change does not diminish a critique of the devastating impact of colonialism, I argue, but effectively repoliticizes decisions that are made today and in the future. As Ursula Heise contends, the fact that "Nature never really

---

36 Beck, "Climate for Change, or How to Create a Green Modernity?," 263.
37 Robbins and Moore, "Ecological Anxiety Disorder," 4.

was separate from human society" means that "whatever baseline for a desirable nature the environmentalist movement sets for itself needs to be chosen from different cultural models and preferences rather than grounding itself simply on the idea of minimal human presence and impact."[38]

Projects undertaken by several contemporary Latin American artists map out how we might challenge hegemonic, Western paradigms of conservation, replacing them with a focus on coexistence, collaboration, and co-evolution. They also demonstrate how dominant discourses of the Anthropocene—and particularly those that posit a future environmental apocalypse—may actually serve the interests of Western globalism and universalism. In Chapter Four, for example, I explore decolonial perspectives on the "global time" of the Anthropocene, which may be understood as a covert means of reinforcing (Western) universalism. I examine texts and images that bring to light the past extinctions that are often erased in discourses of the Anthropocene, which win urgent attention by locating environmental disasters in a future still to come or only just starting to unfold. A decolonial approach to the temporality of environmental change would also be attentive to the challenge of navigating the disjunction between the temporality of Western technomodernity and that of complex natural systems, such as river basins, finding new modes of dwelling in habitats that are subject to periodic change.

Leff calls for a new kind of environmental knowledge that would draw on knowledges and subjectivities that have been marginalized by Western rationalism. This knowledge should not be reduced to the simplifying, objectifying, commodifying approaches to environmental crisis that are commonly found in the natural and social sciences.[39] The artists discussed in this book find multiple ways to expand environmental knowledge beyond the limits of modern science, in order to reconnect laboratory findings with social, political, cultural, and spiritual realms of experience. These may involve the conscious mixing of scientific and popular visual idioms, the promotion of premodern or non-Western conceptions of the natural world, and an engagement with precolonial, colonial, and postcolonial myths and legends. Many of these artworks

---

38 Heise, *Imagining Extinction*, 10.
39 Leff, *Discursos sustentables*, 165, 202.

challenge the apocalyptic imaginaries that are common in Western depictions of environmental catastrophe. For Haraway, a corollary of the fact that natural history and (more recently) the biological sciences have developed within a capitalist, patriarchal framework is that nature has been "theorized and constructed on the basis of scarcity and competition."[40] In this context, to emphasize abundance, reciprocity and successful co-evolution is not only to offer a more positive and hopeful environmental future, but to carve out a feminist and decolonial perspective on environmental change.

An Overview of the Book

Chapter One, "Bestiaries and the Art of Cryptozoology," focuses on artworks and illustrated texts that have reworked the enormously popular mediaeval genre of the bestiary for more contemporary ends. Many twentieth-century Latin American writers—including Jorge Luis Borges, Silvina Ocampo, Juan José Arreola and Wilson Bueno—experimented with the form of the bestiary, adapting it to the fantastic genre or for the purposes of satire. This chapter focuses on the work of twenty-first-century writers and artists who draw on the themes and forms of the medieval bestiary in order to revitalize pre-Hispanic legends, to construct an alternative modernity that embraces plural ontologies, and to explore the changing relationship between humans and animals in the Anthropocene.

The act of (re)imagining extinct and mythical animals takes on a particular poignancy in the context of the current rapid decline in biodiversity across the world. Indeed, as I argue throughout this chapter, the mediaeval bestiary gains a new resonance in the context of global ecological crisis. It offers ways of thinking about the natural world that have been excised from the modern, rationalist, Western standpoint, challenging ideas about human exceptionalism and promoting a view of the universe as intimately interconnected within relationships of reciprocity. At the hands of contemporary writers and artists such as Rafael Toriz and Edgar Cano (Mexico), Claudio Romo (Chile) and Walmor Corrêa (Brazil), Latin American bestiaries of the twenty-first century challenge dominant images of a depleted, fragile

---

40   Haraway, *Simians, Cyborgs, and Women*, 68.

natural world, responding to the need to re-enchant nature in the face of its rationalization and commodification in Western modernity, to revalorize indigenous and popular approaches, and to reconnect animals with human social, cultural, and spiritual lives.

My second chapter, "New Cabinets of Curiosities," presents artistic projects that have revisited the cabinets of curiosities that were fashionable in Europe in the sixteenth century, predating the more systematized approach to collecting and displaying nature that was to characterize the Enlightenment. Cabinets of curiosities employed visual analogies and other effects to raise ontological questions about the natural world and the relationship between art and nature. Pablo La Padula (Argentina) and Cristian Villavicencio (Ecuador/Spain) interrogate the politics of such collections, developing a critique of the relationships that underpin them, between colonialism, capitalist accumulation, and the commodification of nature.

Renaissance cabinets did, however, allow for more creative and diverse entanglings of nature and culture than were permitted in the more systematic collections of the eighteenth century that were to replace them. In his reassemblings of natural history collections, Villavicencio reflects on the link between microscopes (among other technologies of vision) and a commitment to a distanced, "objective" vision that became central to modern scientific techniques. Both La Padula and Villavicencio create opportunities for alternative encounters with the natural world that are embodied and subjective. Like Yuk Hui's concept of "cosmotechnics," these allow us to explore "the different relations between the human and technics inherited from different mythologies and cosmologies" and therefore to generate plural accounts of technological modernity.[41]

Chapter Three, "Floras, Herbaria, and Botanical Illustration," brings us fully into the era of Enlightenment taxonomies. New World plants were exhaustively catalogued in the floras and herbaria produced by the great scientific expeditions led by European naturalists in the eighteenth and nineteenth centuries, such as the Royal Botanical Expedition to New Granada (1783–1816), directed by José Celestino Mutis. Species were primarily illustrated in a way that would allow their identification according to Linnaean taxonomies. Three contemporary artists from

---

41 Hui, *The Question Concerning Technology in China*, 29.

Colombia—Alberto Baraya, María Fernanda Cardoso, and Eulalia de Valdenebro—have reworked the Enlightenment norms of botanical illustration in order to draw attention to their many erasures and to chart environmental change over the past two centuries. Baraya's *Herbario de plantas artificiales* (2002–) celebrates the anomalies and aberrations that were smoothed out in the European quest for a universal system of classification, exposing the relationship between modern Western science and the dynamics of economic and cultural dispossession. De Valdenebro's seed collections contrast the homogenization and commercialization of transgenic varieties with the greater biodiversity of native seeds, whose cultivation has unfolded within a much higher degree of reciprocity between humans and their environment. In *On the Marriages of Plants* (2018), Cardoso reflects on Linnaeus's use of sexual terms borrowed from the human world in her exploration of more recent research into reciprocal relationships between plants, insects, and humans.

I bring these projects into dialogue with a selection of illustrations by Abel Rodríguez (Mogaje Guihu), an artist whose work preserves the ancestral knowledge of the Nonuya and Muinane communities in the Colombian Amazon. Contrasting with Linnaean abstraction, Rodríguez's drawings and paintings depict rainforest ecosystems in ways that cast light on Amazonian concepts of cohabitation and the co-constitution of human and nonhuman subjects. These enter into conflict with two dominant Western paradigms: extraction, on the one hand, and conservation, on the other.

"Retracing Voyages of Science and Conquest," my fourth chapter, focuses on how artists and researchers have re-performed journeys and expeditions as a form of epistemological and aesthetic practice. This allows them to highlight changes and continuities in landscapes and relationships with the natural world, staging a complex interplay of temporalities. A major interdisciplinary and collaborative project discussed here is the *Paraná Ra'anga* expedition (Argentina, 2010), led by Graciela Silvestri and others. Around sixty Spanish and Latin American artists and researchers from different fields retraced the journey undertaken by Pedro de Mendoza in 1536, sailing from the new settlement of Buenos Aires to the interior of the continent, up the rivers Paraná and Paraguay, to found Asunción. Rather than a voyage of conquest, theirs was one that aimed to reinvigorate the riverine culture of Argentina's Litoral region, a socionatural landscape that has been significantly transformed since that first Spanish expedition and is being further changed as a result of a megascale engineering project.

My reading of the texts and images produced by participants in the *Paraná Ra'anga* expedition highlights how they engage with the divergent temporalities of the river. These works carry a critique, I argue, not only of the collusion between global capitalism and environmental destruction, but also of the temporality of the Anthropocene itself. In its linearity and apocalypticism, Anthropocene time as it is constructed in the West often ignores past environmental catastrophes that have already produced the extinction of whole communities and livelihoods. The future tense employed to describe ecological apocalypse also furthers the interests of globalism and economic liberalism by deepening the subjugation of those regions that have already experienced cataclysmic changes to Western technology and scientific rationalism.

Chapter Five, "Albums, Atlases and their Afterlives," is divided into two parts. The first discusses art projects that intervene directly into the books and other materials created by travelling European naturalists of the later colonial period, whose conception of nature has so thoroughly shaped representations of Latin America's landscapes. I explore projects by Rodrigo Arteaga (Chile), Antonio Bermúdez (Colombia), Claudia Coca (Peru), Tiago Sant'Ana (Brazil), Oscar Santillán (Ecuador), and others that stage material interventions or performances in relation to the printed images, atlases, albums, and catalogues that recorded the findings of scientific expeditions in the eighteenth and nineteenth centuries. As well as combating the particular images of Latin America forged in these works, these artists reflect more broadly on the affordances of different material technologies—such as printing, engravings, and the book—used to create and disseminate knowledge.

The second part of the chapter brings together projects that engage with the scientific, commercial, and artistic afterlives of the iconic images that emerged from Humboldt's journey across the Americas (1799–1804). Bermúdez demonstrates how Humboldt's images of Latin American landscapes—such as the famous views of the Chimborazo— live on through different kinds of cultural mediation and commercial accumulation. The relationship between Humboldt's science and extractivism in Latin America, suggested in a poetic mode by Santillán, is explicitly developed in the expansive *Archivo Humboldt* (2011–), a set of performances, documentation, and (mock) archives created by Fabiano Kueva (Ecuador). These remediations and re-enactments recuperate archives of all kinds for decolonial purposes, reworking them in ways that decentre the ocularcentric, logocentric bias of Western modernity while exploring the power of published words and images to represent the colonial other.

The final chapter, "Taxidermy and Natural History Dioramas," selects works that engage with the art and science of taxidermy and the construction of dioramas for museums of the late nineteenth and twentieth centuries. While many artists have rejected taxidermy, given its association with cruelty toward animals, some have reclaimed the practice with the purpose of drawing attention to histories of animal objectification or rethinking human-animal relations. Recent recourses to taxidermy among Latin American artists have provided an opportunity to question of the exhibition practices of natural history museums, while exploring alternative ways of thinking about ecology and the environment. The projects I discuss in this chapter by Daniel Malva (Brazil), Adriana Bustos (Argentina), Rodrigo Arteaga (Chile), Walmor Corrêa (Brazil), and Pablo La Padula (Argentina) remediate, recycle or reuse taxidermy animals within new forms of diorama that construct a critical dialogue with Eurocentric conceptions of nature. They create "afterlives" for taxidermy animals that are held in tension between nature and culture or science and popular myth; they also demonstrate how taxidermy may—paradoxically—be deployed to restore animal agency and to create narratives that are less anthropocentric.

From the Decolonial Neobaroque to Environmental Democracy and the Humanization of Nature

In reworking historical forms and genres, the projects discussed throughout this book create folds in time that trouble linear temporalities, cast new perspectives on the past, and allow us to envision alternative futures. In the conclusion, I relate this argument to Deleuze's observations about the centrality of the "fold" as the "operative function" of the Baroque, proposing that these artworks may be approached as instances of a *decolonial neobaroque*.⁴² Many of the artists explored here stage a tactical return to baroque imaginaries, invoking the historical co-option of the baroque in Latin America as an instrument for anticolonial and anti-institutional expression, while redeploying its excess, heterogeneity, and performativity to explore post-anthropocentric perspectives on science and the living world. Reading their work as part of a decolonial neobaroque highlights ways in which they construct alternative modernities that are less exclusionary, while nevertheless remaining in close dialogue with European scientific, literary, and visual traditions. I mark key differences between the *neobaroque* in Latin America, a category proposed by several scholars that shares many characteristics with the disembedding effects of postmodernism's subversion of authority and linear narratives, and the *decolonial neobaroque* I propose, which is more often a form of historical re-embedding, with the specific aim of constructing a critique of Enlightment epistemologies and Eurocentric modernity.

The ontological and epistemological pluralism to which the decolonial neobaroque is committed also underpins Leff's concept of environmental democracy, which establishes the right of different communities to inhabit biocultural worlds through different rationalities.⁴³ This approach challenges the "one-world" solutions to environmental change that have most often been pursued by Western scientists and engineers. One of those rationalities—one that is explored recurrently by the Latin American artists in this book—is founded on a belief in the fundamental non-separation of humans from the rest of the natural world. If for many Western environmental thinkers and conservationists the "humanization" of nature is to be denounced and reversed, in these artworks (and the philosophies they draw on), the act of (re)humanizing or (re)socializing nature may constitute a more profound response to environmental crisis.

Artists and Curators: A Note

The artists whose projects feature in this book cannot be described as a generation or a movement. Several decades separate the youngest from the oldest; they come from entirely different disciplinary

---

42 Deleuze, *The Fold*, 3.
43 Leff, "Power-Knowledge Relations in the Field of Political Ecology," 243.

backgrounds (or none). Some of them have travelled extensively and are internationally known, while the work of others is much more grounded in local or regional contexts. Walmor Corrêa is wholly self-taught, while others (including Édgar Cano, Laura Glusman, Claudio Romo, Rodrigo Arteaga) have graduated from degrees in photography, sculpture, or fine arts. Few of them have even a low level of insertion into the commercial art world: most sustain their work through other means. Some (like Cristian Villavicencio, María Fernanda Cardoso, Eulalia de Valdenebro) have chosen to develop their artistic work through a PhD programme; some combine artistic practice with university teaching. Pablo La Padula is a research scientist by profession; others (like Daniel Malva) also have a scientific background or (like Oscar Santillán) have collaborated extensively with scientists.

Some of the artists studied here (Alberto Baraya or Abel Rodríguez, for example) have developed a substantial *oeuvre* based on the themes of ecology, nature, and natural history, while others (including Adriana Bustos and Fabiano Kueva) engage with the discourses of natural history as part of a broader exploration of the (colonial) geopolitics of knowledge. Other artists are principally known for their work on other subjects, such as urban culture (Facundo de Zuviría), Afro-Brazilian identities (Tiago Sant'Ana) or race and gender (Claudia Coca). All of them share an interest in exploring how the discipline of natural history as it developed in imperial Europe has served expansionism and extractivism (together with other kinds of resource exploitation), resulting in widespread environmental crisis, but also in how the particular ways in which natural history has perceived and ordered the natural world might be redeemed for very different purposes.

The critical and often reflexive exploration conducted by these artists into the relationship between natural history and the visual arts has been facilitated and promoted by the work of renowned curators in and beyond Latin America. Of the many who would deserve a mention here, chief among them might be José Roca, the Artistic Director of FLORA ars+natura, an independent space in Bogotá that curates exhibitions, runs seminars, and hosts residencies. Other very important exhibition spaces in Latin America for the artists discussed in this book include the Laboratorio Arte Alameda in Mexico City, directed for over a decade by Tania Aedo, and the Centro de Arte y Naturaleza run by the Universidad

Nacional Tres de Febrero in Buenos Aires, under the artistic direction of Diana B. Wechsler. The figure of Humboldt has inspired several significant exhibitions, particularly in commemoration of the 250th anniversary of his birthday, including *La naturaleza de las cosas: Humboldt, idas y venidas* (The Nature of Things: Humboldt, Back and Forth), curated by Halim Badawi at the Museo de Arte de la Universidad Nacional de Colombia (2019), which included works by José Alejandro Restrepo, Antonio Bermúdez, and Óscar Santillán, and *250 Jahre Jung: Celebrating Alexander von Humboldt's Birthday* at the Humboldt Forum in Berlin (2019), which displayed works by Fabiano Kueva, Abel Rodríguez, and José Alejandro Restrepo, among many others.

The art projects brought together in this book should be regarded as a corpus in formation: many of the artists studied here are actively staging new interventions that further reconfigure the relationship between visual art and natural history, while others who are developing very relevant projects could not be included here for reasons of space or thematic coherence. A recent growth of interest in the global history of science, in decolonial critiques of the production of knowledge, and in the relationship between art and nature in times of environmental crisis has created the space for a flourishing scene of artistic practice that is set to continue its expansion.

1. Bestiaries and the Art of Cryptozoology

Mediaeval bestiaries were among the most popular and influential books circulating in Europe in the twelfth and thirteenth centuries. The bestiary was a compilation of the work of diverse authors over time, reaching back to antiquity, and the texts were often richly illustrated.[1] The genre lived on in the chronicles composed by sixteenth-century European travellers to the New World, who borrowed heavily from classical and medieval descriptions of *terrae incognitae* in their accounts of the fabulous creatures they discovered. The bestiary has proved to be eminently reinventable, registering changing beliefs and perspectives with respect to our relationship with animals, our understanding of what (if anything) distinguishes humans from animals, the nature of signs and language, and the principles on which the world may appear to us as ordered or meaningful.

The mediaeval bestiary was ordered in different ways, presenting each animal alphabetically or grouping them in categories such as "beasts of the air" or "beasts of the sea." Their organization was not consonant with the categories of modern Western science, however: bestiary writers and compilers did not distinguish between animals that were commonly to be found, exotic animals from remote lands, and wholly mythical beings. References to the supernatural abilities of animals were meshed together with details of copulation habits,

---

1   The bestiary has its deepest origins in the oral traditions of antiquity, which echoed in the works of ancient historians and philosophers such as Herodotus, Aristotle, and Pliny; these in turn influenced the work compiled by the anonymous writer known as Physiologus around the second to the fourth century A.D. This manuscript was translated many times over and widely disseminated in the Mediterranean world and beyond. Together with Isidore of Seville's *Etymologies* (c. 615–630s), it was an important predecessor of the mediaeval bestiary.

© 2023 Joanna Page, CC BY-NC-ND 4.0   https://doi.org/10.11647/OBP.0339.01

pregnancy durations, and migration patterns that were unexpectedly precise, if not always zoologically accurate. Animal lore gained through observation was also interwoven with etymological analysis (what the origin of an animal's name revealed about its characteristics). Most often, animal behaviour formed the basis of didactic Christian allegories. The writer of a thirteenth-century bestiary tells us that the hedgehog is "a sinner full of vices like spines, skilled in wicked cunning, and in deceits and robberies," as it makes off with food produced by others to feed its own young. When threatened, it curls up into a spiny ball and hides among the rocks. For this reason, the hedgehog becomes "like the man bristling with sins, who fears the judgment to come, and takes very secure refuge in the rock of Christ."[2] To the mediaeval mind, it was less important to know whether an animal existed than to be able to interpret what it might symbolize. The symbolism of bestiaries was highly flexible and even contradictory, with the same animal given positive or negative attributes depending on the context.[3] Writing styles were similarly heterogeneous, with studious notes on animals' behaviour and physiological appearance mixed with fantastical flights of the imagination and stern admonitions to readers.

The bestiary has been serially reinvented in more recent times, not least by writers and artists from Latin America. Although it dispenses with Christian theology, Juan José Arreola's *Punta de plata* (1959) also resorts to allegory in a sceptical exploration of human folly and destructiveness in the modern world.[4] Jorge Luis Borges found the highly intertextual nature of bestiaries, together with their potent medley of fable and fact, popular lore, and classical erudition, to lend itself perfectly to his irreverent literary experiments. His *Manual de zoología fantástica* (1957, with Marguerita Guerrero)—later republished as *El libro de los seres imaginarios* (1967)—is a collection of literary and legendary animals in which brief fables (often attributed to specific authors, such as C. S. Lewis and Kafka) are interspersed with longer texts containing citations from Pliny, Homer, Isidore of Seville, and Milton, alongside a host of

---

2   Barber, *Bestiary* [*MS Bodley 764*], 113.
3   Page, "Good Creation and Demonic Illusions," 37.
4   Arreola's *Punta de plata* was illustrated by Héctor Xavier and published by the Universidad Nacional Autónoma de México; the text was republished in 1972 with additions but without illustrations as *Bestiario*, the title it would carry for subsequent editions.

commentators from China, Scandinavia, South America, and the Islamic world. Rather like his mediaeval precursors, Borges folds together reality and fantasy in a way that defies any rigid separation between ontological orders: thus a chapter on "The Elephant that Foretold the Birth of the Buddha" is joined by one on "Spherical Animals" and another on "An Animal Dreamt by Poe."[5]

Julieta Yelin has explored how twentieth-century bestiaries and animal fictions from Latin America have reimagined the animal in order to question the humanist foundations of Western philosophy.[6] She brings these literary projects into dialogue with the philosophical works of Giorgio Agamben, Jacques Derrida, Gilles Deleuze, and Felix Guattari and others to tease out their incursions into posthumanist thought. My own analysis will focus on Latin American writers and artists of a more recent period, whose reinventions of the bestiary are more centrally focused on the decolonial and the ecological.

The first part of this chapter will present a reading of *Animalia* (Mexico, 2008), written by Rafael Toriz and illustrated by Édgar Cano. *Animalia* draws on the genre of the bestiary in order to revitalize pre-Hispanic legends and to take up some of the philosophical questions that fascinated writers of medieval bestiaries, including the nature of language (human and nonhuman) and the relationship between humans and other species in a world of close interaction and reciprocity. The second part examines bestiaries published by the Chilean artist Claudio Romo Torres, including *Bestiario: Animales reales fantásticos* (with texts by Juan Nicolás Padrón, 2008) and *Bestiario mexicano* (written and illustrated by Romo, 2018). Romo's books resurrect the fabulous beasts described by mediaeval and early modern writers and explorers, adding new variants of his own. They reflect on the exclusions on which European conceptions of modernity and civilization are founded and explore an alternative modernity that is ordered around the plural ontologies of Mesoamerican cosmologies. In the third part, I discuss two series created by the Brazilian artist Walmor Corrêa, *Natureza perversa* (2003) and *Unheimlich, imaginário popular brasileiro* (2005). These

---

5   The chapter titles are taken from the English version of the book, translated by Norman Thomas Di Giovanni. Borges and Guerrero, *The Book of Imaginary Beings*.
6   Yelin, *La letra salvaje*, 15. Among the writers whose novels and short stories form Yelin's corpus are Jorge Luis Borges, Silvina Ocampo, Clarice Lispector, Juan José Arreola, João Guimarães Rosa, Augusto Monterroso, and Wilson Bueno.

portray fantastical animal figures from early colonial accounts and indigenous legends with anatomical precision, reinserting the fabulous, the folkloric, and the popular into the visual idiom of modern Western science. Corrêa's (re)invention of hybrids and cryptids challenges the separation of modern science from popular forms of knowledge and experience, and reappropriates colonial fantasies in order to re-enchant the natural world.

My approach to these texts is guided by a hypothesis: that the bestiary has acquired a new relevance in the twenty-first century in the context of the ecological and existential crisis that pervades the technologically developed, urbanized, globalized world. If the mediaeval bestiary promoted a view of the universe that was intimately interconnected, recent research in biology and ecology has similarly demonstrated the complex interdependence of species and their environments, countering the greater emphasis on individual species in nineteenth- and twentieth-century zoology. We now understand that both signification and knowledge are cognitively and affectively embedded in material environments. At a time when city dwellers have never been more estranged from animals, we are beginning to grasp in a deeper way how integrated our own lives are with those of other species, and how reliant our wellbeing is on their continued existence. Modern-day bestiaries—such as those composed by Toriz and Cano, Romo, and Corrêa—challenge us to question received ideas about human exceptionalism and to imagine our role in a post-anthropocentric era of greater cooperation between different species. They also contest dominant images of an exhausted, frail nature, pointing to the need to re-enchant nature, following its wholesale rationalization and commodification in Western modernity. The popular and indigenous myths that these bestiaries revive and mobilize are not confined to the past or to a timeless present, but actively illuminate the historical and ongoing consequences of colonialism and global capitalism on human and nonhuman animals.

Animalia: The Case for Anthropomorphism in an Age of Mass Extinction

A compendium of short texts, *Animalia* recalls the eclecticism of many mediaeval bestiaries: it includes not only animals—real, extinct, or imaginary—but also philosophers (Cratylus), figures of speech (the *metáfora*), and metaphysical entities (such as the *cronotopo*, which digs immense holes connecting time and space). Like earlier composers of bestiaries, Rafael Toriz supports his observations with citations from Pliny, Aelian, Isidore of Seville, and other authorities of the ancient world. To these he adds several (mostly Latin American) authors to the canon, such as Jorge Luis Borges, Horacio Quiroga, and Julio Cortázar, as well as other sources of knowledge, including Mesoamerican folklore and contemporary neurobiology. Structured on a principle of diversity, the bestiary typically deals with singularities rather than systems; the fragments from which it is composed do not obey a sequential logic. Toriz's aim was to create a similarly diverse space that would accommodate the *transgenérico*, crossing genres and genders.[7]

Appropriately, Édgar Cano's accompanying illustrations do not set real animals apart from legendary ones. Many of the figures are given a dense materiality, unlike the flattened images that adorned the manuscripts of illustrated mediaeval bestiaries or the airy, transparent sketches by Héctor Xavier that accompanied Arreola's *Punta de plata*, perhaps the most important precursor to *Animalia* in the modern Mexican context. The effect of density results from the use of lithography in most of the images to print a heavy, dark background tint, which contrasts with the lighter lines and textures drawn onto the plate. This technique lends a solid verisimilitude to animals that are often described in more mystical or metaphysical terms, such as the *cronotopo* (see Fig. 1.1). These are not naturalistic drawings of the kind one might find in a zoology book, however. While some animal forms are represented with greater precision, starkly figured against a plain background, others emerge as smudges from hazy textures or appear grainy, as if they were images of objects seen through a microscope.

---

7   Luna, "La voz interrogada," 3.

Fig. 1.1 Édgar Cano, 'Cronotopo' from *Animalia*, written by Rafael Toriz and illustrated by Édgar Cano (Mexico City: Vanilla Planifolia, 2015), 15.

Like many bestiaries—especially those that drew extensively on Isidore of Seville's seventh-century *Etymologies*—*Animalia* presents a philosophy of language as well as an account of the natural and spiritual worlds. The inclusion of Cratylus, whose description is falsely ascribed to the *Aberdeen Bestiary*, the *Historia Animalium*, and other ancient texts, brings to the fore the debates over language referenced in *Animalia*. Plato's Cratylus adopts a position of extreme naturalism, claiming that "he who knows names knows also the things which are expressed by them," or in other words, that language faithfully names the essence of things and is not arbitrary.[8] This was the belief that led writers of bestiaries to preface their descriptions with an analysis of the linguistic origins of the animal's name, which encoded the essence of the animal's character and behaviour: to turn to etymology as a source of zoological knowledge.

---

8   Plato, *Cratylus*.

1. Bestiaries and the Art of Cryptozoology　31

Toriz generally parodies the view that human language can tell us something important about animal experience, focusing instead on what animal experience can tell us about human language. In his text on the crocodile, he cites recent research by the neuroscientist Daphne Soares on the pigmented nodules to be found on the skin of some crocodile species. These have been shown to act as sensory organs, allowing the crocodile to detect the presence of a potential meal causing ripples in the water.[9] In *Animalia*, the crocodile informs us that his sensors are not only used for hunting; when the night is beautiful and the waters calm, they also emit a delicate chamber music. Importantly, the crocodile reflects that "*Al igual que los hombres,* mi cuerpo se torna en el primer y último umbral de la significación" (*Just as for humans,* my body becomes the first and last threshold of signification).[10] The act of creating meaning does not take place in a rational mind that is divisible from embodied experience; like all animals, we communicate and understand through our bodies.

A similar reminder of our animal nature comes in Toriz's assertion that "somos descendientes directos del extincto iguanodon y primas terceras de los arcosaurios. Quien mira con detenimiento, observa en nuestro cuerpo el pasado fascinante del planeta" (we are direct descendants of the extinct iguanodon and third cousins of the archosaurs. Whoever looks carefully will observe in our body the fascinating past of the planet).[11] It is an image fit for a post-anthropocentric sensibility, in which human exceptionalism dissolves as we are reminded of our reptilian heritage. As if to emphasize the common ancestry of all mammals and reptiles, Cano's illustrations are notably serpentine, with coiled tails and writhing bodies; even the giraffe's long neck is looped snake-like around its feet (see Fig. 1.2). The absence of colour in these greyscale images—save for a vivid red colour wash on some pages—focuses the eye on the textures they create. Although the illustrations are printed in their entirety in a small format at the back of the book, within its pages we are often only shown an enlarged detail from each, with the images exceeding the margins of the page. This draws us into a close encounter with coarse, wrinkled, scaly, bristly skins.

9　Soares, "An Ancient Sensory Organ in Crocodilians."
10　Toriz and Cano, *Animalia*, 16; my emphasis.
11　Toriz and Cano, 13. Most scientists hold that mammals are not direct descendents of dinosaurs but that we share a common ancestor.

Fig. 1.2 Édgar Cano, 'La jirafa' from *Animalia*, written by Rafael Toriz and illustrated by Édgar Cano (Mexico City: Vanilla Planifolia, 2015), 17.

In classical and medieval times, the bestiary offered explanations of the world in which animals became metaphors for broader natural or divine forces and exemplars in the teaching of morality, such as the swan that holds its neck high "like a proud man drawn along by the vanity of the world."[12] Human qualities of wisdom, timidity, or courage were ascribed to animals in the writings of ancient philosophers that formed the inspiration for many medieval bestiaries. Toriz comically exaggerates the anthropomorphic tendencies of these texts: his wasp, for example, is a brilliant catechist who knows his Seneca well and preaches God's word wherever he can. We have grown suspicious in more recent times of the anthropomorphism that animates so many of our metaphors. In his essay on the alterity of the animal, Derrida asserts that fables should be avoided, as "We know the history of fabulation and how it remains an anthropomorphic taming, a moralizing subjection, a domestication.

---

12 Barber, *Bestiary* [MS Bodley 764], 135.

Always a discourse of man, on man, indeed on the animality of man, but for and as man."[13] A deeply human-centred perspective certainly informs the claim in a thirteenth-century bestiary known as *MS Bodley 764* that nature "brings forth creatures [...] to instruct us and confirm us in the faith."[14]

For John Berger, however, the anthropomorphism of metaphors and fables was an expression of the imbrication of our everyday lives with those of animals. He argues that until the nineteenth century, "animals constituted the first circle of what surrounded man."[15] As a result of this close proximity with animals, "The first subject matter for painting was animal. Probably the first paint was animal blood. Prior to that, it is not unreasonable to suppose that the first metaphor was animal."[16] It was to animals that humans looked for explanations, and animals "lent their name or character" to the qualities of a mysterious world.[17] Until the nineteenth century, anthropomorphism was "integral to the relation between man and animal and was an expression of their proximity."[18] Since the advance of industrial capitalism, however, animals have disappeared from our world, and in this new separation from them, Berger finds that "anthropomorphism makes us doubly uneasy."[19]

In many contemporary bestiaries, Toriz's among them, anthropomorphic techniques are used to re-entwine those human and animal lives that have become estranged through modernization. In the tangled web of correspondences woven in mediaeval bestiaries, however, humans and animals were bound not only by the anthropomorphic but also by the zoomorphic. A figure common to many texts was the honest working woman who imitates the nightingale in her diligent devotion to her children.[20] The zoomorphic also shapes texts in *Animalia*: maenads (the female followers of Dionysius) are described as "animales altamente sociables" (highly sociable animals) but also as sexually voracious flesh-eating hunters.[21] Cano's illustrations draw attention to

---

13   Derrida, "The Animal That Therefore I Am (More to Follow)," 405.
14   Barber, *Bestiary* [*MS Bodley 764*], 121.
15   Berger, *About Looking*, 3.
16   Berger, 7.
17   Berger, 8–9.
18   Berger, 11.
19   Berger, 11.
20   See Barber, *Bestiary* [*MS Bodley 764*], 158; White, *The Book of Beasts*, 140.
21   Toriz and Cano, *Animalia*, 72.

the centrality of animals in human culture and art since ancient times by representing animals as if they had already been inscribed in other forms of media, often painting or sculpture. Some illustrations make use of pointillist effects or evoke the fluidity of water colours, while the darkened tones of many of his images recall the begrimed folds and façades of aged statues or engraving; indeed, the *ahuizotl* is depicted as if it were an Aztec stone sculpture (see Fig. 1.3). This technique of remediation points simultaneously to an absence: these illustrations are images of images that merely evoke the animals they substitute.

Fig. 1.3 Édgar Cano, 'Ahuizotl' from *Animalia*, written by Rafael Toriz and illustrated by Édgar Cano (Mexico City: Vanilla Planifolia, 2015), 76.

Throughout *Animalia*, Toriz describes a natural world—like that of the mediaeval bestiary—that is shaped by myriad imitations and correspondences to such a degree that the essence and character of all animals, including humans, is intensely relational. This means that the loss of a species is not a footnote in the history of evolution but a diminishment of the sensory, cognitive, or affective experience of other species. Toriz expresses this idea in a compelling way in an entry on the *macaco muriquí* (woolly spider monkey), the name given to two species of the largest primate in South America, both now endangered, largely as a result of hunting and deforestation in Brazil. In a playfully alliterative text, Toriz addresses the monkey:

> Mientras mucho masculles más modelas mi memoria. [...] Mejor, mientras mantengas momentos memorables (maravillosos) mantendremos moderados mares, moluscos minúsculos, manifiestos malthusianistas.[22] Mirado minuciosamente, mientras mucho masculles, mejor mundo moramos.[23]

> Your many mutterings mould my memory. [...] Better said, while you maintain memorable (marvellous) moments we will maintain moderate seas, miniscule molluscs, Malthusian manifestos. Monitored meticulously, while you mutter, we dwell in a better world.

Toriz's text follows a poetic logic here rather than a strictly ecological one, of course, but it does convey the interdependence of a world in which the preservation of forests has a direct impact on sea levels. The monkey is described here as moulding human memory in a way that suggests that our cognitive processes are not independent of our relationship with other species.

Until new forms of classification emerged in the seventeenth century, animals tended to be described and categorized with reference to humans: according to their usefulness (for food or medicine) or their value as moral symbols. In his work on changing relationships with the natural world in early modern England, Keith Thomas suggests that the symbolism attached to animals and plants was tied to "the ancient assumption that man and nature were locked into one interacting world." The myriad "analogies and correspondences between the species" meant that "human fortunes could be sympathetically expressed, influenced,

---

22 Today, neo-Malthusianism often takes the form of advocating for population control to limit environmental damage and to protect resources for other species as well as humans.
23 Toriz and Cano, *Animalia*, 18.

and even foretold by plants, birds and animals."[24] In contrast, the new systems of classification developed in the seventeenth and eighteenth century epitomized a new form of looking at things that was "more detached, more objective, less man-centred than that of the past."[25] We are becoming acutely aware of the cost of this detachment, however. In privileging structure over function and separating out objects of study from their place within a complex ecology, modern taxonomies record nothing of the central role that animals have played in shaping human language and experience until very recent times. In this context, *Animalia*—like many other contemporary bestiaries—revives that vision of an interacting world whose importance we are beginning to grasp again.

This world is not devoid of conflict. Toriz's animals do not only live in close relationship with humans but also threaten us, penetrating our bodies to bury themselves in our flesh to live inside us or to reproduce. Toriz builds on the ancient legend of the *rémora* (a suckerfish), thought to attach itself to boats to slow them down. He creates a rather more intimate and sinister variant, claiming that postmortems have revealed that uncaring men live with a tiny *rémora* lodged near the heart. He also replays the myth of the *tlaconete*, in appearance rather like a salamander, which invades unsuspecting women who bathe in the river to lay its eggs in their entrails. In a humorous tone, he warns the reader of the dangers of an escaped *axolotl* armed with large-calibre weapons, a knowledge of terrorist tactics, and a deep-rooted class consciousness.[26]

The many legends in *Animalia* that cast animals as threats to humans seem oddly quaint in an age of mass anthropogenic extinction. (We may note that most species of *tlaconete* found in Mexico are at risk and the *axolotl* is critically endangered.) *Animalia* takes us back to the worldview

---

24 Thomas, *Man and the Natural World*, 75.
25 Thomas, 52.
26 Here Toriz makes ludic reference to the presence of the *axolotl* in previous literary works, in which the creature becomes emblematic of Mexican identity. Echoing the *axolotl*'s description in Bernardino de Sahagún's *Historia general de las cosas de Nueva España*, which emphasizes its biological and sexual ambiguity, Octavio Paz explores in his poem *Salamandra* (1962) the creature's doubling and self-transforming qualities, which also arise from the contradictory legends surrounding the god Xólotl in Aztec mythology. For José Emilio Pacheco in *El reposo del fuego* (1966), the *axolotl* "es nuestro emblema. Encarna / el temor de no ser nadie" (is our emblem. It embodies / the fear of being nobody). *El reposo del fuego*, 48.

of the mediaeval bestiary in which species were engaged in continual battles of wit and might with each other in a world designed to produce a parity of forces. In this world, humans were both the hunters and the hunted. Toriz's description of the hyena, an animal that lives close to cemeteries and deceives humans with its calls for help only to devour them, closely follows the account given in many mediaeval texts, including *MS Bodley 764*. This manuscript is typical of bestiaries of its time in its depiction of a certain kind of harmony that results from a balance of power: "For the Creator of all things has made nothing for which there is not an antidote."[27] Toriz creates a world that is similarly sustained by "el equilibrio de las especies" (the balance between species) and in which humans are not necessarily dominant.[28] He invents the *dongui*, a species more powerful than humans, that will spread across the world in a similar wave of urbanization (Paris, London, New York) with the aim of eradicating humans and their customs.[29] To reimagine an era when animals presented a threat to humans becomes an act of nostalgia or of consolation, perhaps, at a time when our actions are fast producing their disappearance.

Indeed, many of Toriz's animals speak to us from the other side of death, bearing witness to their own extinction as well as to human acts of violence against fellow humans. The *ahuizotl* is a legendary creature from Aztec mythology, rather like a dog, who lived on the edge of the lake and drew people to watery deaths. According to some versions, the *ahuizotl* is the guardian of the fish in the lake. In Toriz's work, the *ahuizotl* becomes an eye-witness to the burning of the "purest civilization," the city on the lake, and the deadly advance of a skin disease among its inhabitants. The reference here is to the conquest of Tenochtitlán (now the site of Mexico City) by Cortés and his men, and the epidemic of smallpox they unleashed. The last of the *ahuizotl* species dies drinking from the poisoned lake, having seen the city in flames and its temples awash with blood. Toriz's rewriting of the myth of the *ahuizotl* thus highlights the historical relationship between colonialism, violence, and ecological destruction.

---

27 Barber, *Bestiary* [*MS Bodley 764*], 184.
28 Toriz and Cano, *Animalia*, 28.
29 Toriz and Cano, 43.

The final image in *Animalia* is a blank page, cut away at the foot to reveal the image of a page from another book (see Fig. 1.4). It is fitting that this highly intertextual bestiary should end with the reproduction of a book by another writer. The author in question is Julio Cortázar, and the text duplicated is from "Polonia y El Salvador: Mayúsculas y minúsculas" (1982). In this essay, Cortázar criticizes the support given by the US to the Salvadoran army, which facilitated even greater violence toward civilians during the Civil War that had started in 1979. He also denounces the little attention paid in the international media to the thousands of deaths and disappearances that were taking place as a result of the conflict. To learn anything about the role of the US in the violence, he laments, "hay que buscar casi al pie de una página interior hasta encontrar algún eco de ese genocidio infinitamente monstruoso" (one has to look almost at the bottom of an inside page to find any mention of that infinitely monstrous genocide).[30] This is the phrase that Toriz allows us to glimpse, partially, behind the page of his own book. The veiled epilogue gives us pause to reflect. What is the truly monstrous here? Hidden, perhaps, in the inside pages of his own text? Amid the various duplicitous and deadly creatures he describes, it is clear that none is capable of the genocide unleashed by Hernán Cortés and his allies in the conquest of Cholula and Tenochtitlán, nor of the ecological and cultural destruction that ensued in the valley of Mexico.[31] *Animalia* harks back to the vibrant imagery of the mediaeval bestiary and its world of signs and wonders. But it is also a text for our own time, one that is increasingly and painfully aware of the terrible cost of our physical, spiritual, cognitive, and affective separation from animals and the rest of the natural world, and how that separation has been sealed with the violence of colonialism and global capitalism.

Claudio Romo: Correspondences and Co-Essences, Myths and Metamorphs

Claudio Romo's illustrated texts evoke the myriad compendia and cabinets of curiosities in which marvels of the natural world were

---

30 Cortázar, "Polonia y El Salvador," 333.
31 On the ecological consequences of the conquest of Mexico, see Melville, *A Plague of Sheep*.

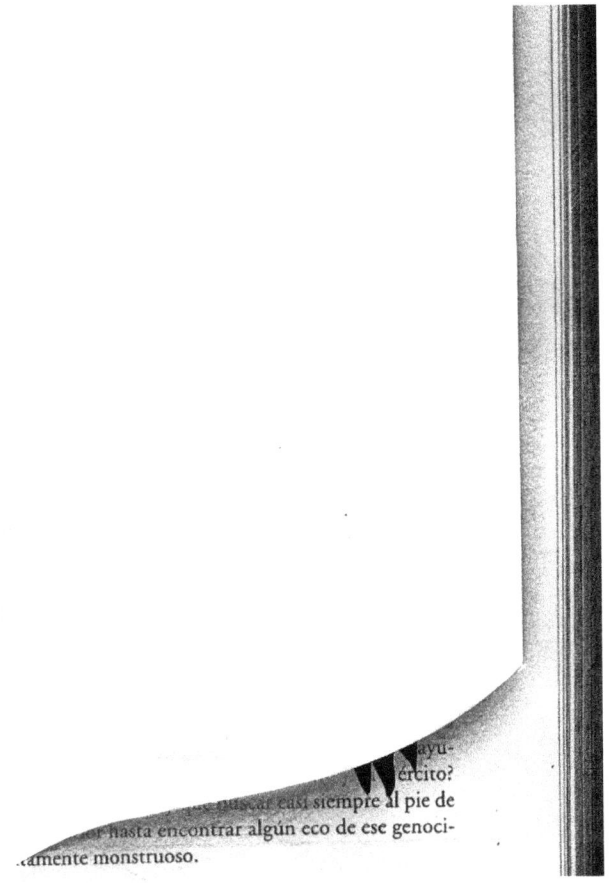

Fig. 1.4 Édgar Cano, 'Merovingio' from *Animalia*, written by Rafael Toriz and illustrated by Édgar Cano (Mexico City: Vanilla Planifolia, 2015), 91.

brought together before the more systematized collections of the Enlightenment period. *Bestiario: Animales reales fantásticos* (Bestiary: Fantastic Real Animals, 2008), a collaboration with the Cuban poet and essayist Juan Nicolás Padrón, is an anthology of legendary beasts and monsters associated with both the Old and the New Worlds. Like Borges's *El libro de los seres imaginarios*, Padrón's texts give prominence to mythology over morality. Padrón and Romo emphasize the diversity of imagined animals, but also point to their capacity to cross boundaries of language, culture, and religion, turning up in slightly different guises over the centuries, as if there were certain constants in the monsters that humans have invented. But the continual translation of these creatures between the animal, vegetable, and mineral realms, between the natural and supernatural worlds, and between different cultures, creates a world that is ontologically plural, dynamic, and relational.

In the mediaeval bestiary, the correspondences that governed the natural world did not only allow animal behaviour to be infused with moral significance; they also emphasized the profound interconnections between living and non-living things that were evidenced in visual analogy. Natural entities often had "physical counterparts" in another stratum of life.[32] Until the end of the sixteenth century, as Foucault explains, emulation expressed "a sort of natural twinship existing in things."[33] Such correspondences still animated the descriptions to be found in early chronicles of the New World. In his monumental *Historia natural y moral de las Indias* (1590), José de Acosta observes that "así como los metales son como plantas ocultas de la tierra, así también podemos decir que las plantas son como animales fijos en un lugar" (just as minerals are the hidden plants of the earth, so we can also say that plants are like animals fixed in one place).[34] This principle of analogy, through which "all the figures in the whole universe can be drawn together,"[35] is everywhere evident in the texts and illustrations of *Bestiario: Animales reales fantásticos*. When it is immobile, for example, we are told that the *aplanador* (rather like an elephant) can easily be confused with an enormous mossy rock. The entanglement of plant, animal, and mineral kingdoms is heightened in many of Romo's illustrations: the unicorn's horn appears as a thorny stem with roses emerging from it, and the form of the mandrake root replicates in minute detail the human digestive system and reproductive organs. This emulation is taken to an extreme by the Gigantic Sloth, which climbs so slowly that its fur fuses with the bark and tendrils of a tree (see Fig. 1.5); for this reason, "podría considerarse una prolongación de los centenarios árboles que abundan en los más intrincados lugares de la Amazonia" (it could be considered an extension of the centenarian trees that abound in the most impassable places of the Amazon).[36]

---

32 White, *The Book of Beasts*, 245.
33 Foucault, *The Order of Things*, 19–20.
34 Acosta, *Historia natural y moral de las Indias*, 97.
35 Foucault, *The Order of Things*, 22.
36 Padrón and Romo, *Bestiario: Animales reales fantásticos*, 49.

Fig. 1.5 Claudio Andrés Salvador Francisco Romo Torres, 'El perezoso' (detail) from *Bestiario: Animales reales fantásticos,* written by Juan Nicolás Padrón and illustrated by Claudio Andrés Salvador Francisco Romo Torres (Santiago: LOM Ediciones, 2008), 48.

In *Bestiario: Animales reales fantásticos,* American creatures (real and legendary) such as the glyptodon, the megatherium, the axolotl, and the plumed serpent Quetzalcoatl are slipped in alongside sirens and satyrs, much in the way that Amerindian legends were worked into Baroque friezes in the New World. Another work authored and illustrated by Romo, *Bestiario mexicano* (Mexican Bestiary, 2018), develops a more explicit critique of coloniality and modernity through the presentation of a series of mythical Mayan creatures. Romo has little interest in excavating these myths to find the most authentic versions; instead, he draws attention to how myths are transformed or hybridized as a consequence of intercultural contact, and even how different mythical figures within the same cultural tradition swap attributes or merge with each other over time. Mayan monsters—like those everywhere—become a sign that refers to "the incessantly changing nature of reality, perceived as proteiform, metamorphic and never fully knowable."[37]

---

37 Romo Torres, *Bestiario mexicano,* 45.

Bestiario mexicano outlines a critique of the exclusions of Western modernity. Romo draws out the similarities between European paganism and Mesoamerican mythology: both are built on the "fusion" of the human world with the animal kingdom that is rejected in the more hierarchical conception of the cosmos inherent in Jewish and Christian traditions.[38] The myth of the "wild man," known in the Yucatán as the *sinsimito* (or the *sisimito* or the *sisimite*), is described by Romo as "foundational" because it represents "the perfect summary of the animality that we wanted to leave behind": the barbarism that we rejected "once we had crossed the frontier between the state of nature and that of culture, once we had built the walls of the City."[39] It is a myth that represents the dark side of modernity: the scapegoats that are repressed and excised in order to erect a divide between nature and culture, allowing certain groups to project a view of themselves as more rational, scientific, and civilized. Nature and culture are however confounded here in Romo's depiction of the hairy *sinsimito* as well-groomed, adorned with the "sumptuous and elaborate hairstyles" that had once been adopted by ancient inhabitants of the region, together with the stone jewels worn by its victims (see Fig. 1.6).[40]

Aníbal Quijano identifies the opposition between the state of nature and the state of civilization as the founding myth upon which Eurocentric narratives of modernity have been built. This myth gives rise to a belief in the unilinear nature of change and progress across human history, and enables Europeans to position themselves at the apex of civilization and to reorganize time, to such an extent that "todo lo no-europeo es percibido como pasado" (everything non-European is perceived as the past).[41] It is this conception of time that allows some societies to be depicted as backward, with their beliefs dismissed as irrational and irrelevant to the modern world. In contrast, myths and local beliefs in Romo's *Bestiario mexicano* are manifestly not relegated to a past that has been superseded by modernity, but exist with and within modernity.

The text describing the *aluxe* provides a clear example. Romo tracks recent claims of the continued activity of these impish demons in

---

38 Cenzi, "La natura del mostro," 4.
39 Romo Torres, *Bestiario mexicano*, 8, 10.
40 Romo Torres, 6.
41 Quijano, "Colonialidad del poder, eurocentrismo y América Latina," 220, 222.

Fig. 1.6 Claudio Andrés Salvador Francisco Romo Torres, 'Sinsimito' from *Bestiario mexicano*, trans. Federico Taibi (Modena: Logosedizione, 2018), 9.

Mexico today. In 2010, when the pop star Elton John was to perform at the ancient Mayan site of Chichén Itzá, part of the stage collapsed the day before the concert, injuring three technicians. Romo observes that the organizers had failed to ingratiate themselves with the *aluxe*. This was, in fact, the explanation given at the time by local Mayan leaders who considered the concert to be an irreverent and inappropriate use of sacred ruins for private profit, with ticket prices aimed at global elites.[42] Significantly, Romo notes that the importance of the *aluxe* in Mayan culture was strengthened with the arrival of the monotheistic Spanish, and that some ethnologists have suspected that they were "imported" by English colonists and pirates, only later to be adopted in indigenous mythology.[43] For this reason, the *aluxe* may not be considered antithetical

---

42 Gordon, "Elton John Concert at Chichen Itza Encounters Opposition."
43 Romo Torres, *Bestiario mexicano*, 18.

to modernity so much as a product of the capitalist-colonialist enterprise of modernity itself. Certainly, current-day *aluxe* in Romo's account have a clear role in drawing attention to cultural (mis)appropriation and structural inequality, helping to define the cultural and social injustices that have been exacerbated by contemporary forms of globalization and neocolonialism. The deployment of mythical Mayan figures as agents in this way opens up the possibility of alternative modernities that are more pluralistic.

Romo presents Mesoamerican ontologies as much more complex and integrated than European ones, particularly in their subtle understanding of the fluidity of relations between humans and nature, and between the natural and the supernatural, terms held rigidly apart in modern European thought since the Enlightenment. This is most clearly evident in the concept of the co-essence, which, Romo explains, is an animal or a celestial phenomenon (such as rain, lightning, or wind) that shares the consciousness of its owner. Such myths bear witness to "the inherent complexity of the Mesoamerican vision of the world, of the innumerable presences that inhabit it, of man himself understood as an integral part of this crowded natural and supernatural space."[44]

This vision of a world in which humans are fully woven into a plural reality, integrated with the natural and supernatural rather than separated from them, is also expressed in the modes of illustration employed by Romo, which continually cross divides between nature and art, nature and technology, myth and modernity. Highly textured, precise line-drawings of each mythical animal in *Bestiario mexicano* make use of techniques of hatching and cross-hatching that were common in early forms of printmaking (in etchings and engravings) and in some scientific illustrations (see Fig. 1.7). These techniques contrast with others that might be found in fantasy graphic novels, children's literature, and other forms of popular art, with rich colours and simple, whimsical designs. The depictions of creatures switch easily between the natural, the cultural, and the mechanical: the *waay pop*, a man who is able to transform himself into a bird, is shown first as a man with wings clearly strapped onto his back and a beak-shaped helmet (see Fig. 1.8); then as the static, stylized representation of a mythical figure, next as a being that genuinely seems to combine characteristics of a man and a bird, and finally fully transformed into a bird. The illustrations thus

---

44 Romo Torres, 45.

Fig. 1.7 Claudio Andrés Salvador Francisco Romo Torres, 'Waay Pop' from *Bestiario mexicano*, trans. Federico Taibi (Modena: Logosedizione, 2018), 37.

Fig. 1.8 Claudio Andrés Salvador Francisco Romo Torres, 'Waay Pop' from *Bestiario mexicano*, trans. Federico Taibi (Modena: Logosedizione, 2018), 38.

encode the ontological ambiguity of the *waay pop* and other co-essences: are these full metamorphoses in which one being is transformed into another, the acquisition of certain characteristics, or simply the donning of a disguise?

Transformations and exchanges in Romo's work often illustrate Amerindian concepts of the relationship between human and nonhuman animals. As the anthropologist Eduardo Viveiros de Castro explains, while Western cosmologies are founded on a "physical continuity" between human and nonhuman bodies (we are all made of the same organic stuff) and a "metaphysical discontinuity" (only humans have spirits or minds), in Amerindian cultures, the reverse is the case. Humans and other beings in the cosmos share the same spiritual nature, while our bodies are what distinguish us.[45] This means that "the animal clothes that shamans or sorcerers use to travel the cosmos are not fantasies but instruments: they are akin to diving equipment, or space suits, and not to carnival masks." The function of animal masks and other clothing is thus not to conceal, to disguise oneself, but to take on the "affects and capacities which define each animal."[46] Romo's illustrations clearly show this dynamic at work, as human wearers of masks and other coverings are not intending to hide their humanness, but to take on the functions and perspectives of other beings.

If myths may (re)animate our world and even articulate critical visions, however, they may also draw a convenient veil over the human origin of violence and destruction by furnishing these with a supernatural explanation. We are told in *Bestiario: Animales reales fantásticos* that the electric eel is responsible for a good number of fires that ravage the Amazon, and that when trees disappear in the forests of South America, the megatherium cannot be far away. Given our knowledge of the real causes of deforestation in the region, these suppositions are highly ironic. *Bestiario* closes with the statement that humanity was created by Quetzalcoatl, the feathered serpent, whose need for human blood explains "tantos desastres" (so many disasters).[47] This submission of human destiny to the will of animals (real or supernatural) affords

---

45 Viveiros de Castro, *The Relative Native*, 260.
46 Viveiros de Castro, 278.
47 Padrón and Romo, *Bestiario: Animales reales fantásticos*, 70.

an alternative perspective on the anthropocentrism of our own era, however, which is nowhere more evident than in our ready assumption of guilt for all forms of ecological change and our self-appointed role as guardians of the future planet. Tim Ingold reminds us:

> a premise of totemic belief and cult is that it was the animals who made the world for man, who originally laid down the order and design of human social existence, and who are ultimately responsible for its continuation. The Western cult of conservation precisely inverts this premise, proclaiming that from now on it shall be man who determines the conditions of life for animals (even those still technically wild shall be "managed"), and who shoulders the responsibility for their survival or extinction.[48]

Undoubtedly wild and beyond our management, the animals of Romo's bestiaries retain much of the agency of which they have been stripped in modern Western imaginaries. They challenge a belief in human supremacy that has caused great damage to the natural world and that continues to underpin our attempts to rescue it.

Walmor Corrêa: Cryptozoology for a Disenchanted World

The legendary beasts created in Walmor Corrêa's artistic projects are often inspired by the letters and chronicles written by sixteenth-century European travellers and missionaries to Brazil. Corrêa's reinsertion of Brazilian popular and indigenous imaginaries within modern scientific modes of illustration mischievously elevates the folkloric and the fantastic, which have been systematically excluded from the canons of modern European knowledge since the Enlightenment. His bestiaries, full of hybrid beings and cryptids old and new, may be read as parodies of the taxonomic and anatomical zeal of eighteenth-century Western science, but also as a more serious attempt to reweave different forms of knowledge together and to recapture a sense of the marvellous that animates early colonial accounts of the New World, sorely needed in a disenchanted modern era.

---

48 Ingold, "Introduction," 12.

In his work, Corrêa has been particularly drawn to the letters of Padre José de Anchieta, a Jesuit missionary who spent several decades evangelizing the Indian population of Brazil in the second half of the sixteenth century. Anchieta is credited with being one of the founders of São Paulo and Rio de Janeiro; he was also a pioneering linguist, ethnographer, and naturalist. In the Jesuit tradition of report-writing, he sent exhaustively detailed letters to his superiors on the customs of indigenous communities and the flora and fauna of Brazil. Corrêa cites one such epistle, the *Carta de São Vicente* (1560), as the motivation for many of his artistic works. Anchieta's account in this letter of a journey into the Mata Atlântica, the forest that extends along Brazil's Atlantic coast, is a pre-Enlightenment medley of methodical observations and fabulous tales. He pays close attention to the animals he encounters—in folktales and in the flesh—and attempts to systematize his knowledge, roughly grouping species together according to their type or habitat.

Maria Esther Maciel finds that such syntheses of animal knowledge in the Renaissance were typically a jumble of precise descriptions, arbitrary classifications, citations, fables, myths, and observations about the possible uses of animals in both medicine and magic, in which new forms of classification—still very much in formation—had not erased a lively interest in the fabulous as explored in the mediaeval bestiary or the zoological findings of natural philosophers from antiquity.[49] Like these, Anchieta's texts were written in an era in which knowledge of the natural and supernatural worlds came from much more diverse sources, and in which marvels were a proper object for scientific exploration, not the target of suspicion.

Having survived the adversities of a stormy sea passage and evaded the attention of diverse and deadly snakes, Anchieta musters a range of superlatives to account for the new and wondrous animals he encounters, which boast the sharpest nails or teeth, the stoutest legs, or the tastiest flesh. Unlike his eighteenth-century successors, who would catalogue species according to European classification systems, Anchieta prefers to use local Indian names. While accounts of scientific expeditions in the later colonial period extracted species from their natural, social, and cultural environments, focusing primarily on their commercial potential for Europe, Anchieta describes the uses the Indians found for each

---

49   Maciel, "Imagens zoológicas da América Latina," 90.

animal: often to eat, but also to make belts or shields, or to incite sexual pleasure. He displays an evident admiration for indigenous medicine and hunting and fishing techniques.

Recognizing that some of the extraordinary incidents he relates may stretch his readers' credulity, Anchieta insists at several points that he and his Jesuit brothers have witnessed them at first hand. An Indian cure for ulcers has been "provado com experiência" (demonstrated by experience); likewise, a snake so huge that it may easily swallow a deer is "observado por todos" (observed by all).[50] The same claims are made about phenomena that stray into the realm of the supernatural. Although Anchieta and his Jesuit brothers attempt to convert the Indians they meet to the Christian faith, they give at least partial credence to local beliefs concerning demons, or strange beasts that threaten them. "É cousa sabida e pela bôca corre" (it is a well-known fact and on everyone's lips) that the Indians are whipped and beaten to death by *corupiras*, and Anchieta affirms that his brothers can testify to this, having seen several Indians killed by them in this way.[51] Equally murderous are the water-dwelling *igpupiáras*, who drowned many members of an Indian community before Christians moved into the area. Indeed, Anchieta believes these monsters to be nothing less than incarnations of the Devil, who oppresses those who do not know God with "cruel tirania" (cruel tyranny) of this kind.[52]

The physical features of the dreaded *igpupiára* and *corupira* (or *curupira*, as it is more commonly known) are not described by Anchieta. Both creatures are minutely portrayed, however, in Corrêa's series *Unheimlich, imaginário popular brasileiro* (Unhomely, Popular Brazilian Imaginary, 2005), alongside other monsters and hybrids that live on in Brazilian folklore and popular culture.[53] In creating these works, Corrêa turned to another important intertext, Luís da Câmara Cascudo's *Geografia dos mitos brasileiros* (1947). He represents the *curupira* in one of the regional versions detailed by da Câmara Cascudo, with its feet

---

50   Anchieta, *Carta de São Vicente 1560*, 19, 17.
51   Anchieta, 34.
52   Anchieta, 35.
53   The full series was first exhibited in 2006 as part of the *Cryptozoology—Out of Time Place Scale* exhibition at the Bates College Museum of Art (Lewiston, Maine) and the H&R Block Artspace at the Kansas City Art Institute (Missouri), curated by Mark Bessire and Raechell Smith.

facing backwards, one eye and no anus (see Fig. 1.9).[54] The figures in the *Unheimlich* series are depicted as they might be presented in an anatomy textbook. A large frontal view of the body dominates a plain white background, often with part of the torso pulled back to show the inner organs or a limb shown without skin to reveal joints and muscles. This central figure is flanked by smaller illustrations in multiple projections, showing details of anatomical structures, each labelled in meticulous handwriting. In this way, Corrêa treats his chimerical creatures with the gravity of a scientific treatise, lending them veracity through anatomical precision.

It has become a commonplace to assert that monsters are often ciphers for that which threatens ontological boundaries and confounds the neat ordering of classification systems.[55] In Corrêa's annotated illustrations, in contrast, science steps up to the challenge of analysing the fantastical. Noting some of the anatomical features that the *capelobo* shares with humans, the written descriptions point to the limited rotation of the head on the neck, given the elongated form of the *capelobo*'s cranium, and explain how the jaw moves to accommodate food when eating.[56] In his description of the amphibian *ipupiara*,[57] Corrêa notes the flexible skeleton but adds coyly that details of the articulation of the flipper will be better understood when it has been properly dissected. To develop his work on the *ondina* (siren), Corrêa consulted medical specialists to explore the possible anatomy of a mermaid.[58] How would its body be able to withstand the higher pressures of deep water? What would its foetus look like? He adds gills behind the ears, near the carotid arteries, to allow the hyperoxygenation of blood flowing to the brain while the siren is below water, and adapts the eye for lower levels of light, removing tear glands as the cornea would be continually washed with water.

Corrêa's *Unheimlich* series therefore takes to an extreme the transcultural and transdisciplinary elements of Anchieta's text, finding

---

55 See, for example, Cohen, "Monster Culture (Seven Theses)," 7.
56 The *capelobo* is given a human frame here, with the long snout of the anteater and the rounded feet that it acquires in some regions of Brazil, according to da Câmara Cascudo. *Geografia dos Mitos Brasileiros*, 404.
57 Da Câmara Cascudo, 254–84.
58 Conversation with the author, 28 April 2019.
54 Da Câmara Cascudo, *Geografia dos Mitos Brasileiros*, 180–82.

1. Bestiaries and the Art of Cryptozoology

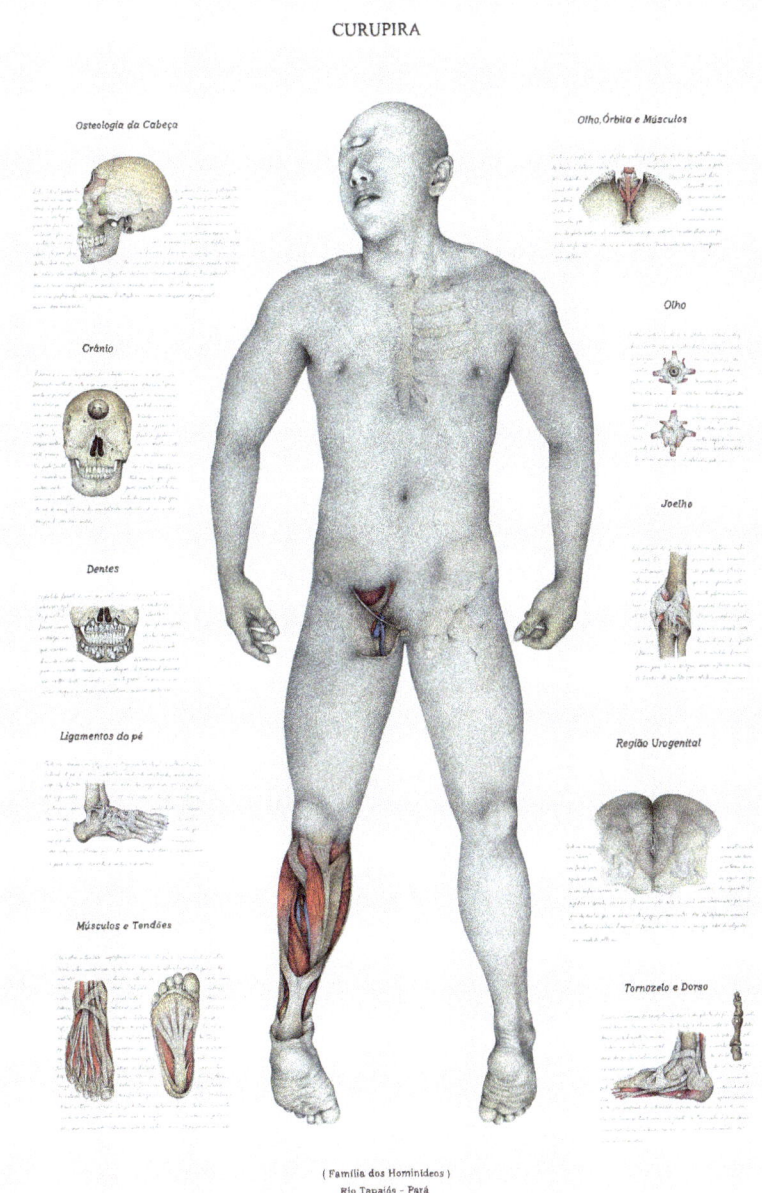

Fig. 1.9 Walmor Corrêa, *Curupira* from *Unheimlich: Imaginário popular brasileiro* (2005). Acrylic and graphic on canvas, 195 x 130 cm.

room within a Western scientific idiom for the popular, the alien, and the supernatural: locating strangeness in the familiar, much like Freud's theory of the *unheimlich* (the uncanny). The effect is utterly incongruous. If, as Jeffrey Jerome Cohen reminds us, "the monstrous body is pure culture" and it is "a construct and a projection,"[59] then the anatomical description of its body parts is comically irrelevant. The irony derives from our understanding that the physiological analysis of a monster's vital organs will tell us nothing of how monsters signify. And yet to render the fabulous creatures of folktales with such zoological rigour and fidelity is also to question how and why scientific modes of expression and analysis have become so estranged from everyday beliefs and lore. It is also to mount a semi-serious—if speculative—investigation into nonhuman forms of perception and knowledge. Maciel finds in the work of Wilson Bueno (a Brazilian writer) and Francisco de Toledo (the illustrator of Borges's *Manual de zoología fantástica*) an intent to develop "uma espécie de *razãoanimal*" (a kind of animal-logic) on the basis of a knowledge that is thoroughly embodied and sensory.[60] Corrêa's interest in the precise anatomies of his creatures, like Toriz's recourse to neurobiological research on the crocodile's sensory organs, stems from a lively curiosity about how knowledge is created through multiple sensory interactions with our environment.

Corrêa had already developed his work on animal hybrids in *Natureza perversa* (*Perverse Nature*, 2003), which adopts the conventions of zoological illustration to explore the possible anatomies of invented species, such as the *pinguisch* (which combines the head of a fish with the lower body of a penguin; see Fig. 1.10) and the *schnabelaffe* (a beaked monkey), and to speculate on their bizarre mating habits.[61] Rekindling a pre-Enlightenment fascination with the monstrous, these inventions speak to an early colonial imaginary in which composites and mixtures were rife, arising from encounters with otherness. Hybridization, along with spontaneous generation, were the two main theories proposed to explain the existence of animals in the New World that did not appear in the Old one, and were therefore unaccounted for in the original

---

59 Cohen, "Monster Culture (Seven Theses)," 4.
60 Maciel, "Imagens zoológicas da América Latina," 95.
61 *Natureza perversa* was exhibited as a solo show at the Museu de Arte do Rio Grande do Sul Ado Malagoli (MARGS) in 2003.

Creation.[62] The continued belief in interspecies hybridization, a matter of lengthy discourse and debate across the ancient, medieval, and early modern periods, is clear evidence of the priority given to theology over zoology in scholarship throughout this time.[63]

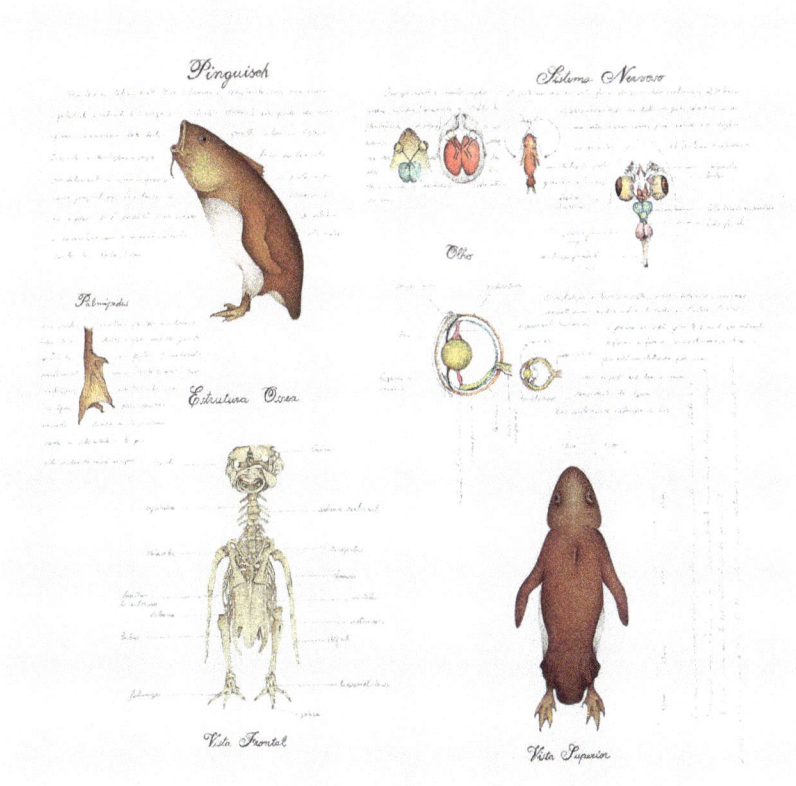

Fig. 1.10 Walmor Corrêa, *Pinguisch* from *Natureza perversa* (2003). Acrylic and graphite on canvas, 80 x 80 cm (photograph by Fabio del Re).

If these creatures largely resulted from the projection of European fears, desires, and theological debates onto the New World, what interest might contemporary Latin American writers and artists have in resurrecting such beasts? For Maciel, the fantastical creatures that swarmed across the pages of European chronicles of the New World

---

62 Enenkel, "The Species and Beyond," 99.
63 See Enenkel, 59, 68–83.

sprang from "uma insuficiência epistemológica" (an epistemological failure).[64] Sixteenth-century systems of knowledge could not assimilate "a *alteridade* radical dos animais latino-americanos" (the radical *alterity* of Latin American animals) within the existing categories of rational knowledge.[65] And yet, Maciel wonders if contemporary revivals of the bestiary in Latin America might hark back in an ironic mode to systems of classification that predate the triumph of scientific rationalism, precisely in order to denounce the failings of modern forms of knowledge.[66] This certainly appears to be a crucial motive in Corrêa's *Unheimlich* series. It is evident that the deficiency signalled here is on the part of modern, post-Enlightenment zoologists, whose expertise in anatomy has been cultivated through an absolute separation of the discipline from other realms of knowledge and experience: cultural, spiritual, and social.

There is also a clear interest in Corrêa's work in finding in the many errors and exaggerations of early colonial accounts something of value for our own time, namely the experience of being overwhelmed by diversity and disoriented by the unexplained. His recycling of colonial fantasies allows us to appreciate the "ideological malleability" that Stephen Greenblatt accords to wonder, as both "a sign of dispossession" and "an agent of appropriation."[67] If in Columbus's account of the New World the language of wonder is central to rituals of possession, Greenblatt wishes to reserve the possibility that it may also signify other kinds of relation with the world, as "the experience of wonder continually reminds us that our grasp of the world is incomplete."[68]

Importantly, Corrêa's work does not only explore the hybrid and fabulous animals that European travellers spied in the Americas, but also those that emerge from indigenous traditions and from the contact between two cultures. Like Anchieta, several early colonial chroniclers assimilated indigenous legends and taxonomies in their descriptions of the natural world. The work of Francisco Hernández (1514–1587), the only scientist to have written a natural history of the New World in the sixteenth century, is a synthesis of European classificatory systems and indigenous nomenclature, often relying on local Indian knowledge of

---

64   Maciel, "Imagens zoológicas da América Latina," 90.
65   Maciel, 90.
66   Maciel, 92.
67   Greenblatt, *Marvelous Possessions*, 24.
68   Greenblatt, 24.

new animals and plants.⁶⁹ Its incorporation of Aztec legends relating to the hidden powers of animals presented no difficulty to his readers, as "The Renaissance image of nature, with its insistence on its plastic power, its 'secrets' and the possibility of its control through natural magic, could accommodate part of the native lore with which many of the conceptual and literary representations of New World animals were invested."⁷⁰

Corrêa's own hybridizing work therefore stretches back to a moment of greater fluidity and exchange, before such beliefs, along with local names and cultural uses, were erased in the Enlightenment bid for objectivity and a universal nomenclature. The use of new Latin names to replace the "vivid vernacular names" that ordinary people had used to refer to the animals and plants around them widened the increasing gulf between learned and popular views of the natural world.⁷¹ Indeed, serious eighteenth-century naturalists became "contemptuous of popular lore."⁷² The imbrication of science and folklore in Corrêa's work constructs an alternative path that modernity might have followed instead, one that is less exclusionary and hierarchical. An emphasis on myths of indigenous origin also characterizes Wilson Bueno's *Jardim zoológico* (Brazil, 1999). But where Bueno seeks to dismantle the taxonomies of natural history in favour of orderings that arise from the subjective, the anecdotal, from memory or from dreams, Corrêa brings the scientific and the mythical together in a more genuine attempt to bridge the chasm that has separated them in modernity. Studying the contemporary bestiaries composed by Bueno and other Latin America writers, Maciel finds that the exoticizing gaze of the New World chroniclers is reappropriated "como traço constitutivo de uma identidade disforme, heteróclita, paradoxal" (as a defining trace of a deformed, heteroclite, paradoxical identity).⁷³ There is little attempt on the part of Corrêa—or indeed, on that of Toriz and Romo—to reclaim hybridity or the fantastic as defining characteristics of Latin American identity, however. Corrêa extends his *Unheimlich* series to include popular figures from US (and global) culture, including Spiderman and the arch villain Penguin from the Batman comics.

---

69 De Asúa and French, *A New World of Animals*, 101.
70 De Asúa and French, 234.
71 Thomas, *Man and the Natural World*, 81.
72 Thomas, 80.
73 Maciel, "Imagens zoológicas da América Latina," 93.

In his analysis of mediaeval animal imaginaries in literary descriptions of American nature, Hernando Cabarcas Antequera argues that early travellers found mysteries and miracles in the New World because they had started to disappear from the Old one. If God was no longer visibly manifest in European nature, in the luxuriant landscapes of America "la naturaleza vuelve a mostrar y a predecir" (nature begins to reveal and to foretell again) and signs of Providence were everywhere to be seen.[74] The monsters that Europeans saw may not only have emerged from the exaggeration of cultural and racial difference, but also from a need to reanimate a world that was fast becoming predictable. Comparing the study of monsters in the ancient world and in the present, Peter Dendle finds that "in the classical period the zoology of the hidden and unconfirmed reflected anxiety about how vast and frightening the world was. This stands in sharp contrast to contemporary cryptozoology, which serves rather as a marker of how weary many people are with a world over-explored, over-tamed, and over-understood."[75]

In the introduction to their exhibition on the art of cryptozoology, Raechell Smith and Mark Bessire note in a very similar vein that we are now not confronted with the unknown so much as "plagued by a weariness of absolute certainties," and that artists who stage a search for new species invite us to engage again in "wonder, speculation, and wishful thinking."[76] Since the mid-nineteenth century, when the last areas of land were mapped, and the start of the twentieth century, when most large species living on land had been catalogued, we have moved into an era in which the populations and habitats of most terrestrial animals are known to us.[77] This has produced a profound change in our relationship with the natural world, as well as with geographical space. Dendle argues that an important role for cryptozoology in contemporary times is "to repopulate liminal space with potentially undiscovered creatures that have resisted human devastation."[78] If there might be species that have somehow escaped human detection, then "we feel a little humbler about our ability to alter the natural biosphere and, perhaps, a little less guilty about the damage we have inflicted on it."[79]

---

74 Cabarcas Antequera, *Bestiario del Nuevo Reino de Granada*, 45.
75 Dendle, "Cryptozoology in the Medieval and Modern Worlds," 193.
76 Smith and Bessire, "Introduction," 11.
77 Dendle, "Cryptozoology in the Medieval and Modern Worlds," 197.
78 Dendle, 198.
79 Dendle, 198.

Many of Corrêa's projects allow us to glimpse this possibility. The texts composed for the *Natureza perversa* series do not only present us with bizarre, undiscovered creatures that shy away from human contact, but also give details of their ingenious survival tactics. The *Apterogiformes Aco II* (a flightless bird) is a hybrid of two almost-extinct species that were able to mate because of their genetic similarity, thus increasing their chances of survival. The *Schnabelspringer* (a beaked bird-rodent with powerful hind legs) shares the care of its young with other mothers on a weekly rota, which is effective in securing the continuity of the species. The *Möve mit Krallem* (Gull with Claws) may even have been the result of genetic experiments carried out by biologists in the Bikini Islands after nuclear testing.

There is a risk, of course, that Corrêa's spirited celebration of all things hybrid might create a utopian vision of liminality and cross-cultural encounters that skips too quickly over the real violence of colonial relations. In 2013, he created another hybrid in the style of the *Unheimlich* series, a woman-lizard entitled *Salamanca do Jarau*, in reference to a legend of some importance in the south of Brazil (see Fig. 1.11). According to the story, a Moorish princess with magical gifts (also called the Teiniaguá) arrives from Spain and is turned into a lizard by indigenous people to demonstrate their superior power; she continues to grant the wishes of those who visit her cave. In developing the work, Corrêa conducted research alongside doctors and a community association based in Barcelona on the health issues experienced by Latin American women immigrants. Common problems included alcoholism, chronic back pain, infertility, and the deformation of hands through too much manual labour. These were shown in red in the relevant area of the figure of the *Salamanca do Jarau*, in a testament to the suffering of current-day migrants for whom the hoped-for fulfilment of their desires has turned into something more monstrous, born of the poverty, inequality, and discrimination that mark reverse migrations from Latin America to Spain within the enduring legacy of coloniality.

Once common currency in colonial accounts of the New World, marking out the frontiers of modern civilization, the monstrous is reclaimed in Corrêa's work for decolonial purposes: to reweave histories of knowledge that have been torn apart in the imposition of a dominant, secular, Enlightenment science, to recreate the natural world as a site of

58   *Decolonial Ecologies*

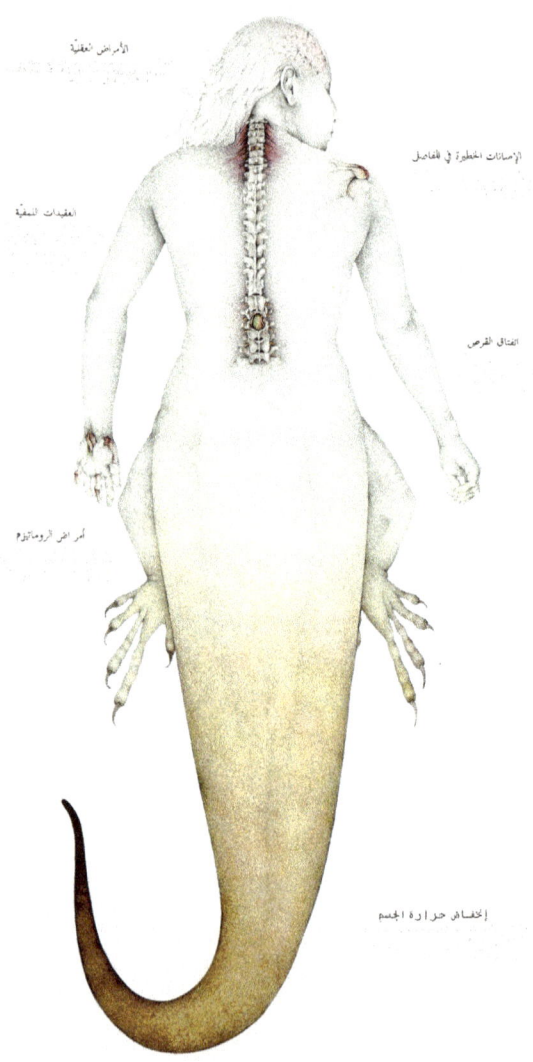

Fig. 1.11 Walmor Corrêa, *Teiniaguá, vista dorsal* from *Salamanca do Jarau* (2013). Acrylic and graphite on canvas, 90 x 110 cm (photograph by Hugo Curti).

excess, entanglement, and enchantment that confounds our attempts to tame it, and also to testify to the human suffering that continues to result from the forms of displacement and dispossession produced by global capitalism.

Conclusion

Twenty-first-century composers of bestiaries in Latin America have borrowed from the imaginaries of mediaeval bestiaries and the imperial fantasies of early New World chronicles in a quest to re-enchant the world, as a vital step toward learning to act differently in relation to it. The images they create and curate point to myths that are continually mutating and available to repurpose for our own times. The format of the illustrated book (or in Corrêa's case, the annotated illustration) heightens the possibilities for polyvalency. Indeed, in mediaeval bestiaries, the illustrations often added to the indeterminacy of meaning, with frequent discrepancies between texts and images that may have been the result of misunderstandings, the incorporation of images from other accounts or even the artist's deliberate attempt to contradict the text.[80] In the bestiaries discussed here, the image often strikes a different tone to the text, making a metaphor literal or lending a fantastical air to a zoological description, or introducing styles of illustration that seem out of time and place. Like the work of Borges's Pierre Menard, who rewrites the *Quijote* three centuries after its publication, to recompose the mediaeval bestiary in the twenty-first century is to lend it an even greater richness and ambiguity.

Perhaps the most surprising tactic used in these bestiaries is a recourse to anthropomorphic fables in which animals take on human characteristics and motives. Anthropomorphism is often associated with the childlike, magical view of the world embedded in fables, in which animals speak, embody human values or become the bearers of moral lessons. As the act of projecting human emotion and experience onto other species, anthropomorphism has come to be considered at best a category mistake, and at worst a perpetuation of anthropocentrism, our incapacity to grasp the otherness of nonhumans and the value of

---

80 Brown, "Bestiary Lessons on Pride and Lust," 54.

their different perspectives and capacities. It remains true, however, that the bestiaries of old often depicted animals as wiser and more skilled than their human readers. Inspired by the Biblical book of Proverbs, *Physiologus* enjoins its readers to emulate the discretion of ants; indeed, "irrational animals and weak reptiles" behave with such prudence that "all are found to be clever and wise."[81] Finding traits in animals that we share, or skills that surpass our own, may help us to recognize our common inheritance and allow us to think about alternative ways of being human.

But more broadly, as Kellie Robertson argues, "the unraveling of the old humanist certainties offers a chance to look afresh at what premodern models of nature have to offer to more recent models of environmental criticism."[82] The common recourse to anthropomorphic personification in mediaeval literature is one case in point: rather than representing a naïve narcissism, Robertson suggests that it often became a critical means "to explore what counts as human and what as nature" as well as "a tool for teasing apart the very subtle ontological threads that link earthly creatures of different kinds."[83] In more recent times, it has perhaps been environmental criticism that has voiced the strongest objections to the personification and humanization of nature. As it was the Enlightenment search for objectivity that demanded the separation between humans and nonhumans, however, Robertson proposes that a hostility toward anthropomorphism "makes strange bedfellows of environmental critics and the Enlightenment thinkers whom they otherwise seek to debunk."[84]

More profoundly, the central revelation of the Anthropocene is, of course, the extent to which humans are indeed becoming the designers and producers of the natural world. In his introduction to *The Book of Barely Imagined Beings* (2012), Caspar Henderson points out that "as we increasingly reshape Creation through science and technology, not to mention our sheer numbers, the creatures that do thrive and evolve are, increasingly, corollaries of our values and concerns."[85] In secular Western

---

81 Curley, *Physiologus*, 21.
82 Robertson, *Nature Speaks*, 342.
83 Robertson, 343.
84 Robertson, 343.
85 Henderson, *The Book of Barely Imagined Beings*, xviii–xix.

societies we may not believe now that animals are manifestations of moral and religious lessons. But in the context of the current extension of our powers over the rest of the planet, "The Enlightenment and the scientific method will, therefore, have made possible the creation of a world that really will be allegorical because we will have remade it in the shadow of our values and priorities."[86]

Toriz and Cano, Padrón and Romo, and Corrêa return to mediaeval and early colonial genres in a quest to re-embed animals in our social and spiritual lives. Reflecting on José de Anchieta's sixteenth-century letters from Brazil, Paulo De Assunção observes that he is not interested in classifying the diverse species he encounters or in analysing the relationships between them. His principal concern is to describe how they may be used for food, or in other words, how they are placed "ao serviço do homem" (at the service of man).[87] For this reason, De Assunção finds that Anchieta's descriptions of the animal world "tendem a reforçar o sentido de posse" (tend to reinforce the sense of possession).[88] We may choose to read Anchieta's descriptions differently, however, if we compare them with modern approaches to zoology since the Enlightenment. Eighteenth-century taxonomies were to describe animals in ways that were more detached and less overtly anthropocentric, striving to classify animals according to their physical characteristics rather than their human uses. This objectivity was to parallel, and to reinforce, the growing separation between humans and animals in everyday life in the technologically developed world. It is this disconnection, born out of a conviction of disparity, that Corrêa, Romo, Toriz, and their collaborators seek to reverse.

---

86   Henderson, xix.
87   De Assunção, *A terra dos brasis*, 179.
88   De Assunção, 183.

2. New Cabinets of Curiosities

The baroque cult of curiosities in Europe crystallized in the form of prized collections, owned by royals, nobles, and wealthy merchants, of fabulous objects drawn from the furthest reaches of the known world. Like medieval collections, which often contained ecclesiastical treasures or objects with magical power, European cabinets of curiosities of the late sixteenth and seventeenth centuries boasted items of high monetary value, such as precious stones, as well as ones to which supernatural powers were commonly ascribed, such as unicorn horns, basilisks, and dragon's blood. Each object was prized for its rarity: its uniqueness, the difficulty involved in bringing it back from far-off lands, the excellence of its craftsmanship.

Unlike the more systematic natural history collections that were to gain ground in the eighteenth century in Europe, cabinets of curiosities emphasized aberrations and transgressions over universal laws and taxonomies. Although the collections were far from unorganized, many of their exhibits were admired because of their resistance to classification. Natural specimens such as coral, which seemed to bridge the animal, vegetable and mineral kingdoms, held a particular fascination for collectors.[1] Similarly, intricately crafted objects (such as carved ivory and wood) and mechanical devices (such as automata) were often included for their capacity to defy the boundaries between art and nature or life and machine. Cabinets of curiosities used techniques of juxtaposition and symmetry to create visual analogies that would provoke ontological questions about the natural world: what unites all living things, despite their immense diversity? What is the relationship between art and nature? Can nature be understood as creator as well as creation?

---

1   Mauriès, *Cabinets of Curiosities*, 89.

© 2023 Joanna Page, CC BY-NC-ND 4.0   https://doi.org/10.11647/OBP.0339.02

In their study of the marvels of European *Wunderkammern*, Lorraine Daston and Katherine Park investigate how such questions helped to transform the understanding of art and nature in early-seventeenth-century natural history and natural philosophy, "undermining the ancient ontology that opposed art and nature, with profound consequences for the early modern understanding of the natural order."[2] In this chapter, I explore the relationships staged between art and nature in the reworkings of cabinets of curiosities and early natural history collections developed by two Latin American artists: Pablo La Padula (Argentina) and Cristian Villavicencio (Ecuador-Spain). I examine what new (or old) ideas about the natural world emerge from their invocations of the aesthetic and conceptual design of early modern collections, and how their own works reconfigure the relationship between art, nature, and science in the twenty-first century. These new cabinets and collections deliver a critique of the relationships between colonialism, capitalist acquisition, and the commodification of nature, as well as the dominance in Western science since the Enlightenment of a certain kind of distanced, "objective" vision. They foster alternative encounters with the natural world that emphasize the affective, the embodied, and the subjective. These allow us, like Yuk Hui's concept of "cosmotechnics," to explore the different relationships between humans and technology that have emerged from different cosmologies, and thus to pluralize accounts of technological modernity.[3]

Cycles of Life in Pablo La Padula's *gabinetes biológicos*

Pablo La Padula has created a series of installations for museums and art galleries that adopt many of the characteristics of the cabinets and collections founded in Europe in the sixteenth and early seventeenth centuries. In his *gabinetes biológicos* (biological cabinets), specimens drawn from the natural world—fossils, bones, shells, dried leaves—are interspersed with figures drawn on transparent sheets of glass and laboratory equipment, including flasks and specimen jars. The objects are arranged on large light tables and enclosed in simple display boxes

---

[2] Daston and Park, *Wonders and the Order of Nature, 1150–1750*, 261.
[3] Hui, *The Question Concerning Technology in China*, 29.

(see Fig. 2.1). Their diversity is extremely engaging for gallery visitors, who pore over them, inspecting them from multiple angles. Like the owners of many early cabinets, La Padula is often present at exhibitions to talk about the objects and their origins.

Fig. 2.1 Installation view of Pablo La Padula, *Zoología fantástica* (2018). Centro de Arte y Naturaleza, Museo de la Universidad Nacional de Tres de Febrero, Buenos Aires, Argentina (photograph courtesy of the Museo de la Universidad de Tres de Febrero).

The cabinets of curiosities that rose to prominence in Europe in the baroque era were highly personal collections, assembled on the whims of individual creators and drawing on their own experiences. In a similar way, La Padula's *gabinetes biológicos* are intimately connected with his travels and his practices as a laboratory scientist. They include a fossil given to him by a friend, stones gathered on a trip away to which particular memories are attached, and old books from his childhood. These objects are not presented for their biological value but for the memories and emotions they evoke for the artist. These are of course opaque to the casual spectator. But as with the baroque cabinets, from these collections' broader principles of selection and arrangement a particular understanding emerges of the natural world and the place of humans in it.

In its impressive abundance and heterogeneity, the European cabinet of curiosities seemed to stand in for the immense diversity of the world. It reinforced a classical and medieval conception of the prodigious variety of nature. It was not ordered systematically according to the logic of later natural history museums, with different genera or habitats enclosed in separate glass cases, which were often dedicated to specific geographical regions or stages in evolutionary development. It would be an error, however, to consider the cabinet as unstructured. Its multiple "frames, niches, boxes, drawers and cases" created a series of systems and hierarchies (see Fig. 2.2).[4] Some of these were based on the four elements, while others represented the chain of being, displayed certain types together or established relationships between disparate objects on the basis of visual analogies. The setting and arrangement of objects inscribed them with additional meanings; as Patrick Mauriès suggests, cabinets and cases were not only intended to preserve items or to keep them secure, but to locate each object "in a vast network of meanings and correspondences."[5] The affinities established between objects from different regions of the world or from different natural kingdoms, or between the creativity of art and that of nature, revealed "the fundamental unity that lay beneath this welter of multiplicity."[6]

The many different objects in La Padula's *gabinetes biológicos* also invite viewers to speculate about the possible logic that might unite them. The artist explains that "El gabinete no va a pretender hacer una explicación del mundo. No pretende generar una narrativa lógica, pretende ser el envés de una narrativa científica. Pretende ser elocuente, poético" (the cabinet does not offer an explanation of the world. It does not purport to generate a logical narrative, it wants to be the reverse of a scientific narrative. It wants to be eloquent, poetic).[7] As he intends, La Padula's exhibitions allow viewers to create their own "adventure" within the universe laid out before them. But they also convey broad scientific principles which relate to the unity and diversity of the natural world. Visual resemblances point to forms or faculties that are shared across species: in *Zoología fantástica* (Fantastical Zoology, 2018), for

---

4   Mauriès, *Cabinets of Curiosities*, 12.
5   Mauriès, 25.
6   Mauriès, 34.
7   Conversation with the author, 22 April 2021.

2. New Cabinets of Curiosities

Fig. 2.2 Francesco Calzolari's cabinet, as shown in the frontispiece to Benedetto Ceruti, *Musaeum Franc. Calceolari iun. Veronensis* (1622).

example, an enlarged illustration of the veins and membranes that make up the architecture of a dragonfly's wings (below, right) is drawn on a plaque placed below the skeleton of a dolphin, whose bone structure also allows it to soar into the air (see Fig. 2.3).[8] The dolphin's branching vertebrae and ribs reproduce the fanned pattern of an image created with smoke on paper (bottom left), which in turn resembles the form of the lobed leaves placed nearby.

Links between all of these objects are also suggested by the graphic representations of molecular structures which are drawn on glass sheets, erected vertically on the light tables. As we look through these transparent plaques to the objects laid out beyond them, the atoms

---

8   *Zoología fantástica* was exhibited at the MUNTREF Centro de Arte y Naturaleza in Buenos Aires, Argentina, between 24 August 2018 and 29 May 2019.

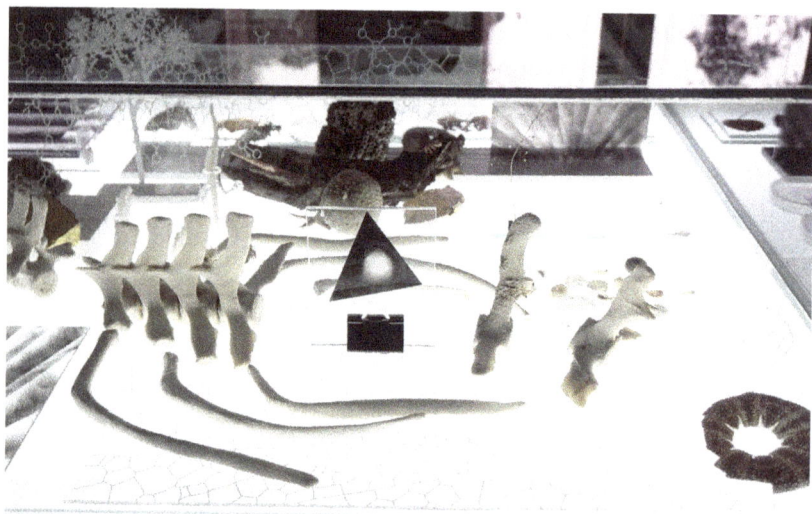

Fig. 2.3 Installation view of Pablo La Padula, *Zoología fantástica* (2018). Centro de Arte y Naturaleza, Museo de la Universidad Nacional de Tres de Febrero, Buenos Aires, Argentina (photograph by Gabriela Schevach, courtesy of REV magazine).

Fig. 2.4 Installation view of Pablo La Padula, *Zoología fantástica* (2018). Centro de Arte y Naturaleza, Museo de la Universidad Nacional de Tres de Febrero, Buenos Aires, Argentina (photograph by the artist).

and chemical bonds stretching out across them seem to unite them, binding together objects of natural and human design; the organic and the inorganic; animal, vegetable, and mineral (see Fig. 2.4). The insertion of illustrations made with candle smoke also points to carbon as the common denominator of life on the planet. Like early modern cabinets, then, *Zoología fantástica* stages the unity of nature and blurs the boundaries between nature, art, and technology. The visual correspondences that intrigued viewers of early cabinets are still present in La Padula's work, but they replace mysterious alliances and occult agencies with the knowledge we now possess of carbon's importance to life and the intimate relationship it creates between the organic and inorganic.

La Padula's artistic explorations with smoke and photography are in part inspired by the great nineteenth-century scientist and inventor, Étienne-Jules Marey, who—like La Padula—was also a cardiovascular physiologist. As well as instruments to capture pulse and blood pressure, Marey invented "smoke machines" to capture the movement of air. Smoke became in this way "una imagen viviente de los procesos en el tiempo" (a living image of processes in time).[9] For La Padula, the significance of smoke also lies in the trace it provides of the process of combustion through which energy is released, to be reconfigured into other material forms.[10] It is a reminder of death, but also of the participation of almost all living things on Earth in the carbon cycle that sustains life. Our continued existence depends on this combustion, which knits us into the planet's dynamic processes, in which all forms are broken down and remade:

> Es en nuestro humo donde la materia, independientemente de su origen y lógica se unifica en un mismo plano de jerarquía. Es en este estado, si se quiere gaseoso y dinámico de la materia, donde se redime de sus divisiones circunstanciales, liberada del aprisionamiento de las formas.[11]
>
> (It is in our smoke that matter, regardless of its origin or form, is united in a single hierarchical plane. It is in this state, gaseous and dynamic, if you will, in which matter frees itself from its provisional partitions, liberated from the imprisonment of form.)

---

9   La Padula, "La red de humo," 63.
10 La Padula, 65.
11 La Padula, 65.

Smoke, then, represents the biogeochemical cycle through which energy and matter are transformed into usable forms to support living organisms and ecosystems. For this reason, La Padula explains, a smoke image is placed next to the skeleton of the dolphin, which has, likewise, undergone a process of mineralization (in which the organic is broken down into mineral forms which are then available as nutrients to be taken up by plants).[12]

Early cabinet-creators were similarly keen to explore transformations in nature; petrifications were often given pride of place as they seemed to offer evidence of metamorphosis.[13] The slow transformation of organisms into fossils suggested the possibility of a conversion from one kingdom (plant or animal) to another (mineral). In the twenty-first century, we understand such transformations not as singular or uncanny, but as part of a complex but ubiquitous cycle that binds all forms of matter together in delicately balanced ecosystems. We have ample additional evidence to support theories of the unity and dynamism of nature that were evoked in the visual correspondences of early cabinets of curiosities.

In many ways, however, the objects chosen by La Padula to symbolize such interconnections are very different from those assembled in early modern cabinets. Measured against the mercantile value of cabinets of curiosities, in which "wonders were also commodities: to be bartered, bought, sold, collected,"[14] La Padula's objects are consciously not chosen for their economic value, or even their value to scientific inquiry. If sixteenth- and seventeenth-century collectors chose precious articles that excelled in their rarity or beauty, La Padula brings together simple forms that are not, by themselves, prodigious or spectacular: stones, leaves, fragments of fossils, discarded biological material. He buys nothing for his *gabinetes*, creating them only with objects he has at home or in the lab, or finds on his travels.[15] He replaces a logic of exceptionality with one of the everyday, selecting objects that have been discarded, are obsolete, or exist only as by-products or incomplete remains.

If baroque cabinets of curiosities turned nature's creativity into objects of artistic and commercial value, La Padula's *gabinetes* invite us

---

12   Conversation with the author, 22 April 2021.
13   MacGregor, *Curiosity and Enlightenment*, 46.
14   Daston and Park, *Wonders and the Order of Nature, 1150–1750*, 67.
15   Conversation with the author, 22 April 2021.

to question value itself. What is the value of an object, if it is merely composed of the recycled matter of another object? How could an object be considered "unique" in this context? In the natural world it is not the rarest element but that which is to be found in the greatest number of compounds—carbon, a waste product—that enables all life. In symbolic deference to the importance of residues and waste in the cycles that structure life on the planet, La Padula includes several objects in his exhibitions that represent by-products of his own scientific and artistic activities. Behind the dolphin's remains are lab flasks holding the candle wax that had dropped when he made the smoke images; nearby is a microscope slide containing proteins that had been used in the process of writing a scientific paper.[16] In nature, nothing goes to waste; here, similarly, La Padula puts to second use materials that might have been discarded according to the values of art or science, in which it is commonly the final result that is prized, and everything else is a means to an end. What is disposed of and overlooked is, of course, essential to the process of producing both art and science. As La Padula puts it, "Porque existe todo ese descarte, es posible la abstracción bella y simple del paper" (the existence of everything that is thrown away makes possible the simple, beautiful abstraction of the [scientific] paper).[17]

Zoología fantástica and the other *gabinetes biológicos* created by La Padula therefore question how objects circulate and acquire value in the different—but entangled—systems of knowledge, culture, and commerce. Sixteenth- and seventeenth-century collections were vastly enriched by objects arriving from the Spanish and Portuguese empires, which offered alluring exotic crafts and unusual specimens. In their search for marvels to display, collectors travelled far afield; as Daston and Park observe, "Wonders tended to cluster at the margins rather than at the center of the known world."[18] Cabinets of curiosities were located at a crucial point of intersection in a burgeoning world system that would entwine natural history (and other disciplines) with capitalism, and with colonial practices of conquest and dispossession. Although collections bore witness to the wealth of individual collectors, Juan Pimentel argues that they should also be understood more broadly as "una interesante

---

16 Conversation with the author, 22 April 2021.
17 Conversation with the author, 22 April 2021.
18 Daston and Park, *Wonders and the Order of Nature, 1150–1750*, 14.

versión de la acumulación capitalista auspiciada por la ciencia moderna y su anhelo por ejecutar su imperio sobre la naturaleza" (an interesting version of capitalist accumulation backed by modern science and its desire to exercise its power over nature).[19] La Padula's collections adopt a very different logic that is not only non-commercial but decolonial, marking a clear difference with European acts of dispossession. While he removes objects himself from the places in which he finds them (national parks, beaches, fields), their small size and number, together with their commercial and scientific insignificance, only throws into relief the massive scale of acquisition programmes conducted by major museums and scientific institutions. His own practice of collecting, by contrast, is pursued entirely outside the capitalist system.

To some viewers, the act of removing stones or fossils from their natural environments to gallery spaces in the city may still constitute a form of extraction, however small-scale and symbolic. But La Padula's cabinets fully espouse a conception of the natural world that is not, and should not be, corralled off from human intervention. Indeed, he denounces the contemporary use of ecology by the Global North to promote the conservation of natural resources (for exploitation by a future Europe). The idea of an "untouched" Nature is being imposed on indigenous communities in the Amazon, for example, in order to "save" natural resources in Latin America from the destruction they have already suffered in Europe.[20] Far from promoting "Nature" as a pristine enclave that should be protected from human activity, La Padula's *gabinetes biológicos* celebrate the artist's personal and embodied encounter with a natural environment and the act of collecting and displaying objects, through which the natural immediately becomes cultural. He defends the right of the artist (unlike the scientist, whose studies are highly regulated by ethics committees and funding bodies) to develop a relationship with the natural world that is based on a direct intervention in it, guided only by an artistic imperative and a personal ethic.

This comparatively unmediated relationship does not conform to the representation of the natural world that is dominant in contemporary media or science museums. Bones in La Padula's collections are

---

19 Pimentel, *Testigos del mundo*, 151, 155–56.
20 Conversation with the author, 22 April 2021.

displayed as fragments rather than reconstructed to form an image of a whole animal (as they might be in a natural history museum); neither is the animal world presented as a dramatic spectacle (as would be typical in a nature documentary). His bones are, instead, the objects of his encounters with real animals and their remains. Each *gabinete* is rooted in a specific geographic territory, with the majority of the objects collected from local sites. The objects take on the power of talismans, able to transport the artist back through time and space to the moment of encounter and discovery.[21] As La Padula states, "Lo que yo quiero rescatar es que todos volvamos a poner en valor el encuentro con la naturaleza tal cual se nos presenta, que es más opaca, menos espectacular, es más sucia, es menos didáctica, es menos grandilocuente, generalmente" (what I want to revive is for us all to value an encounter with nature exactly as it presents itself to us, which is generally more opaque, less spectacular, dirtier, less didactic, less bombastic).[22]

La Padula's *gabinetes* thus aim to return to nature something of the opacity and ambiguity of which it was stripped in Enlightenment collections, with their neatly classified display cases, laid out for educational benefit. His unlabelled collections inspire curiosity and speculation. Miniaturization in Baroque cabinets of curiosities invited a sense of play; in La Padula's collections this is heightened by the inclusion of tiny human figures, rendered in smoke on glass plaques, and positioned in such a way that they appear to be exploring a garden of giant fossils and trees (see Fig. 2.5). If making a small-scale replica of the universe or its kingdoms, of the sort commonly presented in the cabinet of curiosities, offers "a degree of mastery or control,"[23] in La Padula's work the only object that has been miniaturized is, tellingly, the human figure. It is we who need to regain our sense of play, immersed in the diversity of the natural world. The theme of *natura ludens* (nature at play) that inspired many baroque cabinets of curiosities becomes here one of *homo ludens* instead.

Sixteenth- and seventeenth-century cabinets often staged a kind of rivalry between art and nature, in which each emulated the other in its

---

21   Conversation with the author, 22 April 2021.
22   Conversation with the author, 22 April 2021.
23   Weston, "'Worlds in Miniature,'" 44.

Fig. 2.5 Installation view of Pablo La Padula, *Teatro científico* (2020). Fundación Federico Jorge Klemm, Buenos Aires, Argentina (photograph by the artist).

creativity.[24] Rather than simply reflecting the splendour of the divine creator, nature was personified in these wondrous objects "as an elevated

---

24   Daston and Park, *Wonders and the Order of Nature, 1150–1750*, 281.

kind of artisan"; like the goldsmith and the painter of miniatures, Daston and Park argue, she was "freed from the demands of utility."[25] If the Aristotelian tradition found beauty in the economy of nature—"nature does nothing in vain"—"the wonders of the cabinets gloried in superfluity, careless of function and extravagant in expenditure of labor and materials."[26] Although the natural world in La Padula's work is still very much a space of creative transformations, a more sombre, post-anthropocentric perspective accords a greater value to "utility" and the careful use of resources than in earlier periods. A baroque aesthetic of excess is replaced with an ethic of minimalism.

Consciously diverging from the kind of high-tech science and art collaborations that are being exhibited at museums worldwide, La Padula attempts to create an art that is as "paleolithic" as possible: "un arte que tenga el impacto ambiental del hombre de las cavernas" (an art with the environmental impact of a caveman).[27] The simple elegance of the natural forms he displays in his cabinets is matched by his own minimal use of resources. Three-dimensional effects are not created with video technologies but with the straightforward projection of light through drawings on transparent sheets of glass. If art imitates nature here, it is a nature that is sober and rather economical. The effect is anything but austere, however, as the poetic play of light and perspective lends a magical quality to the plainest objects.

As part of their critique of the commodification of the natural world, La Padula's *gabinetes* reveal a crucial disjuncture between the circulation of matter in the natural world and the circulation of commodities in a commercial system. Capitalist circulation, which creates unrecyclable waste and reservoirs of accumulation, is of a different order to the kind of circulation that characterizes the natural world. Humans cannot remove themselves from this kind of circulation, and indeed any attempt to do so results in a conservationism that reinforces a separation between the human and the nonhuman. La Padula insists, "el ser humano es un sistema biológicamente abierto, que vive de incorporar y devolver cosas y transformar el medioambiente" (the human being is an open biological system, which lives by incorporating things and giving them

---

25   Daston and Park, 261.
26   Daston and Park, 277.
27   Conversation with the author, 22 April 2021.

back, and by transforming the environment).[28] The question raised by his *gabinetes biológicos* is not whether such exchanges should take place—they are inevitable—but what *kind* of encounters and transformations will characterize our relationship with the natural world, and what values they will reflect or generate.

Cristian Villavicencio: Cosmotechnics and the Politics of Objectivity

In addition to natural wonders and works of art, cabinets of curiosities of the sixteenth and seventeenth centuries often displayed technical devices, such as microscopes and telescopes, which at the time were radically transforming perceptions of the natural world. Ofer Gal and Raz Chen-Morris argue that the growing reliance on the mediation of lenses, screens and other artificial instruments from the late sixteenth century onwards creates a powerful tension that is "crucial" for an understanding of early modern science.[29] As "a corollary of Baroque fascination with the particular, the detailed and the sensual," a commitment to empiricism—the demand that knowledge be based on experience gained through the senses—is foundational to this new science. At the same time, the increasing use of instruments leads to a rejection of the immediacy of the senses and the recognition that "all empirical knowledge is fundamentally mediated; that nature could only be approached by art."[30]

Cristian Villavicencio's installations display fossils, beetles, bacteria, and plants together with some of the visual technologies that have facilitated our study of other organisms, such as microscopes, cameras, and projectors. His works stage an exploration of the relationship between embodied perception and technology that return, in part, to the "baroque paradox" outlined by Gal and Chen-Morris. Villavicencio alerts us to the significant role played by visual technologies in our encounter with, and understanding of, the world. But he also traces new possible roles for such technologies that diverge from, and challenge, the "objective" view accorded by scientific instruments. In Villavicencio's highly mediated

---

28   Conversation with the author, 22 April 2021.
29   Gal and Chen-Morris, "Baroque Modes and the Production of Knowledge," 7.
30   Gal and Chen-Morris, 7.

collections we can detect a kind of counter-history of Western science and technology, in which the technological mediation of perception does not bolster Enlightenment aims of objectivity and universality but instead provides new opportunities for intimate encounters with the natural world. The remediations of archives and instruments that are at the heart of much of Villavicencio's artistic practice are made even more potent by his choice of exhibition spaces. He often exhibits his work either in spaces dedicated to contemporary art—bringing scientific images and objects into a context in which questions of perception and subjectivity are naturally at the forefront—or in spaces associated with university faculties and institutes, where they may take part in broader debates concerning knowledge production and the relationship between art and science or technology.

Selecciones (Selections, 2019) was exhibited in one such venue, Arte Actual FLACSO, which is linked to the Departamento de Antropología, Historia y Humanidades at the Quito site of the Facultad Latinoamericana de Ciencias Sociales, a renowned Latin American research institution. It is a space dedicated to contemporary art with a transdisciplinary focus, and it promotes art as a form of knowledge production with the potential to transform people and societies.[31] In *Selecciones*, a wooden table is set out with objects borrowed from the Departamento de Biología of the Escuela Politécnica Nacional in Ecuador: a colourful array of butterfly and beetle boxes, the skeletons of a porcupine and a sloth, a snake coiled in a large specimen jar, and a 3D-printed model of a fossil (see Fig. 2.6).[32] While many of these items belong to an archive founded in the nineteenth century and catalogued according to the Linnaean system, their selection, heterogeneous combination and theatricalization in Villavicencio's exhibitions is much more reminiscent of earlier cabinets of curiosities. Several of the specimens on the table are placed on rotating disks and simultaneously filmed by tiny cameras; these moving images are projected onto a screen nearby (see Fig. 2.7). Many of the videos are shot in extreme close-up. Displaced from the scientific archive and released from the classifying gaze of a palaeontologist or a biologist, these specimens take on new

---

31 See https://arteactual.ec/quienes-somos/
32 Images of the work may be viewed at http://www.cristianvillavicencio.net/52_selecciones.html

Fig. 2.6 Installation view of Cristian Villavicencio, *Selecciones* (2019). Arte Actual Flacso, Quito, Ecuador (photograph by the artist).

Fig. 2.7 Installation view of Cristian Villavicencio, *Selecciones*. Exhibited as part of *Tecnologías de la experiencia* in the 15th Bienal de Cuenca, Ecuador (2021) (photograph by Ricardo Bohórquez).

aspects and meanings. Their textures, colours, and patterns come to the fore, exuding a vibrancy that is maintained in death. Their display speaks of their availability, in death, to our gaze; on the other hand, the unfamiliar and unsettling perspectives of the video projections ensure that they do not become an object of our visual domination.

Villavicencio had worked with the archives held at the Escuela Politécnica Nacional previously. Founded in 1869 as Ecuador's first research centre, the Escuela was initially overseen by German Jesuits; its natural history collections bear the imprint of that European influence in their organization, and for Villavicencio, they represent the nation's fervent embrace of Western positivism.[33] He filmed boxes of fossils and insects that had been arranged for him by one of Escuela's researchers. The video, entitled *Especímenes* (Specimens) and shown as part of the *Dimensiones paralelas* (Parallel Dimensions) exhibition in Bilbao (2017), brings into play opposing kinds of vision.[34] In the first, a more distanced view allows us to perceive the size, shape, and colour of each beetle, grasping how each compares and contrasts with the other beetles placed alongside it. This kind of vision sees beyond surfaces and textures to the underlying forms, the structural similarities and differences that are the basis of Linnaean classifications. But the video images soon change to focus precisely on those surfaces, zooming in to the point at which they lose form, or acquire new forms that were not visible to the distanced eye (see Fig. 2.8). The juxtaposition of the two kinds of vision encourages us to focus on what becomes visible or invisible in each: how the use of devices to alter scale and perspective shapes our understanding of what we see. Creating a further series of distortions, the video was projected onto rotating screens that appeared to stretch and shrink the images (see Fig. 2.9). The gyration of the screens was also intended to encourage viewers to move around the exhibition, as they had to shift their position to be able to view the video.[35]

The use of optical devices in Villavicencio's work challenges our association of machines with objective vision, an association that has been fundamental to the development of modern science. To the

---

33 Conversation with the author, 27 January 2022.
34 Sequences from the video may be viewed at http://www.cristianvillavicencio.net/46_dimensiones_paralelas.html
35 Correspondence with the author, 24 November 2022.

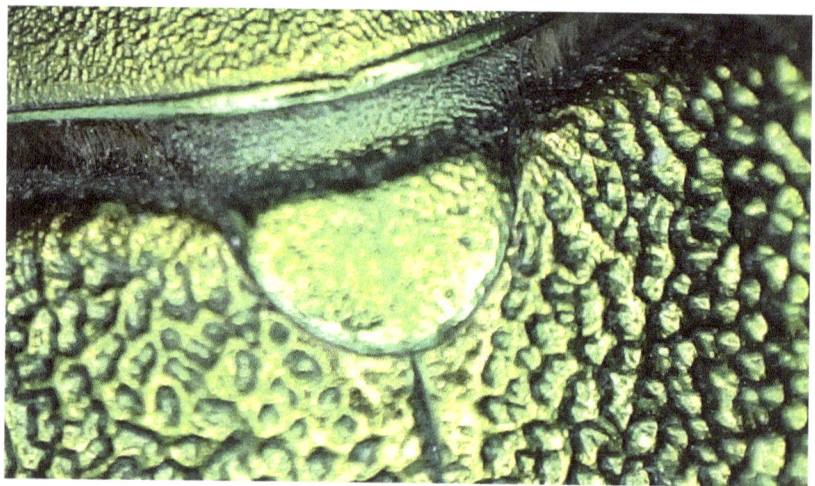

Fig. 2.8 Still from video produced by Cristian Villavicencio for *Dimensiones paralelas* (2017). Fundación BilbaoArte Fundazioa, Bilbao, Spain.

Fig. 2.9 Installation view of Cristian Villavicencio, *Especímenes*, two-channel video projection from *Dimensiones paralelas* (2017). Fundación BilbaoArte Fundazioa, Bilbao, Spain (photograph by the artist).

nineteenth-century scientist, machines seemed to offer freedom from subjectivity, being "ignorant of theory and incapable of speculation."[36] Mechanical objectivity became "a guiding if not the guiding ideal of scientific representation" across many disciplines.[37] Villavicencio's work lends a new role to optical devices, not in erasing the self in our representations of the natural world, but in expanding and deepening our encounters with it. The artist asks:

> ¿Cómo sería una historia alternativa de las superficies microscópicas si rechazásemos el punto de vista de un observador desinteresado? Estas herramientas "clínicas" pueden utilizarse para descubrir cosas que la ciencia occidental no tenía intención de descubrir, o no sabía cómo hacerlo, o cómo buscarlo.[38]

> (What would an alternative history of microscopic surfaces look like if we were to reject the viewpoint of a disinterested observer? These "clinical" tools can be used to discover things that Western science had no intention of discovering, or did not know how to, or how to look for them.)

Dimensiones paralelas assembles works that were both live and mediated, mechanical and digital.[39] These are positioned together in an exhibition space in such a way that viewers are encouraged to move around and between them, understanding them as discrete artworks while reflecting on their potential affiliations. One of the pieces bears the title *Megatherium*, the name of a species of giant ground sloth endemic to South America, now extinct. Discovered in Argentina in 1787, the first megatherium remains were shipped to the Museo Nacional de Ciencias in Madrid, where they are still exhibited. To create his work, Villavicencio used a high-resolution 3D scanner (from the Mechanical Engineering department of the Escuela Politécnica Nacional) to reproduce a fossil from the collection, adding other elements with Rhino 3D software before printing it and covering it with a layer of bacteria (see Fig. 2.8). The bacteria continue to grow over the course of the exhibition, endowing the pale surfaces of the fossil with dark blotches. The piece is thus a

---

36 Daston and Galison, *Objectivity*, 123.
37 Daston and Galison, 125.
38 Villavicencio, "Dimensiones paralelas," 51.
39 Images of the exhibition may be viewed at http://www.cristianvillavicencio. net/46_dimensiones_paralelas.html

fictional, composite creature. The inspiration came from Villavicencio's research in the Archivo General de Indias, where he found references to hybrid beasts in the illustrations drawn by colonial chroniclers, and from a curious image painted on the roof of a museum located in the Iglesia de San Francisco, the oldest church in Quito, which combines the body of an animal with the head of a human.[40] Images such as these were typical in the discrepant accounts of the early colonial period, which purported to present objective descriptions but often overlaid the myths of the Old World onto the New. Villavicencio draws on the capacity of digital techniques to create hybrid images of his own, observing that "el mundo digital está pensado para el remix, la combinación de archivos, una fusión del monstruo" (the digital world is designed for remixes, the combination of archives, a fusion of the monster).[41] Enclosed in a glass dome, Villavicencio's hybridized fossil rotates smoothly on its axis, ensuring that its ridges and cavities continually advance and retract before our eyes.

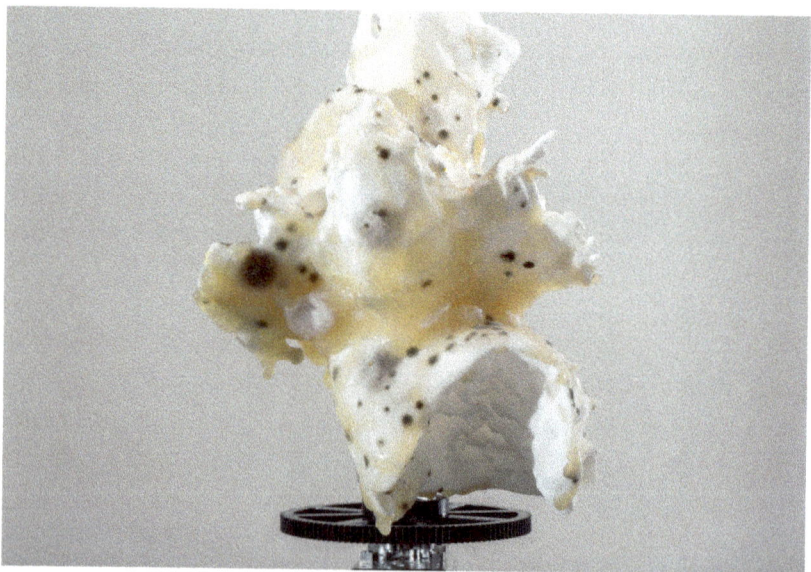

Fig. 2.10 Cristian Villavicencio, *Megatherium*, shown without the glass dome with which it was exhibited, from *Dimensiones paralelas* (2017). Fundación BilbaoArte Fundazioa, Bilbao (photograph by the artist).

---

40 Conversation with the author, 27 January 2022.
41 Zambrano, "Cristian Villavicencio subvierte lo objetivo."

The devices used to render objects mobile in *Dimensiones Paralelas* are both digital and mechanical. Behind *Megatherium,* large hanging banners printed with magnified images of bacterial activity are activated with the aid of electric fans, which cause them to crumple and crease as they respond to the current of air.[42] In putting the objects of scientific knowledge in motion, Villavicencio effectively animates the static gaze of the museum spectator, multiplying perspectives in a way that gestures toward the continually shifting nature of our relations with other organisms and environments. The simultaneous presence of live and mediated elements in Villavicencio's installations demonstrate how visual technologies alter and expand perception. In *Jardín* (Garden), viewers may view from above a small selection of medicinal plants, native to Ecuador, which are presented in wooden boxes placed on the floor; their vision is also augmented by the projection onto a screen, a few feet away, of sequences captured live by a tiny video camera moving in, over and between the plants (see Fig. 2.11). Visual technologies are deployed here to make a greater immersion and dynamism possible, as the close-up shots reveal textures and perspectives that would otherwise be difficult for us to access.

Fig. 2.11 Cristian Villavicencio, *Jardín* from *Dimensiones paralelas* (2017). Fundación BilbaoArte Fundazioa, Bilbao, Spain (photograph by the artist).

---

42   These images are from the *Colonies* project (2016).

As Villavicencio explains, the separation of ourselves from our object of study is only one path that scholars have chosen: another possibility is to "acercarse al punto cero de ese objeto de estudio, donde tal vez no puedas entender ese objeto en su totalidad pero sí puedes fijarte en fisuras o en huellas microscópicas que quedan grabadas en la historia" (move closer to the zero point of that object of study, where perhaps you will not be able to understand that object in its totality but you will be able to detect fissures and microscopic traces that are etched into history).[43] When technologies are deployed to disrupt the smooth, static nature of an "objective" gaze, it becomes more obvious to us how they mediate our knowledge of the world. Villavicencio's devices make visible the "fissures" and "traces" that are obscured in the construction of objectivity.

One of the elements of *Dimensiones paralelas* that achieves this most clearly is *Garden Exercises* (2017), a collaboration with Agata Mergler. The piece includes a seven-minute video filmed in a garden in Quito.[44] It is part of a project designed by Villavicencio and Mergler to explore haptic modes of filmmaking, emphasizing the role of the whole body rather than simply the organ of sight in the production of images. Their aim was to explore how a photographer might move beyond their role as a mere "functionary" (Vilém Flusser) of the apparatus; they envision the artist instead as "an agent capable of modifying and subverting the existing filming apparatus."[45] This subversion is a result of the use of open-source hardware and software to modify devices, defying Flusser's description of the camera as a "black box" whose workings are inaccessible to the photographer.[46] The principal modification made was to build "haptic cameras," which are attached to the user's hands (see Fig. 2.12). In this way, Villavicencio and Mergler wished to explore the possibilities for a more intimate relationship with the objects being filmed that is opened up by the faculty of touch, compared with that of sight, which—as Laura Marks argues—is much more aligned

---

43 Instituto Latinoamericano de Investigación en Artes, "Entrevista a Cristian Villavicencio."
44 The video may be viewed at http://www.cristianvillavicencio.net/31_haptic_visual_identities.html
45 Mergler and Villavicencio, "Collaboration, Media, Praxis," 192. Flusser develops his theory in *Towards a Philosophy of Photography* (1984).
46 Flusser, *Towards a Philosophy of Photography*, 27.

with post-industrial metropolitan experience and with the exercise of control.[47] The displacement of the eye "implies a different approach to distance and a particular way of dealing with space, typical for touch. That is: a fragmentary, not totalizing, way of representing space."[48]

Fig. 2.12 Cristian Villavicencio and Agata Mergler, *Haptic Cameras—4 simultaneous cameras* (2016) (photograph by Cristian Villavicencio).

Macro photography, which was originally developed for scientific research, is here put to very different ends as the lenses hover, spin, and drift unsteadily through the branches and their fruits. The veins of leaves come in and out of focus as hands stray across them. The effect of fragmentation is enhanced by a coded script that turned each camera off and on at certain moments. Operating the cameras was also a collaborative experience in which the participants had to coordinate the movement of their bodies in space. The short length of the cables connecting the cameras to the recording system required them to move in synchrony and close proximity.[49]

---

47 Mergler and Villavicencio, "Collaboration, Media, Praxis," 196. See Marks, *The Skin of the Film*, 198, 244.
48 Mergler and Villavicencio, "Collaboration, Media, Praxis," 195.
49 Mergler and Villavicencio, 198.

The unfamiliar visions generated by Villavicencio's exhibitions encourage us to question how our understanding of the world has been shaped by the totalizing and objectifying perspectives that became central to scientific modes of observation in the eighteenth century. The perspectives generated give us another view of fossils, insects, and plants that undermines their morphological integrity, that is, the particular forms that allow them to be classified as this or another species. Surfaces become abstract textures and our sense of scale is also interrupted. The neutrality of the objective image was, of course, an illusion; these projects allow us to reflect on what kind of world it gave us, and what alternative worlds we might encounter through other kinds of visual or embodied interaction.

In their exploration of the relationship between the eye, the body, and machines, Mergler and Villavicencio found points of contact with the work of Jonathan Crary.[50] Crary maintains that optical devices are not simply material objects; they are "embedded in a much larger assemblage of events and powers." Countering a crude technological determinism, in which modes of perception are reduced to the effects of changing technical practices, Crary argues that optical devices should be understood as "points of intersection where philosophical, scientific, and aesthetic discourses overlap with mechanical techniques, institutional requirements, and socioeconomic forces."[51] Crary's seminal work—*Techniques of the Observer: On Vision and Modernity in the Nineteenth Century* (1990)—excludes any mention of the colonial purposes served by many of the visual technologies he discusses, including photography and cinema. The decolonial impetus of Villavicencio's work emerges most clearly in the tension he creates between the ideals of objectivity, universality, and critical distance to which Western knowledge became bound in the nineteenth century and the more intimate encounters with the natural world facilitated by alternative technologies, many of them associated with indigenous cultures, and which have produced a different kind of knowledge.

In an installation designed for the 2021 Cuenca Bienal (see Fig. 2.13), Villavicencio brought *Selecciones* together with a series of works inspired by the collection of pre-Columbian artefacts held at the Museo

---

50   Mergler and Villavicencio, 195.
51   Crary, *Techniques of the Observer*, 8.

Antropológico y de Arte Contemporáneo in Guayaquil, Ecuador. Moulds were printed from 3-D scans of the original artefacts, which allowed Villavicencio to recreate the pieces in ceramic. Many of these works engage senses other than vision and encourage an embodied response on the part of the gallery visitor, who is permitted to wander between (and sometimes over) them, and to listen to soundscapes that come in and out of audibility as they move through the exhibition space. In *Silbato* (Whistle), two interconnected conical ceramic vessels, joined at the base, are filled with water. As the object is tilted (with the help of a motorized stand), the water moves and the change in pressure creates a whistling sound. The piece is a "relectura" (re-reading) of similar whistling pots exhibited in the museum, many of which take the form of the animal whose sound they reproduce. The *Espejo sonoro* (Resonant Mirror) was also fashioned in a way that recalled the shape of pre-Columbian vessels, some of which recreated the forms of plants or fruit. Its concave shape created an echo as the sound of a hyperdirectional speaker bounced off its surface. The speaker produced an effect of intimacy, as if the sounds were being whispered in the ear; rather than being immersed in ambient sound, the visitor had to stand close to the sculpture to hear them.

The sound transmitted by the speaker was the audio track of a video, *Tecnologías de la experiencia* (Technologies of Experience, 2021), filmed in the Parque Yasuní in Ecuador. It features Fernando Alvarado, an elder of the Alta Florencia community, who had been asked to reproduce with his own voice the sounds of the animals he could hear as he travelled along the river. The astonishing repertoire of sounds that Alvarado is able to articulate is no less impressive than the keenness of his ear, alert to the rich diversity of animal life surrounding him. His imitations become a gesture of reciprocity, an openness to nonhuman signs and languages. They suggest the extent to which sound is a crucial means of orientation among the dense vegetation of the region. Villavicencio wished to capture this reliance on the aural as a way of registering and analysing the natural environment. As he observes, "hay un nivel sónico de entender la realidad, un nivel que no está basado en la visión solamente sino también en lo sonoro" (there is a sonic level at which reality can be understood, a level that is not based on vision alone but also on sound).[52]

---

52 Conversation with the author, 27 January 2022.

Fig. 2.13 Installation view of Cristian Villavicencio, *Tecnologías de la experiencia* (2021). *Tecnologías de la experiencia* (video, back wall); *Silbato*, 50.0 cm x 40.0 cm x 50.0 cm (back left); *Espejo sonoro*, 160 cm x 40 cm x 40 cm (back right); *Resonar/excavar* (foreground). 15th Cuenca Bienal, Cuenca, Ecuador (photograph by Ricardo Bohórquez).

The final piece of the exhibition, *Resonar/excavar* (Resonate/Excavate), comprised a low-lying wooden platform, whose shape echoed the snake coils of *Selecciones*, into which speakers playing sounds of very low frequency had been inserted. Visitors could stand or walk over the speakers and sense the vibrations emanating from them, which produced a kind of "estado alterado" (altered state).[53] Resonance creates relationships that knit bodies and objects together in a complex and reciprocal system. It does not allow for a division between subject and object, expressing instead our thorough entanglement with our environment. Villavicencio reflects on the significance of the resonating body in pre-Hispanic cosmovisions: "el cuerpo danzante, el cuerpo que hace sonido, en este movimiento ritual heterosonoro, es sumamente preponderante" (the dancing body, the body that makes sound, in that hetero-resonant ritual movement, is extremely important).[54]

In creating a dialogue between Western epistemologies and ancestral knowledge in Ecuador, Villavicencio wished to explore the kind of situated knowledges that are embraced in Yuk Hui's notion of "cosmotechnics." Hui argues that "Scientific and technical thinking emerges under cosmological conditions that are expressed in the relations between humans and their milieus, which are never static."[55] Far from understanding nature and technics as opposed, he proposes "cosmotechnics" as a way of unifying the two: as an epistemic project that would seek alternatives to the kind of hegemonic synchronization to which modern technologies are contributing.[56] Cosmotechnics "allows us to trace different technicities, and contributes to opening up the plurality of relations between technics, mythology, and cosmology—and thereby to the embracing of the different relations between the human and technics inherited from different mythologies and cosmologies."[57] It is precisely the relationship between multiple technics and cosmologies that emerges as the underlying theme of Villavicencio's recent work.

Conclusion

Baroque cabinets of curiosities, with their cornucopia of exotic specimens, would gradually be replaced with more systematic collections that swapped the marvellous for the universal and rejected diversity for a narrower focus on specific areas of knowledge. If early

---

53 Conversation with the author, 27 January 2022.
54 Conversation with the author, 27 January 2022.
55 Hui, *The Question Concerning Technology in China*, 18.
56 Hui, 20, 31.
57 Hui, 29.

modern cabinets of curiosities presented the world as a continuum, as "one great unbroken chain" of correspondences and analogies, natural history collections from the eighteenth century onwards placed greater emphasis on differences rather than affinities in their attempt to catalogue the natural world.⁵⁸ Robert Hooke famously called for as full and complete a collection of objects as possible, in which an inquirer might "read the Book of Nature," parsing its varieties with care; such collections should not be for the "Divertisement, and Wonder and Gazing" of viewers with a childlike desire to be pleased.⁵⁹

La Padula and Villavicencio adopt some of the modes of presentation that were characteristic of cabinets of curiosities and natural history collections in order to raise questions about the particular ways in which they ordered nature, as well as to redeem something of value in the encounters they stage. Surekha Davies argues that cabinets "constituted knowledge through processes of compression," bringing diverse things into physical proximity in the same visual and physical space. The series of juxtapositions they created prompted "fresh questions" on the part of viewers, as each visual arrangement "drew attention to different material characteristics, meanings, and uses of things."⁶⁰ In the same way, art installations that rework and remediate collections of objects provoke questions about the relationships between art, science, and nature, and how these have changed over history. The vision of the oneness of the world that is evoked by the visual correspondences of the baroque cabinet is one that regains a particular imaginary force in our own time, as we become more acutely aware of the interconnections between living things and other species and their environments.

Referring to the "compression, ontological disruption, and delight at a world turned upside-down by the shocks of new things" that characterize early modern cabinets, Davies suggests that this "fluidic quality in practices of display" might usefully be deployed in collections of the future to unseat essentialist thinking and to engage more deeply with ethical questions of curation and decolonization.⁶¹ One such question might be directed to the relationship between scientific

---

58 Weston, "'Worlds in Miniature,'" 41.
59 Hooke, *Robert Hooke: The Posthumous Works*, 3:338.
60 Davies, "Catalogical Encounters," 229.
61 Davies, 248.

knowledge and accumulation. Walter Benjamin identifies the "Baroque ideal of knowledge" as one of "stockpiling."[62] It was in this period that many of the great libraries and collections of Europe were founded. As José Ramón Marcaida López argues, "En buena medida, la ciencia moderna podría caracterizarse como el resultado de un ambicioso proyecto de acumulación a todos los niveles" (in good measure, modern science could be characterized as the result of an ambitious project of accumulation at every level).[63] In that process, the collecting of marvels in the Baroque period and their conversion into commodities emerges as a paradigmatic case.[64] Reinserting the Baroque era into the history of science, from which it has largely been excluded, draws attention to this relationship between knowledge, marvels, and the circulation of objects in the early colonial world. It also returns us to the emphasis on the sensory and the material in encounters with the natural world, which predates the relative priority given to texts over images and objects in Enlightenment museums.

Oliver Impey and Arthur Macgregor find in the inclusion of manufacturing tools in early modern collections "an allusion to human ingenuity"; likewise, Elisabeth Scheicher describes rare pieces of fine craftmanship in wood and ivory as a demonstration of "'man's ability to overcome the difficulties" presented by raw materials, and the addition of scientific instruments such as compasses and astrolabes as a testimony to "man's ability to dominate nature."[65] The inclusion of pieces of art and laboratory equipment in La Padula's collections and optical devices in those of Villavicencio do not, in contrast, celebrate the ability of humans to tame and commodify nature. Instead, by historizing how nature has been captured in Western knowledge and culture, they allow us to glimpse the possibility of alternative kinds of encounter. The philosopher Yuk Hui observes that the use of technologies to scale our vision up or down, zooming in through the microscope or out through a telescope, augments our senses in a way that is "about improving the capacity of the senses, but not about developing other

---

62   Benjamin, *Origin of the German Trauerspiel*, 196.
63   Marcaida López, *Arte y ciencia en el barroco español*, 37.
64   Marcaida López, 55–56.
65   Impey and MacGregor, "Introduction," xix; Scheicher, "The Collection of Archduke Ferdinand II at Schloss Ambras," 43.

senses that would allow us to preserve and renew our relations with other beings and the world itself."⁶⁶ In art, Hui finds a space in which the technological augmentation of the senses may be explored and brought into relationship with other forms of sense perception. He contends that "Scientific thinking wants to improve the capacity of the senses, while philosophical thinking wants to develop other senses. It is in art that both can be united."⁶⁷

It is certainly the case that the work of La Padula and Villavicencio creates new or renewed relationships between art and science. While scientists and artists had collaborated closely in the production of illustrations from the sixteenth century onwards, Lorraine Daston and Peter Galison observe that, from the early nineteenth century, "The rise of the objective image polarized the visual space of art and science," as both the self and subjectivity were rigorously purged from scientific images.⁶⁸ The installations created by La Padula and Villavicencio may be read as an attempt to reimbue scientific images and collections with traces of the subjective encounters from which they were never, in reality, separated. They also depict a natural world that is rich in its own creativity. In European cabinets of curiosities, Davies maintains that the juxtaposition of "natural" objects with those wrought by artists "challenge the notion of art as something exclusively made by people."⁶⁹ The separation of the natural and the artificial in later natural history collections responds to a narrower definition of art in which "conscious human fabrication" was central.⁷⁰ Exhibitions by La Padula and Villavicencio explore expanded notions of art and nature in ways that acknowledge the thorough interpenetration of nature and culture in human society. They call for a renewed understanding of the importance of a material, embodied connection with a natural world from which we had thought ourselves disconnected. Early cabinets of curiosities created a world that was thoroughly shaped by human intervention. In a similar way, La Padula and Villavicencio coincide in their refusal to present a positivist vision of "the universe without man," in Baudelaire's resonant phrase.⁷¹

---

66   Hui, *Art and Cosmotechnics*, 62.
67   Hui, 62.
68   Daston and Galison, *Objectivity*, 187.
69   Davies, "Catalogical Encounters," 235.
70   Davies, 248.
71   Baudelaire, "The Salon of 1859," 239.

3. Floras, Herbaria, and Botanical Illustration

The strong ties between botany and medicine in the ancient and medieval worlds gave rise to methods of classifying plants that were based on human uses, giving details of how plants could be used as cures for different ailments and how each should be gathered, preserved, and prepared. Local names for plants prevailed, and the knowledge distilled in medieval herbals was often acquired through personal experience or handed down from previous generations. The indigenous nomenclature that European colonizers found in use in the New World also generally categorized plants according to their culinary, medicinal, or religious uses.[1] European scientists who travelled to the region in the early colonial period often drew on these classifications to produce surveys and compendia of plant life. The Renaissance physician Francisco Hernández de Toledo (1514–1587) travelled to (what is now called) Mexico in 1570; he spent seven years describing and classifying plants and animals, which he organized alphabetically according to Nahuatl names of plants and groupings of plants. In his *Historia general de las cosas de Nueva España* (c. 1577), the Franciscan friar Bernardino de Sahagún also employed Nahuatl terms, paying careful attention to the habitats of the species he lists and their different uses, including their medicinal benefits and hallucinatory effects. He divides his material into categories such as plants that are suitable for eating raw, plants that are eaten cooked, medicinal plants, and poisonous plants. Such forms of classification were later to be rejected by European naturalists in favour of the more abstract, universal taxonomies championed by the Swedish naturalist Linnaeus and his disciples.

---

1 Nieto Olarte, *Remedios para el imperio*, 112.

The overwhelming influx of new botanical material from the colonies in the eighteenth century prompted the search in Europe for more robust and universal methods of organizing knowledge. The sheer number of unknown species, which made classifying them an enormous task, ensured that taxonomy remained a priority in botany for most of the eighteenth century.² In the new system of plant classification developed by Linnaeus, morphology was emphasized over function, behaviour, or evolution: the search for a clear, simple, and unified system of describing plants took priority over more complex questions concerning how they grew or interacted with their environment. The aim was to describe each individual plant in a way that accorded it a place within the diversity of all plants, providing a comprehensive overview of different varieties. Such knowledge was considered to be invaluable in exploiting the economic benefits of plants, which—as Linnaeus wrote—were "of great utility to the human race" and should be "assiduously researched."³

The major scientific expeditions to the New World sponsored by the Spanish Crown in the second half of the eighteenth century were indeed primarily designed to ascertain what economic benefits could be derived from plants in the region. Botanists were sent to research the potential medical and commercial uses of plants that did not exist in Europe.⁴ In Spain, more than in any other European nation, a knowledge of medicinal plants and the promotion of a pharmaceutical industry became central concerns of the State.⁵ Scholars have emphasized the importance of botanical art in facilitating a relationship between science and commerce. This was again particularly marked in the case of the Spanish Empire, whose expeditions resulted in a much greater production of images.⁶ As Mauricio Nieto Olarte explains, once plants were removed from their habitats and either dried or drawn, they became types, which could more easily be examined, compared, and reordered. The act of illustrating nature allowed its complexity to be simplified, domesticated, and made intelligible.⁷ Daniela Bleichmar describes the Spanish natural

2   Schiebinger, "Gender and Natural History," 171.
3   Linné, *Linnaeus' Philosophia Botanica*, 307.
4   Nieto Olarte, *Remedios para el imperio*, 12.
5   Nieto Olarte, 12; Cañizares-Esguerra, *Nature, Empire, and Nation*.
6   Bleichmar, *Visible Empire*, 21.
7   Nieto Olarte, *Remedios para el imperio*, 63.

history expeditions as "visualization projects," designed to make nature "movable, knowable, and—ideally—governable."[8]

As mentioned above, from the eighteenth century, plants were classified in Western science in ways that located them in systems of similarities and differences with *other* plants, not in relation to humans or to the broader ecosystems in which they participated. The four artists introduced in this chapter—all from Colombia—create images and collections of plants or seeds that bear witness instead to the entanglement of plant and animal (including human) lives, particularly with respect to agricultural practices. Each allows us to read human agency with respect to plant life in rather different ways, however.

In Alberto Baraya's work, the global circulation of plants traces patterns of dispossession, as the (neo)colonial management of agriculture produces and deepens racial and economic inequalities. His *Herbario de plantas artificiales* (2002–) exposes these inequalities and suggests (symbolic) forms of reparation. He gathers highly commodified reproductions of flowers, which have been dispatched across the world in search of new markets, and reinserts them in other circuits of meaning to highlight the many cultural, social, medicinal, and spiritual values that plants have acquired in human societies. Eulalia de Valdenebro documents and performs human-plant encounters that demonstrate how humans have shaped the evolution of plants, for good and for ill. *Del páramo al desierto, 19–21* (2009) brings to the fore that which tended to be erased in early nineteenth-century botanical illustrations, which showed an idealized portrait of nature devoid of human influence. *Heterogéneas/Criminales* (2014) denounces the loss of biodiversity and food sovereignty that has resulted from genetic engineering in agriculture. In her illustrations, De Valdenebro forges relationships of greater equality and equivalence between her own body and that of the plants she paints. In *On the Marriages of Plants* (2018), María Fernanda Cardoso gives vibrant expression to Linnaeus's account of plant sexuality, but also highlights the intimate relationships with many other species that are crucial to reproduction and survival, creating a much more integrated understanding of nature that ultimately suggests limits to human agency. Illustrations by Abel Rodríguez (formerly known as Mogaje Guihu) give us insight into the reciprocal relationships that bind

---

8   Bleichmar, *Visible Empire*, 7.

humans with the forest and its other inhabitants in the crop-growing practices developed by indigenous communities in Colombia. His work points to the potential in polyculture to increase biodiversity, mapping out a much more positive and collaborative role for humans in shaping forest ecosystems and producing a vision of the forest in which the natural, the social, and the spiritual are fully integrated.

Directly or indirectly, all four artists challenge the unified, simplified systems of eighteenth-century botany. Baraya, De Valdenebro and Cardoso work to reconnect plant taxonomies with other forms of knowledge and experience that were discredited during the Enlightenment, while Rodríguez articulates a very different approach to plant life that has not, unlike many Western concepts of nature, been forged on a division between humans and the rest of the natural world. This division has led to ecological degradation on a vast scale but re-emerges in the principle of conservation, which defines nature as something that needs special protection from human activity. In the practices and relationships Rodríguez depicts—and brings into being—in his work, we glimpse a version of anthropogenic ecological change which is far from catastrophic, and from which many species benefit.

Alberto Baraya: Botanical Expeditions, Herbaria, and the Natural History of Capitalism

Alberto Baraya frames several of his projects with reference to the Royal Botanical Expedition to New Granada (1783–1816), led by José Celestino Mutis, a Spanish mathematician, botanist, and physician.[9] The expedition, which employed dozens of scientists and artists, investigated aspects of natural history, geography, zoology, astronomy, and mining. The exquisite illustrations that catalogued the region's flora stretched to almost 6000 folio drawings. Although they were more stylized than most, the images produced generally adhered to the norms of botanical illustration in the eighteenth century in Europe. The figure at the centre of a typical plate demonstrated the "habit" of the plant (its general appearance and architecture), with details and transverse sections of

---

9 The *Expedición Botánica al Virreinato de Nueva Granada* covered an area that now comprises Colombia, Ecuador, Panama, parts of northern Peru and northern Brazil, and other smaller states.

the calyx, petals, and fruit often arranged at the foot, allowing the plant to be successfully identified according to the Linnaean system.

This format is employed for many of the plates designed for Baraya's *Herbario de plantas artificiales* (Herbarium of Artificial Plants, 2002–), with the rather significant difference that the specimens shown are not of native flora but artificial flowers, the great majority made in China, fashioned from plastic, fabric, and wire. Baraya collects his samples from the environments in which they are often to be found: cafés, offices, hotel bathrooms, churches, airports, and shop windows. The flowers dominate the plate, with dissections arrayed below; a handwritten label details the origin of the plant and the materials used for its petioles, stamens, and other parts.

In many ways, then, Baraya's plates imitate the design of the illustrations produced for the New Granada expedition. Those plates did not typically represent real, individual plants, either: they were composite images that smoothed out the accidental and the anomalous to create a single, idealized version of the plant.[10] The quest for a universal taxonomy of plants led to an approach that was zealously exact in its depiction of the essence of each plant but disregarded the imperfections of a particular specimen or any characteristics that were not considered common to the species. In the eighteenth and early nineteenth centuries, an allegiance to what might be called "truth-to-nature" obliged the naturalist to be "steeped in but not enslaved to nature as it appeared."[11]

The perfect specimens Baraya uses are not abstracted from their contexts in a quest for a universal type, however: they are surrounded by texts, photographs, and other illustrations that celebrate the local, the contingent, the subjective, the affective, and the cultural nature of our relationship with plants and flowers. Some of the *Herbario* plates include a photographed "comparative study" in which a plastic fruit—designed to represent the recognizable essence of a coconut or a cacao pod—is held next to a real one, showing the deviations in colour, form, or texture of the genuine article in comparison with its idealized reproduction. Photographs tie specimens to specific places or people that Baraya meets on his travels, demonstrating how his artworks arise from chance

---

10 Bleichmar, *Visible Empire*, 67.
11 Daston and Galison, *Objectivity*, 59.

connections and discoveries. In *Taxones Tabatinga*[12] (*Tabatinga Taxons*, 2014), for example, Baraya catalogues the different kinds of artificial plants and flowers he finds in a decorative display in a hairdressing salon owned by Nicolasa, who appears in a photograph placed next to the species identified, brandishing her bouquet with a coquettish smile (see Fig. 3.1).

Fig. 3.1 Alberto Baraya, *Taxones Tabatinga* (2014) from the *Herbario de plantas artificiales*. Found object "Made in China," photography and drawing on cardboard, 56.0 x 82.0 cm (photograph by the artist).

In a similar way, other *Herbario* plates contain photographs showing the shop windows or market stalls where flowers were found or the cultural uses to which they are put. Such references to specific natural or human environments are entirely absent from the illustrations commissioned by Mutis and other leaders of New World expeditions. Baraya's plates reconnect the natural and cultural histories that were torn apart in eighteenth-century abstractions. In a plate dedicated to an artificial reproduction of a *Brugmansia* or *Datura* species (*Borrachero Doble*; *Double Devil's Trumpet*, 2014), he includes photographs of the

---

12 Tabatinga is a frontier city in the Brazilian Amazon, located on the border with Colombia.

natural environments in which the real plants, which contain toxic hallucinogens, are typically found, as well as notes on their use in Europe and America by magicians and shamans for the healing of wounds or the divination of a patient's illnesses (see Fig. 3.2). By contrast, the elegant *Datura* illustration produced for Mutis (see Fig. 3.3) is full of botanical information that would aid identification, folding flowers and spiny fruit into its design, but it reveals nothing beyond the morphology of the plant, which is set against a plain white background.[13.]

As Mary Louise Pratt affirms, the European exercise of natural history "elaborated a rationalizing, extractive, dissociative understanding which overlaid functional, experiential relations among people, plants, and animals."[14] In an operation that was deeply appropriative at heart, life forms across the planet "were to be drawn out of the tangled threads of their life surroundings and rewoven into European-based patterns of global unity and order."[15] While this process is erased in the handsome compositions of the New Granada plates, Baraya traces very plainly how his own specimens are caught up in patterns of global trade and consumption. Next to the dense green foliage and sepia petals of the *Orquídea viajera* (Travelling Orchid, 2013), we find a map of its "commercial and cultural routes," linking the artificial flowers market in Yiwu, China, to retail outlets from Madrid to Miami; a further series of connecting lines trace the flowers' artistic reinsertion into landscapes during Baraya's journeys to New Zealand, Machu Picchu, and elsewhere.

As well as simplifying nature, making it more legible and fit to enter a pre-established system of classification, the illustrations made during expeditions to the Americas allowed specimens to transcend time and space, protecting them against the decay they would otherwise suffer on the long journey across the ocean. Through the creation of permanent inscriptions on paper, the immense variety of nature could be condensed, flattened, and shipped back to Europe, to be measured, compared, ordered, and assigned values. As Mutis famously claimed, his illustrations characterized each plant so fully and accurately that no one viewing them would actually need to travel to search for them in their native environment.[16] For Latour, these and other "immutable mobiles"

---

13 See http://www.rjb.csic.es/icones/mutis/paginas/laminadibujo.php?lamina=2875
14 Pratt, *Imperial Eyes*, 37.
15 Pratt, 31.
16 Uribe Uribe, "Los maestros pintores," 102.

Fig. 3.2 Alberto Baraya, *Borrachero doble* (Double Devil's Trumpet, 2014) from the *Herbario de plantas artificiales*. Found object "Made in China," photography and drawing on cardboard, 112.0 x 82.0 cm (photograph by the artist).

Fig. 3.3 Juan Francisco Mancera, *Giganton. Datura* from the *Drawings of the Royal Botanical Expedition to the New Kingdom of Granada*. Image from the digitalization project of the drawings of the Royal Botanical Expedition to the New Kingdom of Granada (1783–1816) directed by José Celestino Mutis: http://www.rjb.csic.es/icones/mutis. Real Jardín Botánico-CSIC. Reproduced by kind permission of the Real Jardín Botánico.

played a vital role in the rise of capitalism and the European domination of other cultures.[17] As such inscriptions were "superimposed, reshuffled, recombined, and summarized" in Europe's "centers of calculation," merchants, engineers, cartographers, and others drew benefit from the new ideas and phenomena that emerged, which remained "hidden from the other people from whom all these inscriptions have been exacted."[18]

The economic exploitation of America that was the ultimate aim of the New World expeditions may have been suppressed in the illustrations produced for Mutis, but it was a prominent reference in correspondence about the project. The huge expense of such expeditions was primarily justified by the financial gains that an increased knowledge of its colonies' natural resources was likely to secure for Spain. Writing to his King in 1763, Mutis reaffirms the profit and the glory that would surely derive from his expedition. Following some complaints about the discomforts of the "verdaderamente austera y desabrida" (truly austere

---

17 Latour, "Visualisation and Cognition," 12.
18 Latour, 30.

and unpleasant) life of the naturalist, he lists the many riches that the land of America offers the Spanish crown, from gold and precious stones to wood and plants of many kinds: all produced "para la utilidad y el comercio" and "para el bien del genero [sic] humano" (for use and trade; for the good of the human race).[19]

The decolonial thrust of Baraya's work emerges most powerfully in a series that attends to this relationship between natural history and commerce, together with the racial politics of (neo)colonialism. As part of an expedition to Tumaco, a city in the Pacific lowlands of Colombia, Baraya produced a series of plates on cacao, one of the main crops grown in the region. *Cacao, beso de cacao* (Cacao, Cacao Kiss, 2018) features the longitudinal cross-section of a cacao pod made—as the description below tells us—of thermoformed plastic with a heart of polystyrene foam (see Fig. 3.4). Below, where we would normally expect to see smaller illustrations of the plant's characteristic features, Baraya inserts wrappers for a chocolate-covered candy manufactured by Nestlé called "Beso de negra" (black woman's kiss).[20] The bold red packaging is adorned with images of voluptuous lips and an alluring black woman in a shoulderless dress. As Baraya notes in a label below, the sensual experience offered by the combination of cacao and sugar is promoted via an exoticizing depiction of racial difference.

In *Cacao, conguito* (2018), another plate in the series, the artificial red fruit of a cacao tree is accompanied by a small reproduction mounted on cardboard of a black, round-bellied cartoon character. The image forms part of the branding for a range of products marketed in Spain under the name of Conguitos by Chocolates Lacasa, a Spanish confectionery company. The name *conguitos* is the diminutive version of a Spanish term for a black person (which derives from the country name Congo). The caricatured black character has full red lips and is carrying, as Baraya observes, "una lanza tipo tribal" (a tribal-style spear). This jaunty, exotic figure is used to promote the brand in Spain in a way that implicitly celebrates the racial dynamics of cacao production, as cacao growers tend to be black. Many African slaves were brought to work on plantations in Colombia and other countries in Latin America; today's

---

19 Mendoza, *Expedición botánica de José Celestino Mutis al Nuevo Reino de Granada*, 80, 77.
20 In the wake of the protests that followed George Floyd's death, Nestlé announced that it would rename the sweets as part of a broader review of racialized product names. Gretler and Whitley, "Nestle Pulls Beso de Negra, Red Skins Candy in Racial Review."

3. Floras, Herbaria, and Botanical Illustration 103

Fig. 3.4 Alberto Baraya, *Cacao, beso de cacao* (2018) from the Tumaco Expedition, *Herbario de plantas artificiales*. Found object, drawing and photography on cardboard (photograph by the artist).

cacao farm labourers in former colonies in West Africa also work in conditions that approach those of slavery. Baraya's plate exposes the operation of structural racism in global agricultural production, in both colonial and more recent eras.

The close relationship between racism and the emergence of a modern world-system based on extractivism is clearly outlined in the work of the Peruvian sociologist Aníbal Quijano. Ethnic categorizations were "the inevitable cultural consequence of coloniality" and were used to justify different kinds of labour control, including slavery and other forms of coerced labour.[21] Quijano argues that modernity itself only emerges in Europe as a result of its imperial ventures in America: its constitution as a modern power rests historically on the wealth extracted from the region—gold, silver, potatoes, tomatoes, tobacco—as a result of the free labour of Indians, *mestizos*, and African slaves.[22] In this sense, "The Americas were not incorporated into an already existing capitalist world-economy. There could not have been a capitalist world-economy without the Americas."[23] By the eighteenth century, however, Europeans had not only persuaded themselves that they had independently forged their own civilization, but that they were naturally and racially superior to other civilizations, as evidenced by their imperial domination over them.[24] It is this story—of the basis of modern capitalist European society in colonialism and racism—that is laid bare in Baraya's works.

As José Roca points out, Baraya's purloined plants—stolen from hotel receptions, restaurants, and shops—rehearse the thefts of colonial scientists engaged in acts of "collecting." As well as bearing witness to a history of dispossession through forms of re-enactment, however, these expeditions also perform acts of restitution. For his *Proyecto árbol de caucho* (Latex Tree Project, 2006), Baraya travelled to the Acre region of Brazil, the scene of intensive rubber production and the expansion of European colonization in the nineteenth and early twentieth centuries. He worked with local rubber tappers to cover the surface of a thirty-metre rubber tree with liquid latex that had been extracted from other rubber trees, and then peeled off the cast. Exhibited at the XXVII São Paulo Biennial, the empty, flaccid rubber skin spoke to the boom and bust cycles of rubber production and their enormous and lasting social and environmental impact on the region.

Baraya's absurd quest to collect and identify every type of artificial plant in the world mimics the overweening ambition of Enlightenment

---

21 Quijano and Wallerstein, "Americanity as a Concept," 550–51.
22 Quijano, "Colonialidad del poder, eurocentrismo y América Latina," 221.
23 Quijano and Wallerstein, "Americanity as a Concept," 549.
24 Quijano, "Colonialidad del poder, eurocentrismo y América Latina," 221.

natural histories, but replaces their austere language with baroque proliferation and theatricality. For Severo Sarduy, the "obsessive repetition of a useless thing [...] determines the Baroque as *play*, in contrast to the determination of the classical work as a labor."[25] Other elements of Baraya's plates also bear affinities with baroque aesthetics. While they are relatively simple in design, they employ the quintessential baroque technique of *trompe l'oeil* in their presentation of artificial plants that often trick the viewer into believing that they are real. They present matter as "folding, unfolding, refolding" in ways observed by Gilles Deleuze in his work on the baroque,[26] as they recycle and rework themes and forms from the past, trouble the division between the artist as subject and object, entangle the spiritual and the cultural with the material and commercial, and interweave the artificial and the organic, artistic convention and its critique. These recyclings, restitutions, and re-entanglements become part of a symbolic form of reparation in Baraya's work, in response to the dissociative and dispossessive violence of global capitalism.

Domestication and Diversity: Human-Plant Entanglements in the Work of Eulalia de Valdenebro

In 2009, De Valdenebro was appointed to undertake a series of botanical illustrations, to be completed in a classical style. They were commissioned for a permanent exhibition on Francisco José de Caldas (1768–1816), a Colombian naturalist, mathematician, lawyer, and engineer whose work is celebrated in a museum bearing his name in central Bogotá. She agreed to provide the illustrations on the condition that she would create them *in situ*, according to her usual practice. The botanical illustrations produced for the famous Spanish expeditions to the New World were largely created by artists based in workshops, on the basis of ink sketches made quickly in the field or specimens brought back by naturalists or plant collectors.[27] In contrast, De Valdenebro works entirely from direct observation, completing as much as possible of her illustrations in the location where each plant is found. In the company

---

25 Sarduy, "The Baroque and the Neobaroque," 288.
26 Deleuze, *The Fold*, 137.
27 Bleichmar, *Visible Empire*, 83, 91.

of a self-taught naturalist, Mateo Hernández, she undertook a journey through many of the different climate zones in Colombia, selecting flowers from native plants to illustrate the texts by Caldas that would feature in the exhibition.

Del páramo al desierto, 19–21 (From the Paramo to the Desert, 19–21, 2009) was conceived by De Valdenebro as the "negative" of the series of illustrations that she produced for the Casa Museo Francisco José de Caldas.[28] This alternative exhibition, shown simultaneously at the Museo de Arte Moderno in Bogotá, included sketches and photographs from De Valdenebro's journey through Colombia's climate zones. Instead of representing the pristine, idealized nature of nineteenth-century botany, however, she depicts a natural world that is thoroughly imprinted with human activity. Large-scale black-and-white photographs of the branches and twigs that have been carried along by the force of the Río Patía demonstrate the heightened flood risk caused by deforestation.[29] Other photographs in colour provide snapshots of other kinds of human intervention. One shows how a cactus has grown to incorporate the rusting barbed wire that encircled it (Fig. 3.5), while another reveals how a climbing plant has twisted itself around a wire fence, using it as a support to reach further from its roots (Fig. 3.6). In a further photograph, grasses are starting to grow over a pile of abandoned beer bottle tops. Although the presence of barbed wire transecting plant tissues is disconcerting, these images do not ultimately direct our attention to the human devastation of nature; indeed, they testify more to the resilience and ingenuity of plants in adapting to, and even taking advantage of, artefacts of human culture. Above all, they bring into focus the condition of coexistence that binds humans and plants together, as closely as a vine wrapped around a length of wire.

The photographs are interspersed with unframed sheets of paper used to produce sketches, handwritten notes and colour tests for the botanical illustrations created for the Caldas exhibition (see, for example, Fig. 3.7). These notes and sketches are the result of an individual encounter with a plant; here they act as a deconstructed version of the final portrait, the proof—as De Valdenebro writes—that "el trabajo posterior es la construcción de un simulacro" (the work that ensues is the construction

---

28 See https://www.eulaliadevaldenebro.com/paramo.html
29 Conversation with the author, 20 April 2022.

3. Floras, Herbaria, and Botanical Illustration 107

Fig. 3.5 Eulalia de Valdenebro, photograph of cactus from *Del páramo al desierto, 19–21* (2009). 50 x 70 cm.

Fig. 3.6 Eulalia de Valdenebro, photograph of climbing plant from *Del páramo al desierto, 19–21* (2009). 50 x 70 cm.

of a simulacrum).[30] It is this simulacrum of a pure, idealized, abundant, nineteenth-century version of nature that De Valdenebro finds to be responsible for the illusion of our separation from the natural world, which has allowed us to treat nature as a landscape to be "colonizado o admirado" (colonized or contemplated).[31] Her counter-exhibition asks us to recognize our lives as fully imbricated in the natural world, enjoining us to take "un viaje urgente del 19 al 21" (an urgent journey from the nineteenth century to the twenty-first).

This recognition of the deep integration between human culture and what we consider to be the natural world is also evident in *Heterogéneas/Criminales* (Heterogeneous/Criminales, 2012). The work is composed of two sets of illustrations, painted in watercolour: one of maize seeds (see Fig. 3.8) and the other of beans. In each, the upper series shows eight different varieties of the same species, while the lower line consists of eight digital reproductions of a transgenic seed, one identical to the next. A clear contrast is introduced between the surprising diversity of maize seeds and beans, of different colours, shapes, and textures, and the monotony of the transgenic versions below. Handwritten words accompany each series. The labels given to local varieties include "contenedores de vida," "nativa," and "heterogénea" (containers of life, native, heterogeneous). The local seed is "inestable" and "variable" (unstable, variable) but also "autónoma" and "soberana" (autonomous and sovereign). Reference is made to the practice of seed-swapping among farmers of different communities, as the seed is "única" and therefore "intercambiable" (unique, exchangeable). A contrasting set of terms is assigned to the transgenic seed. This is "global" and "homogénea" (global, homogeneous) as well as being "uniforme" (uniform), which may be a guarantee of "calidad" (quality). However, it is also for that reason "patentable" and leads to a "monopolio" (monopoly).

The upper series represents the values of agroecology; the lower series, of agribusiness. Maristella Svampa and Enrique Viale summarize the antagonism between the two models in this way:

---

30   See https://www.eulaliadevaldenebro.com/paramo.html
31   See https://www.eulaliadevaldenebro.com/paramo.html

Fig. 3.7 Eulalia de Valdenebro, sketch from *Del páramo al desierto, 19–21* (2009). 30 x 25 cm (photograph by the artist).

mientras la agroecología apela a la autosuficiencia tecnológica, promueve el diálogo de saberes, se practica a través de un uso diversificado, apuesta a un modelo de pequeña escala, en reciprocidad con los procesos naturales; el agronegocio promueve la dependencia tecnológica, pretende el dominio epistemológico, defiende el uso especializado con tendencia al monocultivo, es sinónimo de concentración de la tierra y grandes propiedades y pretende controlar los procesos naturales.[32]

(while agroecology has recourse to technological self-sufficiency, fosters a dialogue between knowledges, supports diverse practices, works on a small-scale, local level in operating in a relationship of reciprocity with natural processes; agribusiness promotes technological dependency, claims to be the only source of knowledge, defends specialist practices with an inclination for monocultures, is synonymous with the concentration of land ownership and huge properties and aims to control natural processes.)

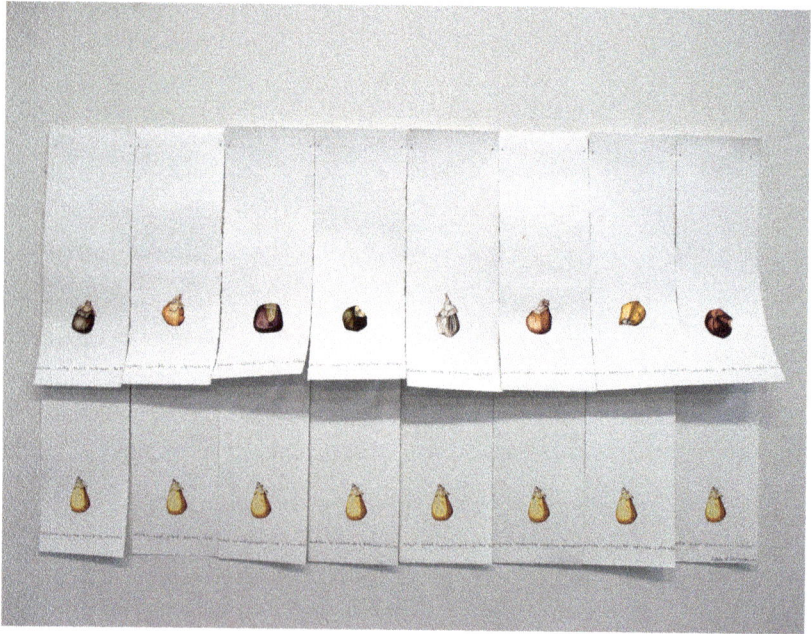

Fig. 3.8 Eulalia de Valdenebro, *Heterogéneas/Criminales* (2012). Watercolour on paper for heterogeneous seeds, digital reproduction from original in watercolour for homogeneous seeds (GMO), 120 x 60 cm (photograph by the artist).

---

32 Svampa and Viale, *El colapso ecológico ya llegó*, 256.

De Valdenebro's piece was created in 2012 in response to an attempt made by the Colombian government to introduce Law 1518 and Resolution 970, which effectively penalized the use of local seeds and criminalized farmers working with them, forcing them to buy patented seeds from transnational companies. De Valdenebro notes that although the law is currently in force, it is not legally binding.[33] Indeed, it has been deemed to be unenforceable as it affects the constitutional rights accorded to indigenous peoples and other protected minorities.[34]

Although it presents a clear denunciation of the patenting and homogenizing of seeds, *Heterogéneas/Criminales* does not censure human intervention in plant cultivation and crop improvement *per se*. The native seeds illustrated in the top row of each of De Valdenebro's series owe their striking diversity to the domestication and selective breeding of different varieties by indigenous and peasant farmers of the Americas, a process that has taken thousands of years. The exchange of seeds in local communities (often through barter) aids the conservation of diversity and enables farmers to select varieties that are most suited to local climates and conditions. As Darwin observed, selection in plants and animals after domestication has produced enormous diversity that far outstrips variation in their wild ancestors.[35] The domestication of crops is considered "one of the most successful of all plant–animal mutualisms."[36] Humans have benefited from more varied and reliable sources of food, with crops better adapted to local climates and cooking practices, while plants have benefited from a selection that has, as Darwin stated, more speedily "fit them for infinitely diversified conditions of life, to avoid enemies of all kinds, and to struggle against a host of competitors."[37] Transgenic seeds, on the other hand, produced to a universal formula, are often poorly adapted and must be protected through a greater use of pesticides. De Valdenebro's work thus celebrates the history of symbiotic relationships between humans and plants, while subjecting to critique the loss of diversity that has resulted from the appropriation and homogenization of native seeds by biotech companies.

---

33 See https://www.eulaliadevaldenebro.com/heterogeneas.html
34 Grupo de Investigación en Derechos Colectivos y Ambientales (GIDC), Colombia, "El despojo de la propiedad intelectual a través del Convenio UPOV 91."
35 Darwin, *The Variation of Animals and Plants under Domestication*, 2:406.
36 Purugganan and Fuller, "The Nature of Selection during Plant Domestication," 843.
37 Darwin, *The Variation of Animals and Plants under Domestication*, 2:412–13.

A rejection of the universal and the homogeneous also guides many of De Valdenebro's more recent works of botanical illustration, which attempt to trace alternative encounters between humans and plants that are not ones of subordination and standardization. *Frailejonmetría comparada esc 1:1* (Comparative Frailejonmetry scale 1:1, 2020) shows a *frailejón* (*Espeletia grandiflora*), a plant that grows in Colombia's high-altitude *páramos* and is endemic to this ecosystem (Fig. 3.9).[38] In many ways, the illustration has been produced according to the traditions of botanical art: every detail of the plant's appearance—its yellow flowers, the green leaves curling upwards, and the brown-grey marcescent leaves that droop below to form a skirt around the trunk—is richly and meticulously rendered in watercolour, and the proportions of its different parts have been reproduced with precision.[39] What is unexpected is the scale, as the plant is drawn at life-size, standing almost two-and-a-half metres tall. In another departure from convention, De Valdenebro completed the entire illustration on location in the *páramo*, travelling there every week for around a year.[40] But perhaps most striking is the artist's decision to map her own body onto the paper, with the subtle contours of her head in profile just visible in a lighter tone in the head-like rosette of the *frailejón*.

For De Valdenebro, the extended encounter with the *frailejón* in its habitat and the decision to work at a 1:1 scale was a response to a plant that has often been anthropomorphized: it is a common experience, she explains, to feel that they are humanlike in their form and their distribution in small groupings.[41] Drawing a specimen at full size was a logistical challenge in the extreme weather of the *páramo*: the illustration had to be composed in a number of smaller sections that were later assembled for exhibition.[42] If *antropometría* is the study of the dimensions and proportions of the human body, and comparative anthropometry was a powerful tool of racial discrimination in colonial science, *Frailejonmetría* suggests the possible recuperation of this exercise for a more horizontal, egalitarian act of comparison and encounter between

---

38 *Páramos* constitute a neotropical high-altitude ecosystem of exceptional biodiversity. They are found along the Andean mountain range, and especially in Colombia.
39 See https://www.eulaliadevaldenebro.com/fraile2.html
40 Conversation with the author, 20 April 2022.
41 Conversation with the author, 20 April 2022.
42 https://www.eulaliadevaldenebro.com/fraile2.html

Fig. 3.9 Eulalia de Valdenebro, *Frailejonmetría comparada esc 1:1* (2020). Watercolour on paper, 240 x 160 cm.

humans and plants. This act of anthropomorphism is simultaneously an act of phytomorphism.

This relationship of horizontality and reciprocity is emphasized in a related project by the same artist, *Mapa de relaciones táctiles esc 1:1* (Map of Tactile Relations Scale 1:1, 2020).[43] Against a series of concentric circles traced on an enormous sheet of paper, which map out the plant seen from above, De Valdenebro imprinted different parts of her own body alongside those of the *frailejón* to show the relative size of each. She covered her hand, arm, foot, calf, ear, and face with dark red ink before pressing them onto the paper, placing them next to similar impressions made from the leaves and flowers of the *frailejón* (see Fig. 3.10). Hand-written inscriptions compare the dimensions of human and plant parts.

---

43 See https://www.eulaliadevaldenebro.com/mapa2.html

The length of the petiole equals the width across the four knuckles of her hand, for example, while the petiole with its leaf are the same length as her outstretched forearm and hand. A flower head has the same size as her metatarsal bone and her eye socket, while the length of her arm measures the radius of seed dispersal from the trunk.

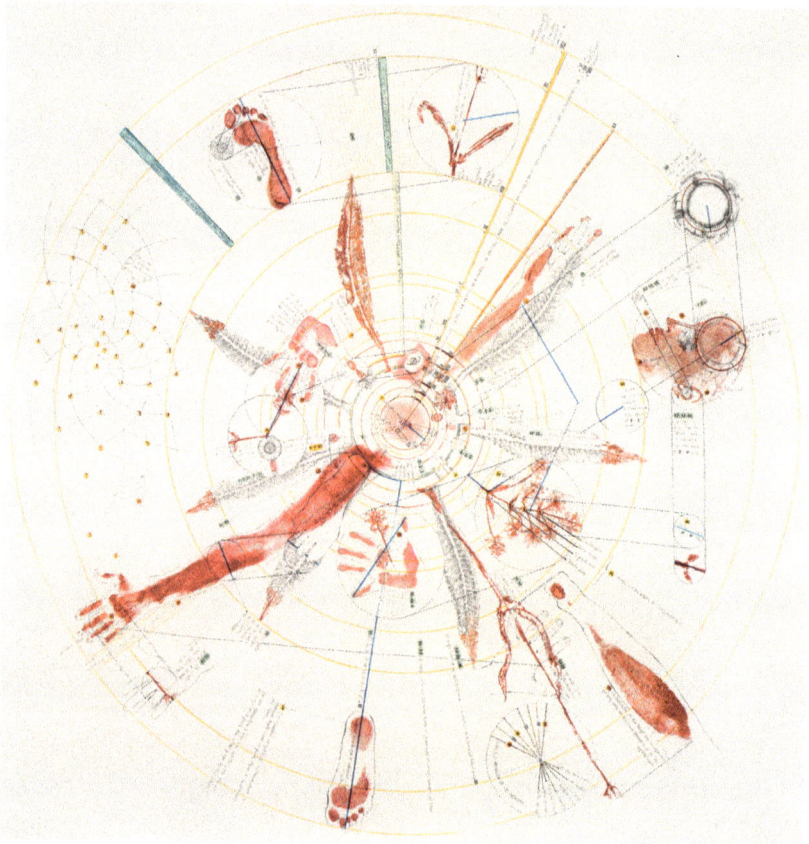

Fig. 3.10 Eulalia de Valdenebro, *Mapa de relaciones táctiles esc 1:1* (2020). Ink prints on paper. 160 x 160 cm.

The startling precision of the measurements, the neatness of the circumferences and annotations, and the comprehensive inclusion of so many different body parts create—as De Valdenebro suggests—a parody of the scientific method.[44] In direct contrast to the use of

---

44 https://www.eulaliadevaldenebro.com/mapa2.html

universal measurements, which would objectify and dissociate the plant, she seeks body-to-body comparisons that are purely proportional and relational. This was an intentional move to situate herself in "en un momento premoderno" (in a pre-modern era), before the invention of the metre in the eighteenth century and its eventual adoption as a universal unit of measurement.[45] From the combination of a series of one-to-one comparisons emerged a common unit which De Valdenebro used to cut the paper used for *Frailejonmetría comparada esc 1:1* into segments of a manageable size.

De Valdenebro's work emerges from the local, the relational, from an intimate, embodied encounter between human and plant which is founded on affinity and equivalence. Rewriting the humanist principle that "Man is the measure of all things," she creates an assemblage of human and plant in which each becomes the measure of the other. The many performances De Valdenebro has carried out in the *páramo* for her extended *Cuerpospermeables* project (Permeable Bodies, 2013–2021) also respond to a desire to configure performance differently, in a way that does not (solely) ascribe action to the human body, using the landscape as a backdrop. Instead, she allows her body to be traversed and permeated by the wind, the fog, and by other forces and forms of life, in an attempt to "ser intervenida en lugar de intervenir" (be intervened rather than intervene).[46]

Although Linnaeus's system for classifying plants went on to become the global standard, he himself advocated that "measurement should be made by the hand or stature of a man" rather than by geometrical rule.[47] It is a curious method, perhaps, to find recommended in the work of a scholar who has been so widely associated with the eighteenth-century turn toward objectivity and universalism. But Linnaeus judged approximate comparisons of this kind to be more convenient for a botanist in the field, and more appropriate given the variability of dimensions between two plants of the same species.[48] Linnaeus's use of anthropomorphic comparisons was intended to allow even amateur botanists to participate in the classification of plants. As he wrote, "no

---

45   Conversation with the author, 20 April 2022.
46   De Valdenebro, "CUERPOPERMEABLE: Conocer el páramo en el cuerpo," 135.
47   Linné, *Linnaeus' Philosophia Botanica*, 282.
48   Linné, 282.

simile is to be used, other than those derived from the external parts of the body, such as the ear, finger, navel, eye, scrotum, penis, vulva or breast; and not from the internal parts of the body, which are well known only to anatomists."[49] His recommendations point to the fact that plants have always been known to us via comparison with animal (including human) bodies. In De Valdenebro's work, this is taken as a starting point for an expanded expression of affinity, parity, and reciprocity. Her work suggests a kind of bioegalitarianism that does not erase the differences between species but finds in them a radical commensurability that is immediate and embodied.

María Fernanda Cardoso: Human Desires and Plant Sexuality

María Fernanda Cardoso's exhibition *On the Marriages of Plants* (2018) draws on scientific research to create detailed photographs and rigorously precise three-dimensional models of the reproductive systems of plants. In her work, Cardoso engages explicitly with Linnaeus's work on botanical classification, but in a way that emphasizes the most ludic and piquant elements of his work. She returns to Linnaeus's provocative analogies between plant and human sexuality to suggest potential re-readings from feminist and post-anthropocentric perspectives.

Cardoso's projects attempt to revive the theatricality of cabinets of curiosities, which was lost in the classificatory zeal of natural history collections. They also take inspiration from popular museums of the nineteenth century that used "technological innovation and technical virtuosity" to construct a "vivid visual language" with which to introduce novel facts and ideas to broad audiences.[50] *On the Marriages of Plants*, shown at Sydney's Powerhouse Museum (Museum of Applied Arts and Sciences) as part of a broader exhibition entitled *Human non Human*, develops some of the ideas and techniques that she had explored in earlier projects, particularly in the *Museum of Copulatory Organs* (2012).[51] In creating intricate three-dimensional models of animal

---

49 Linné, 251.
50 Cardoso, "The Aesthetics of Reproductive Morphologies," 39, 30.
51 *Human non Human*, curated by Katie Dyer and Lizzie Muller, was exhibited between 7 August 2018 and 27 January 2019 at the Powerhouse Museum, Sydney, Australia.

genitalia, Cardoso sought to draw attention to a world of extravagant diversity that is little known beyond the biology laboratory, as well as to understand the relationship between morphology and evolution: the theories that have been proposed to account for the astounding complexity and rapid divergence of genital forms.[52]

On the Marriages of Plants was a celebration of the seductive beauty of the reproductive organs of flowering plants. A huge display cabinet was filled with silk blooms of many colours, shapes, and textures, lit dramatically in a darkened space to accentuate their vivid hues (Fig. 3.11). These flowers are not only aesthetically appealing, but also accurate scientific models, with the anatomy of their petals and reproductive parts rendered with precision. Erected around the cabinet were "walls" made of large sheets of black fabric, onto which had been printed enlarged photographs of flowers with their petals removed, showing their stamens and pistils, responsible for producing pollen and ovules respectively (Fig. 3.12). Lighting was installed behind the fabric, shining through the flowers to give them a glowing luminosity. These "undressed" specimens had been photographed for an earlier project entitled *Naked Flora* (2013). Cardoso chose flowers from her local neighbourhood, stripped them of their petals, and used a macro lens combined with a technique called "focus stacking," in which multiple photographs are blended to extend the depth of field of any single image. These images were magnified for display in *On the Marriages of Plants*. The result was a stunning rendition of the spectacular colours and exotic forms of plant reproductive systems, towering above human viewers.

These glamorous images were given titles according to the classification system laid out by Linnaeus in *Systema Naturae* (1735). In his *Praeludia Sponsaliorum Plantarum* (*Prelude to the Betrothal of Plants*, 1729), Linnaeus had already explained plant reproduction with an effusive metaphor borrowed from human society, describing petals as an opulent marriage-bed, "perfumed with many delightful fragrances," ready for the nuptials to be celebrated between bridegroom and bride.[53] The analogy is made even more explicit in *Philosophia Botanica* (1751), where Linnaeus spells out: "the CALYX is the bedroom, the COROLLA

---

52   Cardoso, "The Aesthetics of Reproductive Morphologies," 11, 56.
53   Linné, *Prelude to the Betrothal of Plants*, 81.

Fig. 3.11 Installation view of María Fernanda Cardoso, *On the Marriages of Plants* (2018) from *Human non Human*. Powerhouse Museum, Sydney, Australia (photograph by Carlos Velásquez).

Fig. 3.12 Installation view of María Fernanda Cardoso, *On the Marriages of Plants* (2018) from *Human non Human*. Powerhouse Museum, Sydney, Australia (photograph by Carlos Velásquez).

is the curtain, the FILAMENTS are the spermatic vessels, the ANTHERS are the testicles, the POLLEN is the sperm, the STIGMA is the vulva, the STYLE is the vagina, the [VEGETABLE] OVARY is the [animal] ovary, the PERICARP is the fertilized ovary, and the SEED is the egg."[54] In his *Clavis systematis sexualis* (Key to the Sexual System), published in *Systema Naturae*, Linnaeus used terminology that thoroughly humanized plants within a lexicon of marriage, moving from defining parts as male or female to referring to them as *andria* and *gynia*, derived from the Greek for "husband" and "wife." [55] Plant marriages ranged from the decorous *monandria* (one husband in marriage) to the licentious *icosandria* (twenty husbands, often more) and the even more wanton *polygamia* (husbands live with wives and concubines in different beds).

It is generally agreed that Linnaeus's provocative nomenclature—thrillingly scandalous in the cultural context of the eighteenth century—continued a tradition of pornographic analogies in the teaching of botany.[56] Linnaeus was certainly not the only (or the first) botanist to have drawn heavily on an understanding of animal copulation to ground his theories on analogies between the sexual organs of plants and those of animals.[57] To extend the metaphor even further with references to the specifically human social convention of marriage suggests a degree of anthropomorphization that most plant scientists would now reject as inaccurate or unhelpful (Linnaeus's nomenclature considerably added, for example, to the eighteenth-century overestimation of the importance of heterosexual reproduction in plants). But what if Linnaeus's aim in producing his "sexual system" was to comment on human society as much as to describe plant morphologies? In a lecture to his students, he described sexual activity as a necessity of nature that could not be subject to moral control without damage to health:

> No dropsical person will be called drunkard, even if always thirsty. No child greedy and avaricious because it wants to eat. Hence no girl unchaste that wants men, since once the egg (*ovum*) swells she feels desire, and it would be a miracle should she not feel it.[58]

---

54 Linné, *Linnaeus' Philosophia Botanica*, 105.
55 Linnaeus, *Systema Naturae. Facsimile of the First Edition*, n.p.; see also Schiebinger, "Gender and Natural History," 167.
56 See Fara, *Sex, Botany, and Empire*, 11–12; Müller-Wille, "Linnaeus and the Love Lives of Plants," 309.
57 Schiebinger, "Gender and Natural History," 165.
58 Linné, *Diaeta naturalis, 1733: Linnés tankar om ett naturenligt levnadssätt*, 109; cit. Müller-Wille, "Linnaeus and the Love Lives of Plants," 311.

In the twenty-first century, Cardoso's exhibition delivers a similar critique of the enduring and widespread convention of monogamous marriage in many human societies, as she—like Linnaeus—stretches the single, inadequate term "marriage" to cover the immense variety of different and evolving reproductive arrangements that plants have created in their bid for survival. *Naked Flora* and *On the Marriages of Plants* celebrate the spectacular creativity involved in that enterprise, which is entirely beyond the reach of moral censure. "Nature is amoral," Cardoso explains: "Whatever we do isn't right and wrong, it just is. It doesn't matter how many husbands you have."[59] Rather than lapsing into lazy anthropomorphisms, then, Cardoso—like Linnaeus himself, perhaps—reverses the rhetoric, asking us to measure the strictures that often govern human procreation against the exuberant ingenuity and diversity of vegetal forms of reproduction.

The excitement surrounding the discovery of plant sexuality in the seventeenth and eighteenth centuries outstripped a knowledge of how fertilization actually took place.[60] Linnaeus himself did not progress far in his understanding of the role of insects in pollination, believing that self-pollination was the rule, although he was also aware of the part played by the wind carrying pollen in certain cases.[61] In this respect, Cardoso's *On the Marriages of Plants* focuses on key revisions to Linnaeus's theories, drawing on more recent research to stress the crucial role in plant sexual reproduction of reciprocal arrangements between different species that have co-evolved over millennia. Near her vivid array of silk flowers, Cardoso positioned further display cabinets, made in dark wood and glass, of nineteenth-century origin. These housed microscopes and *papier mâché* models of flowers and insects that were used to teach anatomy, all from the Powerhouse Museum collection, alongside enlarged models of different kinds of pollen grain that Cardoso had produced for her *Museum of Copulatory Organs* (Fig. 3.13). The importance of interspecies reciprocity in plant reproduction was also conveyed through a work of sound art commissioned for the gallery, which brought the space alive with the buzzing and chirping of bees, birds, and other pollinators.

---

59   Conversation with the author, 27 April 2022.
60   Schiebinger, "Gender and Natural History," 165.
61   Eriksson, "Linnaeus the Botanist," 104–5.

3. *Floras, Herbaria, and Botanical Illustration* 121

Fig. 3.13 Installation view of María Fernanda Cardoso, *On the Marriages of Plants* (2018) from *Human non Human*. Powerhouse Museum, Sydney, Australia (photograph by Carlos Velásquez).

Humans are also important pollinators of plants. The sheer beauty and seductive quality of Cardoso's photographs points to the possibility that it is not only insects, birds, and other animals who are the intended audience for these displays of floral loveliness, but humans as well. This is also tacitly acknowledged in Linnaeus's marriage-bed metaphor, which is effective because we are easily wooed by his alluring description of the flowers' heady scents and the voluptuous softness of their petals. Indeed, plants may manipulate their human pollinators just as successfully as other species. The exhibition text for *On the Marriages of Plants* suggests that Cardoso's work echoes Michael Pollan's hypothesis that plants recruit us, by stimulating our taste and desire for beauty, to ensure their own survival.[62] Flowers have evolved in a highly individuated way to attract specific insects, birds, and mammals by appealing to a range of senses (sight, touch, and smell). As Pollan writes, "We automatically think of domestication as something we do to other species, but it makes

---

62 The text was written by curators Katie Dyer and Lizzie Muller. See https://mariafernandacardoso.com/documentaries/nature-in-art/on-the-marriages-of-plants-at-human-no-human/

just as much sense to think of it as something certain plants and animals have done to us, a clever evolutionary strategy for advancing their own interests."[63]

However we understand the relationship between humans and plants to have evolved, it is clear that Cardoso's work underlines the intricate alliances and synergies that have allowed species to thrive by partnering with others. Linnaeus's projection of human desires and cultural conventions onto plant morphologies and functions betrays an important truth: that in a world that has been shaped through myriad co-evolutionary relationships, the changing desires and tastes of each species are inseparable from the destinies of others.

In curating *Human non Human*, Katie Dyer and Lizzie Muller sought to explore "how humans and our environment and everything that we're involved with are in a constant process of bringing each other into being through interaction." They selected artists, Cardoso among them, "who could move knowledge into a sensory experience."[64] Cardoso's projects enable us to understand the profound connection between these two aims. Her work cannot be reduced to a quest to make science visually appealing and entertaining for a mass audience, worthy though such an aim might be; it also reveals the extent to which it is our sensory immersion in the world that has thoroughly shaped the evolution of human biology and culture, just as we have shaped other species in turn. For the philosopher Emanuele Coccia, the plant is "the paradigm of immersion" in its total and constant exposure to the world around it; this immersion is not a passive experience but the "mutual compenetration between subject and environment, body and space, life and medium."[65] Cardoso's recreation of the "visual y vivencial" (visual and experiential) language of pre-Enlightenment science, with its greater focus on a mode of communication that is "corporal y participativo" (embodied and participatory),[66] is a fitting way to probe how plant sexuality enlists the sense perceptions and actions of other species, and to reflect on the intricate interspecies entanglements that turn all evolution into co-evolution.

---

63   Pollan, *The Botany of Desire*, xiv.
64   Dyer and Muller, "Objects, Energies and Curating Resonance across Disciplines," 257, 258.
65   Coccia, *The Life of Plants*, 53, 5, 37.
66   Cardoso, "Matrimonio entre ciencia y arte," 180.

Abel Rodríguez and the Storied Worlds of Plant Cultivation in the Amazon

Abel Rodríguez (Mogaje Guihu) is a member of the Nonuya community, which has traditionally occupied lands to the south of the Cahuinarí River in the Amazonas region of Colombia. Formerly very numerous, the community is now reduced to fewer than one hundred, with only four members able to speak the Nonuya language with competence. During the rubber boom at the end of the nineteenth century and beginning of the twentieth, the Nonuya—along with other people groups of the region—were enslaved, tortured, and murdered, with the remainder displaced to another part of the Amazon; this violence, added to the effects of multiple epidemics, caused their near-extinction, and the few who returned to their original territory had to merge with other communities.[67] Mogaje Guihu was brought up speaking Muinane and served his community as a *sabedor de plantas*, with extensive knowledge of the great diversity of native plants and how they interact with other elements of the Amazonian ecosystem. He later adopted the name Abel Rodríguez and moved to Bogotá in the 1990s to escape new forms of violence. There, he took up drawing and painting, having been encouraged to document his knowledge in this way by a Dutch NGO working to protect the Amazon (and for whom he had previously worked as a guide).

Rodríguez signs his botanical paintings with his two names, and often labels plants and animals in both Muinane and Spanish. While he reasserts the local names that have often been dismissed by Western biologists, this practice also brings into view a much broader relationship between biodiversity, culture, and language. The concept of "biocultural diversity" seeks to describe these profound interconnections; it "comprises the diversity of life in all of its manifestations—biological, cultural, and linguistic—which are interrelated (and likely co-evolved) within a complex socio-ecological adaptive system."[68] Traditionally, Rodríguez would have used his knowledge of plants within his own community, passing on through oral transmission what he knew

---

67 Dirección de Poblaciones del Ministerio de Cultura, "Estudios de la lengua Nonuya."
68 Maffi and Woodley, *Biocultural Diversity Conservation*, 5.

about ecological relationships through cycles of time. His recourse to ink and paper marks an estrangement from the land of his childhood, and testifies to a cultural and linguistic crisis suffered by the Nonuya, Muinane, and other people groups of the area that is also, simultaneously, an ecological crisis. The destruction of habitats in which indigenous groups live—or their expulsion from them—has a disastrous effect on the languages and cultures that are interwoven with those places. The reverse is also true: as Daniel Nettle and Suzanne Romaine remind us, tropical environments need to be managed with the kind of care and knowledge that often only indigenous people are able to provide, with their experience accumulated over hundreds of generations. However, as they affirm, much of this knowledge about local ecosystems "is encoded in indigenous language and rapidly being lost."[69] For this reason, "It is not coincidental that language endangerment has gone hand in hand with species endangerment."[70]

Rodríguez's illustrations, which are painted from memory, distil a knowledge of biology and ecology that has been passed down through generations and sharpened through patient observation. Unlike classical botanical plates, they place individual species within a broader ecosystem in a way that depicts the natural world as one of continual flux and interaction, in constant conversation with social and spiritual worlds.

A number of Rodríguez's botanical drawings and observations have been compiled in an open-access digital publication entitled *Las plantas cultivadas por la gente de centro en la Amazonia colombiana*, produced by Tropenbos Colombia, the Dutch NGO mentioned above.[71] In one chapter, Rodríguez includes illustrations of several different kinds of cassava, a shrub that is traditionally cultivated in the Amazon and a staple of indigenous diets. Each plate typically shows the full-grown shrub, a leaf, seeds, and flowers, as well as the edible root (peeled and unpeeled) and often an animal that feeds on it. As well as aiding the identification of this species, then, Rodríguez gives information about its human and

---

69 Nettle and Romaine, *Vanishing Voices*, 166.
70 Nettle and Romaine, 14.
71 Rodríguez, *Las plantas cultivadas por la gente de centro en la Amazonia colombiana*. The volume may be downloaded via this link: http://tropenboscol.org/recursos/publicaciones/the+plants+cultivated+by+the+people+from+the+center+in+the+colombian+amazon

animal uses as a food source. The *Yuca brava de sangre*, for example, attracts the *boruga*, a local rodent; the *yuca* root is brown when harvested but cream-coloured once it has been prepared for cooking (39). The brief texts included in the book also contain information relevant to the sowing and harvesting of plants and their particular value for the community, indicating a medicinal use or identifying which birds come to feed when a tree's fruit is ripe. The value that is attributed to each plant is therefore one of use rather than exchange, its purpose being to sustain the communities (human and animal) that live in the forest, rather than to generate revenue through trade.

Botanical illustrations produced since the eighteenth century have tended to depict a timeless version of a plant, showing in a single image the different appearances the plant takes on during fruiting and flowering periods. Rodríguez's work, in contrast, focuses precisely on those changes and how they interact with other cycles in the forest environment. For this reason, many of his illustrations are part of larger series showing an evolution over time. He has created several collections of illustrations that chart the seasonal variations of the Amazon river basin. His *Ciclo anual del bosque de la vega* (Seasonal Changes in the Flooded Rainforest, 2009–2010; 2015–2016) is a series of twelve ink and watercolour paintings that show how the forest is transformed over the year, as different seasons are marked by rising flood waters, the fruiting of trees, the flowering of bromeliads, and the appearance of certain birds, fish, and mammals.[72] The periodic flooding of the Amazon basin has created the conditions for unparalleled biodiversity, as floodwaters bring sediments from the Andes to enrich the soil and provide new food sources for animals.

Rodríguez's illustrations draw out the myriad interrelations that bring this forest-world into being. The cycles of plant and animal lives are interwoven with changes wrought in the terrain by the sun, the moon, and the tides. The particular way that each of these beings draws energy from its milieu and navigates its changing conditions makes other worlds and practices possible. These life forms do not occupy a landscape as if it were some kind of container or backdrop, but actively contribute to its evolution and that of every other living being that

---

72 The 2015–2016 series may be viewed online at https://www.banrepcultural.org/coleccion-de-arte/obra/ciclo-anual-del-bosque-de-vega-12-ap6170

inhabits it. In a world of continual flux and entanglement, "living beings of all kinds constitute each other's conditions for existence," creating, as the anthropologist Arturo Escobar maintains, "a relational ontology [...] in which nothing preexists the relations that constitute it."[73]

Another series by Rodríguez published in *Las plantas cultivadas por la gente de centro en la Amazonia colombiana* describes the *Ciclo de la chagra* (The Chagra Cycle, 2009), showing in four paintings the successive stages of the cultivation of a community plot. The intricate designs in green and brown ink are accompanied by a key showing the placement of each kind of plant.[74] They demonstrate the enormous variety of crops grown and the attention paid to how they grow alongside each other, in combinations that allow each to flourish and to be harvested at different points. This cycle has been carefully managed so that each plant receives the right nutrients to mature at the right point, as all crops "tienen su tiempo de ser" (have their time of being).[75]

These are designs, or perhaps more accurately co-designs, that lay out how humans might weave their own practices into the web of coexistences and interrelations through which the forest and its inhabitants are co-constituted. Rodríguez adopts the relational perspective Escobar articulates when he describes the important conversations that take place in the community before work on the *chagra* is begun: "En ese momento, se habla de la creación, de crear muchas cosas, de cómo crear la chagra y cómo la chagra crea personas" (at that time, we talk about creation, about creating many things, about how to create the *chagra* and how the *chagra* creates people).[76] The people and the plot each come into being as a result of the way that the other comes into being. This understanding contrasts starkly with the kind of knowledge generated by European botanists in the employ of colonial (and neocolonial) states, which has facilitated practices of extraction and exploitation. It also differs markedly from Western discourses of conservation, which promote an illusory vision of an "untouched" nature, affirming instead an alternative form of coexistence between humans and the forest.

---

73 Escobar, *Pluriversal Politics*, 71–72.
74 Rodríguez, 18–21; 24–27.
75 Rodríguez, 50.
76 Rodríguez, 10.

The agricultural practices described by Rodríguez are very different from the monocrop farming methods that have led to widespread deforestation across many parts of the world. The *chagra* is carved out of the forest by felling trees and burning vegetation to produce a layer of fertile ash. This is the method that has been used for millennia to grow crops in the Amazon, where the soil is naturally thin and lacking in nutrients. It creates a plot of land that will be productive for one or two years; after the last crops are harvested, the plot reverts to the wild and a new plot will be cleared in order to start again. Rodríguez explains this process as one of substitution, replacing life with life, wild species with cultivated ones:

> Yo no voy a jugar con la selva y mucho menos con los árboles, porque eso tiene vida, yo no voy a destruir por destruir. Así como destruyo la selva tengo que reponer con frutales, así como destruyo la yuca silvestre, tengo que reemplazarla con yuca propia, con otros tubérculos [...].[77]
>
> (I am not going to play with the forest and certainly not with trees, because there is life there, and I am not going to destroy for the sake of destroying. If I destroy the forest I have to put fruit trees in its place, if I destroy wild cassava shrubs, I have to replace them with domesticated ones, with other tubers [...].)

The *chagra* is in fact a motor of biodiversity. The act of creating a clearing brings similar benefits to those that are reaped in the natural cycle of the forest when old trees fall and let in light, which leads to a regeneration of the area, as new plants can grow and benefit from nutrients recycled from dead branches.

The *chagra* depicted in Rodríguez's work is an example of polyculture, the practice of growing several different crops together. As in many polycultures in Latin America, trees are grown together with crops, providing shade as well as additional nutrients when they shed leaves or fruit, and preventing soil erosion. Polyculture systems are often much more sustainable than other forms of farming. The diversity of crops grown together makes them more resistant to pests and diseases, so they do not require the large amounts of fertilizer and pesticide needed for monocultures. They also share available nutrients more efficiently. Polycultures join a much larger set of strategies that have been grouped

---

77 Rodríguez, 12.

under the term "reconciliation ecology." The term was coined by Michael Rosenzweig in 2003, but some of the practices it involves date back for millennia. Rosenzweig proposes the strategy as a necessary complement to the two more dominant approaches that have been adopted in conservation biology. The first of these, "reservation ecology," fences off those small and fast-vanishing areas of the world that contain natural habitats. The second, "restoration ecology," attempts to return areas that have been developed to a more natural state. The problem is that very little land is available for either reservation or restoration. Rosenzweig uses the term "reconciliation ecology" to describe practices that conserve or increase biodiversity in places where humans live and work, using land "in a way that reconciles our needs with those of wild, native species."[78]

By the third illustration of Rodríguez's *Ciclo de la chagra* series, which is entitled *Chagra un año* (Chagra One Year), the neat rows of plants have become an exuberant tangle. The last, *Chagra un año y medio* (Chagra One and a Half Years), shows how the plot is already being reclaimed by the forest. Rodríguez describes how trees, lianas and grasses "se van apoderando de todo" (take over everything).[79] The *chagra* is a temporary occupation, a parenthesis in the life of the forest, which recolonizes the earth once its human farmers have moved on. And yet of course the forest will not be the same afterwards, as the palm trees and fruit trees will remain for some time, enriching the uncultivated vegetation that grows back around them. The abandoned *chagra* becomes a rich hunting-ground, as animals are attracted to the plants and trees that remain there. Indeed, ecologists have found that some long-lived tree species in particular may persist in secondary forests in the Amazon for decades or even centuries.[80]

The extent to which humans were already modifying landscapes and transforming biodiversity before the industrial revolution has been significantly underestimated. Nicole L. Boivin and her co-authors argue that "even before the Age of Discovery, cumulative human activities over millennia resulted in dramatic changes to the abundance and geographic

---

78 Rosenzweig, *Win-Win Ecology*, 1, 7.
79 Rodríguez, *Las plantas cultivadas por la gente de centro en la Amazonia colombiana*, 23.
80 Clement, McCann, and Smith, "Agrobiodiversity in Amazônia and Its Relationship with Dark Earths," 172.

range of a diverse array of organisms across taxonomic groups."[81] It is now known that the Amazon, which has often been viewed as a "pristine" forest, was home to dense populations that modified its soil to make it more fertile and, well before the arrival of the Europeans, produced "large-scale transformations to forest plants, animals, and wetlands" in some areas.[82] Far from pristine examples of an untouched nature, "Most landscapes are palimpsests shaped by repeated episodes of human activity over multiple millennia."[83] As William M. Denevan puts it, bluntly, "There are no virgin tropical forests today, nor were there in 1492."[84] Denevan argues that the wildernesses described and painted by European travellers to Latin America in the eighteenth and nineteenth centuries were an invention, but one that came from a misreading of the landscape that was "in part understandable."[85] This was caused by the large-scale demise of indigenous populations between 1492 and 1750 (he estimates that the population of the Americas in 1750 was only thirty percent of its total in 1492). Areas that had been densely populated before European colonization had undergone significant reforestation since that time, such that, by the eighteenth century, they seemed considerably "less humanized" than they had been previously.[86] More recent studies have shown that forests in Amazonia and elsewhere are "largely anthropogenic in form and composition."[87]

Focusing on this much longer history of human-led environmental change allows us to understand that not all anthropogenic processes have been catastrophic: human actions have sometimes increased species diversity, especially through controlled fires.[88] Human disturbance of ecosystems is not necessarily destructive: ecosystems do not evolve to their greatest maturity and highest point of diversity *without* disturbance, in fact, which may come in natural forms, such as floods or hurricanes, or as a result of human interventions.[89] It would be a mistake to assume that all indigenous interventions into the landscape

---

81   Boivin et al., "Ecological Consequences of Human Niche Construction," 6388–89.
82   Boivin et al., 6392.
83   Boivin et al., 6393.
84   Denevan, "The Pristine Myth," 375.
85   Denevan, 379–80.
86   Denevan, 371.
87   Denevan, 373.
88   Balee, "The Research Program of Historical Ecology," 77.
89   Balee, 81–82.

have been ecologically beneficial, as this is not the case.[90] But Rodríguez's illustrations point to the existence of the kind of mutualist relationships that are central to the sustainable use of forests.

These practices are founded on a radical understanding of how all living beings—including humans—co-constitute each other and their habitats. They are not based on an ontological separation between humans and the rest of nature, which in Western modernity has generated concepts of landscape and environment as depeopled terrains or passive backdrops for human activity. Rodríguez's illustrations contrast clearly with the forested landscapes painted by travellers to the Amazon in the eighteenth and nineteenth centuries. A typical scene, *Forêt Vierge du Brésil* (Virgin Forest of Brazil, 1819), was painted by the French scholar and artist Comte de Clarac and circulated widely in the form of engravings in Europe. It depicts the diversity of the rainforest, rendered overwhelming in the absence of any horizon or sky. The indigenous figures are, by comparison, tiny; given the title of the painting, one assumes that they do not count as agents with the power to shape their landscape.

In Rodríguez's illustrations, the entanglement of multiple species does not produce a undifferentiated mass; instead, each species is picked out carefully, drawn in its fullness rather than partly obscured by vegetation, so that it is easily identifiable. The semi-transparent quality of ink is used to draw leaves against trunks, trunks against leaves, in such a way that the identity of each individual form is still visible through and against the dense foliage that surrounds it. As well as documenting the identity of each species woven into the forest system, this method also grants each plant and animal a subjecthood that would be at least partially erased if the scene were depicted realistically from a single (human) perspective. There is no single perspective from which all these species could be visible. This is not a synthesized view of a landscape, in which everything merges together to produce a harmonious effect, or a backdrop for human adventure, but the space of what Escobar might call a "pluriverse," a world into which many worlds fit.

---

90 Denevan notes that indigenous changes to the landscape were not always "benign" and resources were not always used in a "sound ecological way," but their impact was certainly not "localized" or "ephemeral." Denevan, "The Pristine Myth," 370.

Rodríguez also renders visible other subjects and actors that have a role in forging the forest world and its cosmovision. In *Territorio de Mito* (Territory of Myth, 2017), a *maloca* (communal house) is painted in a small clearing in the dense forest.[91] The labelling of the two human figures nearby as the Sun and the Moon clearly indicates that this is also the scene of a mythical encounter. The donning of human form by nonhuman actors (and vice versa) is a commonplace in Amazonian stories and rituals and points to a very different conception of personhood that is not restricted to the human. Eduardo Viveiros de Castro explains that "The attribution of humanlike consciousness and intentionality (to say nothing of human bodily form and cultural habits) to nonhuman beings has been indifferently denominated 'anthropocentrism' or 'anthropomorphism'," while in fact these "denote radically opposed cosmological outlooks."[92] In this case, the Sun and the Moon are anthropomorphized, but the vision communicated is far from an anthropocentric one: as Viveiros de Castro puts it, "if sundry other beings besides humans are 'human,' then we humans are not a special lot."[93] Rodríguez's painting brings the natural and the spiritual into the social, extending the social beyond the human. De Castro defines animism in this way as "an ontology which postulates the social character of relations between humans and nonhumans."[94]

The elegant and precise illustrations of botanical species carried out by European and *criollo* artists and naturalists render plants as objects, as if they existed separately from what they do or independently of their relations with other species and their environment. Indeed, many biological classifications are based on observed structural (or these days, genetic) similarities. Tim Ingold, working at the intersections of anthropology and ecology, finds that "An understanding of the unity of life in terms of genealogical relatedness is bought at the cost of cutting out every single organism from the relational matrix in which it lives and grows."[95] How genetically related a species may be to another similar species tells us nothing about how it has co-evolved with other

---

91 The work may be viewed at https://institutodevision.com/visionarios/abel-rodriguez/
92 Viveiros de Castro, *The Relative Native*, 245.
93 Viveiros de Castro, 245.
94 Viveiros de Castro, 232.
95 Ingold, *Being Alive*, 163.

life-forms. Ingold argues that it is stories that *"always, and inevitably, draw together what classifications split apart."*[96] In a "storied world," we can only understand things as they are brought together in an ongoing field of activity, as "things do not exist, they occur."[97] Rodríguez's botanical illustrations create "storied worlds" in exactly this way, showing how human lives and practices have been shaped by multiple encounters that unfold in a place, binding all things together in a shared history.

In a classic essay of the 1970s on Caribbean literature, Sylvia Wynter distinguished between the values of the plot and those of the plantation, with the former based on use-value and the second on exchange-value. While she recognized that there could be no going back to a society based on "folk culture," she pointed to its importance in providing "a point outside the system" and "a focus of criticism against the impossible reality in which we are enmeshed." Although he acknowledges that indigenous models of nature are not unified, Escobar contrasts them with modern Western constructions of nature, with their "strict separation between biophysical, human, and supernatural worlds." Rodríguez's illustrations demonstrate the continuity between these spheres, which, as Escobar observes, are "embedded in social relations that cannot be reduced to modern, capitalist terms."[98]

Conclusion

The Colombian philosopher Santiago Castro-Gómez refers to the New Granada botanical expedition as a kind of "second conquest," not executed directly by Europeans but by *criollo* botanists, their American descendants.[99] *Criollos* pursued scientific knowledge in a way that was consonant with their own bid for power. If Linnaeus's system created controversy among naturalists in Europe at the time, it was also rejected by many *criollo* scientists in New Spain, for whom its efficiency and claim to universality came at the cost of disregarding local circumstances.[100]

---

96 Ingold, 160 (original emphasis).
97 Ingold, 160.
98 Escobar, "Whose Knowledge, Whose nature?," 61.
99 Castro-Gómez, *La hybris del punto cero*, 214. Apart from Mutis himself (who had been living in the region for almost thirty years), all the scientists and artists who took part in the expedition were *criollos*. Castro-Gómez, 214n28.
100 Lafuente and Valverde, "Colonial Botany," 136.

These naturalists were much more likely to defend the value of indigenous and local knowledge, and to insist on the importance of biogeography in understanding plant life. José Antonio de Alzate y Ramírez (1738–1799) railed against the kind of knowledge that resides in committing plant names to memory rather than understanding their uses.[101] Caldas, a key figure in Mutis's expedition, argued for the radical influence of climate on plants, which he found to be "sujetas a las leyes imperiosas del calor y del frío" (subject to the imperious laws of heat and cold) as well as to many other environmental forces.[102]

As Antonio Lafuente argues, at the core of the many debates that raged over botany in New Spain was the fact that, under imperial politics, botany became "a form of biopolitics" that had little to do with biology and everything to do with the governance of empire.[103] Rather than understanding the works of Baraya, De Valdenebro, Cardoso, and Rodríguez as twenty-first-century rejections of colonial-era botany, it would be more accurate to see them as an important continuation of historical forms of resistance mounted by *criollo* naturalists to metropolitan over-simplifications and expropriations. Universal taxonomies are little suited to accounting for change over time or the influence of soil and climate. With the help of more recent research into (co)evolution and historical ecology, these artists' emphasis on the entanglement of plant histories with other stories—such as those of cultural biodiversity, the domestication of crops, imperial politics, and global capitalism—deepens a critique that had previously been articulated in Spanish America by Alzate, Caldas, and many others.

The work of all four artists discussed in this chapter demonstrate how deeply the plant life we perceive around us has already been transformed by human desires, customs, and cultures. As Pollan suggests, "human desires form a part of natural history in the same way the hummingbird's love of red does, or the ant's taste for the aphid's honeydew."[104] Although Baraya and De Valdenebro chart the destructive effect of human activity, particularly in the construction of plantations, there is no attempt to promote the conservation of a unspoiled nature,

---

101 Alzate y Ramírez, "Carta satisfactoria dirigida a un literato por don José de Alzate," 21–23.
102 Caldas, "Del influjo del clima sobre los seres organizados," 89–90, 119.
103 Lafuente and Valverde, "Colonial Botany," 141.
104 Pollan, *The Botany of Desire*, xvi.

free from human intervention, but instead a desire to understand our integration within it and to promote deeper and more egalitarian forms of encounter. De Valdenebro, Cardoso, and Rodríguez study shared histories that bring together humans and plants in ways that emphasize co-evolution, mutual compenetration, and reciprocity. Not all anthropogenic modifications of other species and the environment have been negative: some have increased the possibility of symbiotic coexistence.

Rodríguez's work reminds us that human-wrought changes to plant life and landscapes far predate the agricultural revolution. Why is it important to be aware that humans have radically transformed their environment for much longer than we might have thought? Does this not effectively weaken a major strand of decolonial critique that dates the beginning of the Anthropocene to the deadly collusion between colonialism and capitalism, leading to widespread extractivism? I would contend instead that it opens up ways of politicizing and decolonizing the Anthropocene. Firstly, recognizing the extent to which indigenous people have transformed their environments returns to them an ecological agency that they have been denied. The representation of indigenous peoples in the New World as "incapable of making their environments flourish" was part of the historical justification for colonization.[105] Secondly, it helps us to understand that there is nothing inevitable about the West's dissociative, extractivist relationship with nature, which has led to dominant (unsustainable) forms of agribusiness. Large populations were sustained in pre-Hispanic America with traditional polyculture methods, which—over time—may create higher yields than monocultures.

And thirdly, the deep history of ecological management by indigenous people shifts the terms of the debate: if there is no pristine nature to which we could return, addressing environmental crisis becomes less about the science of how to reconstruct past ecosystems and more about the ethics of what kind of ecosystems we wish to live in in the future. This helps us to contest the "post-politics" of the Anthropocene.[106] It moves us from questions of a purely scientific, technical, and managerial

---

105 Rivera-Núñez, Fargher, and Nigh, "Toward an Historical Agroecology," 294.
106 Swyngedouw, "Depoliticized Environments," 266. See the discussion of the "post-political" nature of the Anthropocene in this book's introduction.

variety to ones of politics, culture and ethics, enabling us to see that our relationship with the natural world is historically and culturally contingent, and therefore open to change. Studying art alongside environmental history and agroecology sharpens our understanding of the depth and importance of that contingency. It helps us grasp the vital connection between biological diversity and cultural diversity—which has been demonstrated empirically—and to imagine new environmental futures that might be shaped by other ways of living on the earth.

4. Retracing Voyages of Science and Conquest

A profound relationship connects the pursuit of knowledge in the Enlightenment with the many transcontinental voyages undertaken in the period. These expeditions were often promoted and funded by states or new academic institutions in Europe. But more than that, as Juan Pimentel suggests, the journey itself made possible—and visible— the forward movement toward intellectual knowledge and growth that lay at the heart of Enlightenment thinking.[1] These voyages were no longer those of conquest but of scientific discovery, although the surveys and studies undertaken were often commissioned with the aim of strengthening imperial control and maximizing the production of raw materials in the colonies, to be shipped back to Europe. In the neat summary provided by Guadalupe Carrasco González and others, "Se podría decir que ha terminado el tiempo de los conquistadores y comienza el de los comerciantes, el de los contables y el de los científicos" (one could say that the era of the conquistadors had come to an end and that of traders, accountants and scientists was beginning).[2]

Daniela Bleichmar points to the important role of artists, working closely with scientists, in making manifest this new knowledge: their work became part of "a much larger project of making the empire visible in order to know and exploit it."[3] This chapter focuses on the work of recent Latin American artists who have re-performed elements of these expeditions, while the next discusses projects that rework the physical albums, atlases, illustrations, and other materials that were

---

1   Pimentel, *Testigos del mundo*, 14–15.
2   Carrasco González, Gullón Abao, and Morgado García, *Las expediciones científicas en los siglos XVII y XVIII*, 9.
3   Bleichmar, *Visible Empire*, 9.

published as a result of these journeys. Many of these artists adopt a critical perspective on the collusion between science, commerce, and empire, demonstrating the continued legacies of this relationship for Latin American republics through Independence to the present day. They also perceive much of value, however, in the close collaborations such expeditions forged between scientists and artists, and their projects may be read as attempts to recuperate the transdisciplinary nature of these endeavours.

Several of the journeys that Alberto Baraya has conducted in search of new species for his *Herbario de plantas artificiales* (see Chapter Three) retrace the paths of colonial-era Spanish botanists, such as Hipólito Ruiz López, José Antonio Pavón Jiménez, and José Celestino Mutis, or more recent ethnobotanists from the US, Richard Evans Schultes and Wade Davis. Baraya's performances often draw attention to the complicity between science and empire, and science and commerce. But they also move beyond the unveiling of acts of dispossession and exploitation to compose gestures of symbolic reversal and reparation. To some of the plates created for his *Herbario de plantas artificiales*, Baraya adds photographs showing the use of anthropometric callipers, often used in nineteenth-century race studies to measure head and body size in colonized subjects. The measurements obtained by such instruments often led to dubious "scientific" conclusions, used to affirm the superiority of Europeans over other races and to justify the exercise of power. Reversing this objectifying procedure, Baraya asks local people he meets on his expeditions to measure his own head. In *Orquídea Vanda y 4 antropometrías artificiales* (Vanda Orchid and 4 Artificial Anthropometries, 2013), photographs taken during an expedition to Peru show the artist's head being measured by indigenous women and by another tourist in the ancient Incan sites of Ollantaytambo, Cusco, and Machu Picchu (see Fig. 4.1).

Baraya proposes that the journey should not only be understood as an artistic theme, but also as a method. If the scientific expeditions of the New World forged an intimate connection between journeys, progress, and knowledge, Baraya defends the practice of art as a form of knowledge production in our own time. It is not to be compared with scientific knowledge, however, as it represents "otra manera de adentrarse al conocimiento" (another way of entering into knowledge).[4]

---
4   Conversation with the author, 12 February 2019.

4. *Retracing Voyages of Science and Conquest* 139

Fig. 4.1 Alberto Baraya, *Orquídea Vanda y 4 antropometrías artificiales* (2013) from the *Herbario de plantas artificiales*. Found object, photograph and drawing on cardboard, 60 x 45 x 5 cm (photograph by the artist).

The journey, for Baraya, presents an opportunity to distance ourselves from the intricate cultural constructions on which our social lives, our work, and our traditions depend, and to contrast these with other perspectives and other realities. "Y al confrontar nuestro entorno con otros entornos, una parte de los discursos de esas construcciones se tambalea, e inmediatamente se desvelan las estrategias de lo ficticio que constituyen nuestro ser" (and when our surroundings are brought face to face with other surroundings, part of the discourses of those constructions begin to totter, and that immediately reveals the strategies of fiction that make up our being).[5] This process of defamiliarization is heightened by his decision to view cultures and landscapes through the eyes of previous explorers to the regions he visits. Armed with Wade Davis's account of his recreation in 1974–1975 of the Amazonian journey undertaken by the botanist Richard Evans Schultes in 1941, Baraya retraced those retracings in an expedition carried out in 2004 along the Putumayo River.[6] Like all of these, his own journey is always already mediated by the writings of a chain of other travellers and botanists stretching back to Mutis, Humboldt, and beyond.[7]

For other artists, it is not primarily cultural difference that emerges from their re-performings of the voyages of explorers and scientists, but forms of political or environmental change or continuity. Fabiano Kueva, whose *Archivo Humboldt* (2011–) is discussed in Chapter Five, retraces Humboldt's steps in order to show how the (European) quest for a universal science obscures and deepens injustices born of imperialism, and how extractivist practices developed in the colonial era continue to shape Latin America's unequal insertion into the global economy today. In his video installation *Paso del Quindío II* (The Quindío Pass II, 1999), José Alejandro Restrepo draws attention to the continued existence on Colombia's Pacific Coast of *cargueros*, porters who carry travellers and their belongings on their backs. They had been frequently depicted in the chronicles and images produced by nineteenth-century travellers, including Humboldt.

For Walmor Corrêa, the opportunity to take part in the reconstruction of a journey undertaken in Brazil in 1817–1818 by the Austrian painter Thomas Ender allowed him to reflect on changes in the region's flora. Ender had been commissioned as a painter to accompany a large team of eminent naturalists charged with exploring the culture, fauna, flora, and other natural resources of Brazil as part of the Österreichische

---

5 Narro, "El artista Alberto Baraya se inventa herbarios con flores artificiales [interview with Alberto Baraya]."
6 See Davis, *One River*; Davis, *El Río*.
7 Baraya, "Leí *El Río* en el río."

Brasilien-Expedition (Austrian Expedition to Brazil, 1817–1835). For the collective project *The Brazilian Expedition of Thomas Ender—Reconsidered*, Corrêa travelled in 2004 with Mark Dion and a team of other artists from different countries to the places that Ender may have visited.[8] Corrêa had been asked to take on the role of the German botanist Carl Friedrich Philipp von Martius, who had also travelled down the Amazon in one of the journeys reconstructed by Baraya. Having taken with him pages featuring reproductions of Ender's watercolours, Corrêa superimposed onto them new sketches of the birds and trees he came across in each place. He jotted down various observations, noting which species were still in evidence and which had disappeared. The exhibition of these pages drew attention to the palimpsestic nature of these expeditions, which—as Baraya also demonstrates—are so often reprises, rewritings, and recreations (a phenomenon that will be explored more fully in Chapter Five). But it also brought into focus the important theme of environmental change. Discounting those species that Ender had not painted, Corrêa whittled down his findings to a selection of plants that were native to Brazil and were still to be found in Ender's locations. For these, he created a set of fictional seed packets to form a *Sementeiro* (Seed Collection, 2004), with planting instructions and advice on plant care inspired by the many myths and mistakes made by European travellers to Brazil and Latin America.[9]

The themes of environmental change and misreadings of landscapes and flora that structure Corrêa's contributions to *The Brazilian Expedition of Thomas Ender—Reconsidered* are also central concerns of the major collaborative project discussed below, a journey along the River Paraná conducted in 2010 by around sixty artists and researchers from many different disciplines. The journey retraced the route taken by European colonizers and scientists who travelled up the river to explore a vast area of the South American continent. The repetitions, retracings,

---

8   The project was jointly organized by the São Paulo Biennial Foundation and the Vienna Academy of Fine Arts. Mark Dion was later to undertake a similar journey to trace the footsteps of the eighteenth-century American botanist and explorer William Bartram through the southern part of the United States. This project was given the title *Travels of William Bartram—Reconsidered* and it was first exhibited in 2008.

9   The artworks developed during the expedition were first shown at the Bienal de São Paulo from 25 September to 19 December 2004 and then at the Academy of Fine Arts in Vienna from 21 January to 20 March 2005.

and comparisons drawn between past and present—and indeed, future—that are made possible through this re-enacted journey allow a series of reflections to emerge on nonhuman temporalities and on the temporality of the Anthropocene, which I explore in the light of decolonial perspectives on environmental change.

Expeditions Through Time Along the Río Paraná: Decolonial Perspectives on Environmental Change

After founding Buenos Aires in 1536, Pedro de Mendoza assembled those of his men who had not died from starvation or in combat with Querandí warriors and sailed up the rivers Paraná and Paraguay to establish Asunción. With him travelled a German explorer, Ulrich Schmidl, whose account of the journey provides the first written history of the Río de la Plata region. This route was to become the favoured point of entry for Europeans exploring the interior of the South American continent. In his chronicle of the expedition, Schmidl gives a typically crisp account of the slaughter of one group they encountered on the shores of the river, the Mepenes, who numbered around 100,000 men:

> Esta gente nos salió al encuentro por agua en son de guerra, con 500 canoas o esquifes, pero sin sacarnos mayor ventaja, les matamos a muchos con nuestros arcabuces, porque hasta entonces no habían visto arcabuces ni cristianos.[10]

> (These people came out to meet us in a warlike manner, with 500 canoes or skiffs, but they were not able to use them to gain advantage over us and we killed many of them with our arquebuses, as until then they had seen neither arquebuses nor Christians.)

In 2010, around sixty artists and researchers from Argentina, Paraguay, and Spain set out on an expedition to retrace Schmidl's journey up the river from Buenos Aires to Asunción, but with very different intentions.[11] Their principal aim was to explore and reinvigorate the riverine cultural

---

10 Schmídel, *Viaje al río de la Plata, 1534–1554*, Chapter XVIII.
11 The project was funded by the Agencia Española de Cooperación Internacional para el Desarrollo (AECID), with the participation of the Centro Cultural Parque de España in Rosario, the Centro Cultural de España in Buenos Aires, the Centro Cultural de España in Córdoba (Argentina) and the Centro Cultural de España Juan de Salazar in Asunción (Paraguay).

heritage of Argentina's Litoral region, a socionatural landscape that has been densely inhabited for many centuries and thoroughly transformed by colonialism and capitalist development, but that remains part of a wetlands system of huge environmental significance.

Originally conceived by Martín Prieto, the *Paraná Ra'anga* expedition brought together geographers, anthropologists, sociologists, historians, engineers, ecologists, architects, musicians, visual artists, filmmakers, linguisticians, poets, and philosophers.[12] During the journey, which took several weeks, they organized activities such as poetry readings, practical astronomy sessions, and musical recitals in conjunction with local communities and cultural centres at ports along the route. Artworks and studies related to the expedition were later exhibited in several countries and collated in a book (with accompanying CD and DVD) compiled and introduced by the architect Graciela Silvestri, one of the expedition's organizers. Although the journey was initially designed to retrace the route taken by Schmidl, the travellers also sought inspiration from other historical expeditions along the river and through the broader region. In particular, they wished to revive the integrated, interdisciplinary approach to knowledge that often characterized Romantic-era voyages of exploration in Latin America. The participants of this twenty-first-century expedition were chosen precisely for their interest in entering into dialogue with other kinds of knowledge and expression, crossing the frontiers between disciplines.[13]

Together, their works bring into view how the river convenes multiple converging and diverging temporalities. They allow us to approach the landscape of the Río Paraná in multiple ways: as a territory forged by geological and hydrological processes, as a living ecosystem, and as a historical place shaped by human activity. Each of these brings into play a very different timescale; the *Paraná Ra'anga* project adds to these the diegetic time and space of the journey itself, and the journey as an opportunity for reflection and projection. As its chroniclers observe, "El viaje—todo viaje—es diálogo con el pasado y el futuro (the journey— every journey—is a dialogue with the past and the future).[14] The expedition is a palimpsest, a retracing of a route that does not fully

---

12 The name given to the expedition uses the word for "form" or "figure" in Guaraní, an indigenous language spoken by around five million people in the region.
13 Silvestri, "La historia de una idea," 32.
14 Gangui, Silvestri, and Vena, "La expedición Paraná Ra'anga," 103.

erase those expeditions that have been taken place before it. This allows us to glimpse recurring forms of experience over time, entangling the past time of empire with the present time of global capitalism. But it also draws attention to past extinctions that are typically effaced in today's discourses of the Anthropocene. In discussing the expedition and the different texts and images it has inspired, I am interested in how decolonial perspectives on environmental change may unfold in an attentiveness to temporalities that are often erased in dominant narratives of the Anthropocene.

Anthropocene time is already a folding-in of two very different timescales, the almost inconceivably deep time of geology and the much shorter history of capitalism.[15] But Anthropocene time remains almost entirely linear in its conception. This is nowhere more evident than in the Climate Clock, installed in New York City, Berlin, Seoul, and other major cities around the world, which counts down to the deadline at which zero emissions need to be reached to keep global warming below the critical threshold of 1.5°C.[16] The approaching destiny of the planet is measured here in empty, homogeneous, globalist clock time, gathering all of humankind together in a synchrony and a universality that are fundamentally illusory.

In their quest to pluralize the Anthropocene from the perspective of international relations, Jack Amoureux and Varun Reddy observe that "the 'future' is the hierarchically privileged horizon in the grammar of the Anthropocene." With the future progress promised by "normal politics" at risk, global efforts must be turned toward averting impending disaster. The past, they argue, is discounted as a mere "point of narrative curiosity"; "the present is the realm of action but always in service of the future."[17] Anthropocene time thus ignores the fact that experiences of environmental change are plural and that apocalypse is not reserved for some future event that it might be possible to avoid: it has already transformed the lives of billions of the world's inhabitants. More concretely, as the geographer Kathryn Yusoff states, the future tense used to configure the Anthropocene fails to recognize the many extinctions already suffered by black and indigenous peoples.[18]

---

15 See Chakrabarty, "Anthropocene Time," 6.
16 See https://climateclock.world
17 Amoureux and Reddy, "Multiple Anthropocenes," 936.
18 Yusoff, *A Billion Black Anthropocenes or None*, 51.

In my reading of the texts and images produced by members of the *Paraná Ra'anga* expedition, I will bring out the encounters they stage between divergent temporalities and how these can be read as a critique, firstly of contemporary global capitalism and its foundations in colonialism, and secondly, of the temporality of the Anthropocene itself, which can in some ways be understood as the latest rhetorical means of furthering the interests of globalism and economic liberalism.

The *Paraná Ra'anga* project was first devised as a response to cultural decline and environmental deterioration in the regions traversed by the River Paraná and the River Paraguay. These processes are already in evidence but they are set to intensify. Silvestri explains that the waterway between Buenos Aires and Asunción was, until the late twentieth century, "ruta privilegiada de migrantes, turistas, mercancías e ideas" (a route favoured by migrants, tourists, merchandise and ideas). As all transport along the rivers is now largely restricted to commercial barges, these no longer operate as a "corredor cultural" (cultural corridor).[19] This decline began when passenger boats stopped plying the route between Asunción and Buenos Aires in the last century and it may deepen, given the works being undertaken to create the Hidrovía Paraguay–Paraná–Río de La Plata. This megascale engineering project was initially launched in 1991 but many of the most important phases have yet to be executed. It has been designed to reconstruct the waterways between Asunción and the Atlantic Ocean, making them more easily navigable by larger ships exporting agricultural and mining products. This reduces transport costs and makes trade more competitive. The shipping zone centred on the port of Rosario is already the largest agro-export hub in the world.[20] The works involve removing riverbank vegetation, blasting rocks and small islands, changing the course of the rivers to make them straighter and wider, and dredging them to make them deeper. Since the 1990s, the Hidrovía has been founded on three key ideas: privatization, efficiency, and regional integration. It has already brought some

---

19 Silvestri, "La historia de una idea," 30.
20 See Bergero et al., "El Gran Rosario es el nodo portuario agroexportador más importante del mundo." In 2019, the last year before the Covid-19 pandemic, the port of Rosario dispatched seventy-nine million tons of soy, maize, and wheat products.

important economic benefits, but so far these have largely been reaped by transnational companies and international financial groups.[21]

As one might expect, the World Bank's report on the Hidrovía project welcomes the economic gains that the project will bring. What is perhaps less expected is that it also recommends the project on the basis of its potential environmental benefits. These will mainly come from the transfer of freight transport from roads to the region's waterways, which will reduce greenhouse gas emissions.[22] On the other hand, the writers of the report express a concern that improved access to the rivers is likely to bring changes to land use that will effectively cancel out any environmental improvements. They caution that "If land use changes follow the pattern of expanding frontier regions in Latin America, this may imply increases in deforestation, forest fires and habitat fragmentation." They note further that there is no evidence that an institutional framework is being developed by any of the countries involved to manage this.[23] The region is a growing focus for environmental campaigns, with protests being carried out against the dredging of the river and the enormous recent damage caused by widespread forest fires, and repeated calls for a *Ley de Humedales* (Wetlands Law) that have, to date, been unsuccessful.

In this context, one of the main purposes of the *Paraná Ra'anga* expedition was to register images of a river that is changing and very likely to change further. Its original premise might therefore seem to be founded on a relatively straightforward—if deeply troubling—narrative of cultural and environmental decline as a result of accelerating economic development. But this is not the only story that emerges from the experiences of the expeditioners and the texts and images they created. Many of these works may be read precisely as a challenge to such linear narratives. As well as throwing light on a history of multiple extinctions, catastrophes, and renewals that is often elided in global discourses of the Anthropocene, they also help us to imagine what kinds of dwelling,

---

21 Rausch, "Privatización, eficiencia e integración," 152. In late 2021, the Argentine government brought the Hidrovía under state control, ending a period of twenty-six years in which private conglomerates had been responsible for governing and maintaining the waterway.
22 The World Bank, "Southern Cone Inland Waterways Transportation Study," ix, 46.
23 The World Bank, 54.

past and future, have allowed (or will allow) humans to navigate the ebbs and flows of fluvial time, which subjects the morphology of the landscape to continual change.

If the purpose of the Hidrovía project is to speed up the time taken to export goods, overcoming the obstacles of time and space, the *Paraná Ra'anga* expedition sought explicitly to restore these for its travellers.[24] Their experience was deeply marked by the slow speed of travel up the river on the *Paraguay*, an old repair ship donated to the Paraguayan Navy which had been reconditioned as a cruise ship. The sluggish pace of five miles per hour (at most) was often interrupted by setbacks and unplanned stops, to allow a storm to pass or a mechanical fault to be fixed.[25] For many of the voyagers, time and space seemed to stretch out when they were on board, advancing through a landscape that changed only subtly hour to hour.[26]

This expansion of time and space was to shape the twenty-four images composed by the Argentine photographer Facundo de Zuviría.[27] In an exhibition text, Zuviría refers to the strange sensation of almost complete immobility as the boat travelled slowly upriver and the effect of this creeping pace on urban eyes, so used to the variety and speed of stimuli in the city (Zuviría is best known as a city photographer). In part, his images recall landscapes painted by travelling artists in Latin America in the nineteenth century, such as those of the Río Paraná designed by Hermann Burmeister for his *Vues pittoresques de la Republique Argentine* (1881) (see Figs 4.2 and 4.3), which—as the title acknowledges—followed the picturesque style often used in this period.

Zuviría's photographs magnify the pleasing sweep of the river shore in a similar way, through the use of wide angle and distant focus; the inclusion of an occasional little boat adds the kind of artistic touch that many picturesque painters considered to bring out the natural beauty of a scene (see Fig. 4.4). The "ruggedness" that William Gilpin, one of the first theorists of the picturesque, also identified as crucial to the genre is present in the blustering clouds and the ruffled surface of the

---

24   Silvestri, "La historia de una idea," 34.
25   Conversation with Graciela Silvestri, 1 October 2021.
26   See, for example, Silvestri, "La historia de una idea," 35.
27   *Paraná ra'anga / Imagen del Paraná* (2010–2013). The images may be viewed at http://www.facundodezuviria.com/parana-raanga-2010-2013

148   Decolonial Ecologies

Fig. 4.2 Hermann Burmeister, *El Rio Paraná entre el Diamante y el Rio Carcarañal*, from *Vues pittoresques de la République Argentine: XIV planches avec 36 figures, dessinées la plupart d'après nature et accompagnées de descriptions* (1881), Plate III, Figure 5. Reproduced by kind permission of Cambridge University Library.

4. Retracing Voyages of Science and Conquest 149

Fig. 4.3 Hermann Burmeister, *La Punta Gorda en el Rio Paraná y el pueblo Diamante*, from *Vues pittoresques de la République Argentine: XIV planches avec 36 figures, dessinées la plupart d'après nature et accompagnées de descriptions* (1881), Plate III, Figure 6. Reproduced by kind permission of Cambridge University Library.

water in several photographs (see Fig. 4.5).²⁸ In colonial contexts, critics have tended to see the picturesque, which encompasses irregularities within a harmonious whole, as a tool "to domesticate the unknown and organize the unstructured."²⁹ The exhibition of Zuviría's photographs as a series, however, produces a rather different effect. As we shift our gaze from one photograph to the next, the changes evident between them highlight the agency of nature, unfolding over time before the static, passive gaze of the viewer. They depict a landscape that is constantly changing and that resists capture in a single iconic arrangement. The striking use of black and white lends drama and dynamism to the riverscapes by accentuating the play of light, the swirling or scudding of clouds, and the rippling of the waves below. The eye is drawn to the horizon of each photograph, positioned exactly at mid-height: that line separating water from sky that becomes sharper or softer or disappears altogether as atmospheric conditions change. At the same time, the photographs represent, for Zuviría, "algo inmutable en la naturaleza, un tiempo detenido ante ella, el silencio" (something unchanging in nature, a time that is arrested in its presence, silence).³⁰ They represent a kind of permanence through change that is the antithesis of modern constructions of time as progress and supersession.

This altered experience of time that brings to the fore the protagonism of the natural world is also explored in *Amba. Una especie de paraíso* (Amba: A Kind of Paradise), a video created by Laura Glusman, a visual artist born in Rosario, Argentina.³¹ Glusman overlaid sequences that she filmed from the boat with audio recordings of reflections by different members of the expedition. She asked each person how they imagined the future of the landscape through which they were travelling. As in Zuviría's photographs, the fixed position and angle of Glusman's camera brought out variations in light and vegetation. Recorded mainly along the more remote stretches of the Paraná, the sequences show riverbanks rich with plant life (see Fig. 4.6), with canoes or tiny figures on the shore only rarely entering the frame. Slow fades to and from black separate the sequences and the voices that accompany them, evoking the passing of

---

28 See Gilpin, "On Picturesque Beauty," 7.
29 Diener, "The Traveler Artist," 28; see also Auerbach, "The Picturesque and the Homogenisation of Empire."
30 See http://www.facundodezuviria.com/parana-raanga-imagen-del-parana/
31 The video may be viewed at https://www.youtube.com/watch?v=YHXY9A-KPgY

4. *Retracing Voyages of Science and Conquest*   151

Fig. 4.4 Facundo de Zuviría, black and white photograph from *Paraná Ra'anga: Imagen del Paraná* (2010–2013). 16.6 x 24 cm.

Fig. 4.5 Facundo de Zuviría, black and white photograph from *Paraná Ra'anga: Imagen del Paraná* (2010–2013). 16.6 x 24 cm.

days and nights. In the long pauses, the sound of birds and sometimes howler monkeys may be heard above the low, even drone of the boat's engines. The perspective of an unseen, disembodied spectator surveying the riverbank affords little of the sense of visual mastery that it might in another context, as the viewer is subjected to the slow pace of travel and the emptiness of a space unmarked by singular features, with the boat's progress almost imperceptible against the barely changing landscape.

Fig. 4.6 Still from Laura Glusman, *Ambá. Una especie de paraíso* (2010). Video available at https://www.youtube.com/watch?v=YHXY9A-KPgY

Against this backdrop, Glusman's travelling companions share their predictions about the river's future, turning the landscape into a space of imagination and debate. Some interviewees express a pre-emptive nostalgia, acutely aware that they are experiencing and recording a river that may soon cease to be as it is now. Others are more open to possible transformations of the region and the opportunities this may present. But oddly, given the initial purpose of the journey, the theme that emerges again and again in their reflections is the difficulty of believing that this landscape could really change. One after another, the interviewees affirm that they cannot imagine the river being subject to radical human intervention, given its immensity and its persistence through time, appearing now, they presumed, much as it must have done at the Conquest and since time immemorial.

Their reflections bear witness to a powerful experience of the diminishment of the human in comparison to the magnitude of the natural world. This sense of timelessness and permanence provides an important counterbalance to the belief in human dominance through technology that is ingrained in a mega-engineering project like the Hidrovía. It is also a useful corrective to the aggrandizing of human agency in many Anthropocene discourses that ascribe to humans the capacity to destroy or to save the planet. In part, it is the monumental dimensions of the river that invite us to view it as a permanent and unchanging geological feature, and to revise our estimation of human power, to remember—as one interviewee admits—that "el hombre no domina todo" (man does not control everything). As another respondent states, "remontar al río devuelve al ser humano la condición de ser parte de la naturaleza [...] una parte ínfima de un universo que no le pertenece" (going up the river returns humans to being part of nature [...] an infinitesimal part of a universe that does not belong to them).

In his own reflections on the Río de la Plata region, published in *El río sin orillas* (The River Without Banks, 1991), the Argentine writer Juan José Saer relates the sensation of looking down on the Paraná Delta from above and seeing it acquire an illusory immobility and a geometrical definition that belies its dynamism:

> El triángulo de tierra, de un verde azulado, apretado por las dos cintas inmóviles casi incoloras, yacía allá abajo, en medio de una inmensa extensión chata del mismo verde azulado, inmóvil, inmemorial y vacía, de la que yo sabía, sin embargo, mientras la observaba fascinado que, como todo terreno pantanoso, era una fuente inagotable de proliferación biológica.[32]

> (The triangle of land, bluish-green, pressed between the two unmoving, almost colourless, ribbons, lay down below, amid a vast, flat expanse of the same blue green, motionless, immemorial and empty, but that I knew, while I observed it with fascination, to be, like all marshlands, an inexhaustible source of biological proliferation.)

The first impression, that of the immobile and the immemorial, is the one conveyed by so many of Glusman's interviewees. It is, however, an illusion. This is firstly because, as Saer recognizes, the Paraná is a highly mobile landscape in which the boundaries between land and water

---

32 Saer, *El río sin orillas*, 15.

cannot easily be drawn, as the river's beds and banks are continually changed by the sediment carried in its flow. As a result of the large volume of sediment it carries, the Paraná Delta is continually advancing. This is one of the reasons that the river presents significant challenges for navigation for boats of all kinds. Its strong winds and currents are not always registered by monitors or projections, and its maps need to be constantly updated as islands and sandbanks form, reform, shift, or disappear. Such changeable conditions formed a significant part of the expeditioners' experience on the river. The logbook entries tell of new islands that had formed overnight while they were asleep and an unplanned stop to remove from the boat propeller one of the dozens of tree trunks they saw hurtling down the river.[33] If the expedition held out the promise that its members might encounter the slow time of nineteenth-century and early twentieth-century travel by boat, they were also exposed to a dynamic environment constantly being reshaped by multiple forces.

The illusion of timelessness that the river's landscape may create also stems from our inability to detect anthropogenic change in landscapes that might appear natural but have been drastically changed through farming practices and the introduction of non-native species. It shows how much easier it is for urban dwellers to grasp social change than environmental change, and our tendency to reserve for nature a place beyond temporality rather than to grasp the complex ways in which organisms and environments co-evolve. The descriptions of untouched nature recorded on Glusman's video contrast strongly with the findings of the expedition's ecologists, who observed significant changes in flora and fauna that bear witness to a series of radical transformations of the landscape over time.

The Chaqueña region of Argentina, which borders the Río Paraná and the Río Paraguay, was the area most affected by an enormous wave of deforestation in the late nineteenth century and the first half of the twentieth, with timber mostly used for railway sleepers or tannins for the leather industry and whole swathes of forest cut down to make room for the cultivation of cereal crops or grazing cattle.[34] The secondary forests

---

33 Silvestri et al., "Diario de bitácora: El Paraná Medio," 129; Silvestri et al., "Diario de bitácora: Río Paraguay," 148.
34 Zarrilli, "Bosques y agricultura," 92.

that have regrown in some places do not share the same characteristics as primary forests and are generally degraded.[35] At present, it is estimated that ninety-three percent of the remaining forested areas in the region show signs of deterioration as a result of human activity.[36]

The historical accounts of European travellers' journeys upriver are a rich source of comparison that allow environmental changes to be tracked over time. Ágatha Bóveda, a biologist and photographer from Paraguay and one of the members of the *Paraná Ra'anga* expedition, compared and contrasted aspects of land use, flora and fauna in today's river landscape with those described by travelling naturalists in the past. She focused particularly on texts published by the great French naturalist Alcide d'Orbigny, who travelled along the Paraná in 1827–1828 as part of an eight-year voyage in South America. In *Voyage dans l'Amérique méridionale* (1835–1847), D'Orbigny describes the extraordinary biodiversity and abundance of the river's ecosystems, which were able to support a wide variety of fauna, including deer, monkeys, tapirs, and jaguars.

Of the many different birds spied in vast numbers by d'Orbigny, Bóveda notes that only great egrets are now to be seen in large flocks along the Paraná, with other species seen rarely or not at all.[37] For Bóveda, the fact that no capybaras were observed was of particular concern, as they are a common species, and their absence would indicate low environmental quality.[38] Indeed, the only mammal that Bóveda was able to identify from the boat in 2010 was a species introduced in the region in the sixteenth century by early European settlers, namely the cow.[39] Cattle ranching has in fact been the main cause of the loss of habitats for native species in the region, exacerbated by increasing urbanization, agriculture, and the use of natural resources for construction.[40]

In his own essay, the geographer Carlos Reboratti points to the environmental cost of the loss of huge tracts of forested land in order to make way for grazing cattle, which has also resulted in the retreat of other large animals that used to populate the area.[41] D'Orbigny's

---

35 Zarrilli, 93–94.
36 Zarrilli, 96.
37 Bóveda, "Lo que cambia y lo que permanece," 248.
38 Bóveda, 251.
39 Bóveda, 250.
40 Bóveda, 248.
41 Reboratti, "El Paraná: una pequeña geografía," 48.

account already registers the damaging effect of prescribed fires used to make charcoal and to improve grazing for cattle (as they encourage forage regrowth), with dramatic descriptions of the infernal spectacle he witnessed.[42] The accounts composed by Bóveda and Reboratti draw attention to the enormous and ongoing environmental impact of cattle-farming since the early colonial period.

This historicizing approach encourages us to make crucial links between the colonial-era economic system and Argentina's current reliance on export commodities (as epitomized in the Hidrovía project), and to think more broadly about the relationship between imperialism and environmental change. The enormous biological and ecological impact of what Alfred Crosby called the "Columbian Exchange"—the vast intended and unintended transfer of plants, animals, microbes, and materials of all kinds between the Old and New Worlds—is exemplified in the rise of the cattle industry in colonial America. In Río de la Plata, hides from vast herds of cattle were the chief export of the colonial era, with a million hides a year being sent to Spain by the end of the eighteenth century.[43]

Colonialism represents Europe's first attempt to reengineer the environment on a vast scale: to transform landscapes and to move plants, animals, and minerals around the world, forever changing its ecologies. Viewing the Anthropocene from the perspective of colonial history allows us to see that environmental change is not an unintended and unanticipated byproduct of modernity but its very objective. In the future-oriented discourse of the Anthropocene, past extinctions and slow extinctions are often erased. When it is the fate of global humanity that is seen to be at stake, what goes unseen is the apocalypse that has already been forced upon millions of indigenous lives. Eduardo Viveiros de Castro and Déborah Danowski suggest that indigenous people may have "something to teach us" about apocalypses, demographic catastrophes, and the ends of history, as "for the native people of the Americas, the end of the world already happened—five centuries ago. To be exact, it began on October 12, 1492."[44]

This past experience of apocalypse means, Kyle Whyte argues, that "Indigenous persons and allies examine climate change less as

---

42   Orbigny, *Voyage dans l'Amérique méridionale*, 1:92.
43   Crosby, The Columbian Exchange, 91–92.
44   Viveiros de Castro and Danowski, "Humans and Terrans in the Gaia War," 191.

a future trend, and more as the experience of going *back to the future*. For anthropogenic climate change is an intensified repetition of anthropogenic environmental change inflicted on Indigenous peoples via colonial practices that facilitated capitalist industrial expansion."[45] It is for this reason that Yusoff is deeply suspicious of the past innocence that Anthropocene discourses often posit: the suggestion that we are only now realizing the repercussions of past actions and that "these violences were an unforeseen by-product or excess of these practices and not a central tenet of them."[46]

In this light, putting a date on when the Anthropocene begins is not only of scientific importance; it also affects the broader stories we tell about how human society has developed. Among the many dates proposed for the dawn of the Anthropocene, Simon Lewis and Mark Maslin choose 1610, the year that marks the end of a sudden dip in atmospheric carbon dioxide caused by the deaths of more than 50 million people in the Americas over a few decades, killed by Europeans and particularly the diseases that they carried with them.[47] Although Lewis and Maslin ground their theory in geological records and other data, they also emphasize the political significance of the narrative supported by their choice of date, pointing as it does to an intrinsic relationship between long-term planetary environmental change and the history of colonialism, slavery, and profit-driven capitalism.[48] This narrative about the Anthropocene, unlike others that do not pay attention to the differentiated workings of power, "tells of people having the agency to change the world, but our abilities to do so being far from equal."[49]

An important impetus in the global campaign against climate change stems from the desire to turn back the clock, to recapture the carbon we have released into the atmosphere. Looking at environmental change through a decolonial lens shows us that there are events that are simply not reversible, especially given the close relationship between environmental change and the decline and extinction of people groups that wove their lives into a particular landscape.

---

45 Whyte, "Indigenous Climate Change Studies," 156.
46 Yusoff, *A Billion Black Anthropocenes or None*, 26.
47 Lewis and Maslin, *The Human Planet*, 13.
48 Lewis and Maslin, 326.
49 Lewis and Maslin, 319.

But as well as highlighting the eco-genocides of the past, decolonial approaches may also bring into view alternative modernities that might allow the coexistence of multiple worlds and their divergent temporalities. It is revealing that many of the interviewees on Glusman's video preferred to imagine a future Paraná without significant human presence. More often than not, we find it difficult to imagine landscapes in which humans may coexist in more peaceable, sustainable ways with their environment. It is much easier either to assume that we should remove ourselves from nature or to lament the inevitability that we will "ruin" it (in the words of one of Glusman's interviewees); both options effectively reaffirm an essential separation and discord between humans and the natural world. However, the last interviewee does envision a different way in which humans may inhabit this fluctuating riverine environment in the future. He welcomes the greater presence of humans in the region—there is so much space that they could easily be accommodated, he thinks—as long as their interventions remain modest. He imagines floating mobile cities on the river that would allow it to be inhabited by people rather than simply managed as a route for transporting goods. A similar desire for greater integration of humans in this environment is expressed by Bóveda in the conclusion to her ecological study. She writes:

> tal vez sea posible que los relatos de futuros viajeros de nuestra valiosa Cuenca de la Plata cuenten historias de una humanidad que coexiste con su entorno en lugar de una existencia aislada de la riqueza natural que nos caracteriza como continente.[50]

> (perhaps it is possible that the accounts of future travellers to our valuable La Plata basin will tell stories of a humanity that coexists with its environment, instead of an existence that is isolated from the natural riches that define our continent.)

Recent human settlements in the region have catastrophically failed to negotiate a successful coexistence. Contemporary forms of river management rarely seek to accommodate the pulsating flow that characterizes rivers. Karl Wantzen et al. find that the use of metaphors such as "taming the floods" and "correcting the river course" show that river management is still considered "a war against nature" rather than

---

50 Bóveda, "Lo que cambia y lo que permanece," 248.

"a harmonious coexistence."⁵¹ The highly dynamic nature of the Río Paraná has not been properly taken into account in planning human development along its shores. A photographic series by Glusman entitled *Casas rotas* (2005–) charts the collapse of houses into the river as the banks are eroded. María Laura Bertuzzi points out that constructions have caused problems with drainage and, despite claims that they are located on securely reinforced ground, they are still vulnerable to rises in water levels and continual changes in the river's course.⁵² The river's variability has been viewed as "una desventaja, una alteración, una anomalía" (a disadvantage, a disorder, an anomaly). She proposes instead that it could be understood as an important factor in the design of new, amphibian forms of development that are "cada vez más aliados con los procesos de la naturaleza" (increasingly aligned with natural processes).⁵³ She suggests, for example, the possibility of erecting buildings that are intended for temporary occupation or designed to coexist with the changing morphology of the river.⁵⁴

Mega-engineering projects such as the Hidrovía configure hybrid landscapes composed of water, technologies, people, discourses, and relationships of power.⁵⁵ But "natural" landscapes inhabited by humans have always been created through close interactions between the biophysical, the technological, the social, and the cultural. Early accounts of expeditions along the Río Paraná, such as those kept in the expedition's impromptu on-board library, give us a glimpse of how other communities have inhabited this landscape. The fact that most of the land's pre-Hispanic settlers were nomadic or semi-nomadic enabled them to live successfully in a landscape that was subject to periodic flooding. Intermittent flooding has offered many advantages to human societies in the past, which have benefited from the much greater biodiversity afforded by wetlands. This has historically been the case along the Río Paraná and the broader Pantanal region, but the buildings that are constructed today, and current ways of living in them, typically fail to establish a mutualist relationship of this kind, to the detriment of human dwellers and their environment alike. In this context, the

---

51 Wantzen et al., "River Culture," 11.
52 Bertuzzi, "La costa del río Paraná," 77–78.
53 Bertuzzi, 78.
54 Bertuzzi, 77.
55 Rausch, "Privatización, eficiencia e integración," 144.

question that Glusman's video asks is crucial, as it provokes us to consider alternative ways in which humans might inhabit this changing landscape.

Conclusion

The ways in which scientific expeditions have been reimagined and re-enacted in recent art projects draw attention to forms of environmental change and continuity. As I have shown, they stage important reflections on how humans have dwelt in dynamic ecosystems and promote new ways of thinking about our future relationships with them. Writing in the context of another settler colonial state, Australia, Nigel Clark finds that integrating social history with geological or evolutionary history enables a kind of thinking that may "supplement environmental apocalypticism."[56] Focusing on those who have inhabited a region for tens of thousands of years brings into view the question of "how to live on an earth that is subject to localized shifts and changes of state."[57] For aboriginal communities in Australia, this often involved the expert management of fire to increase flora and fauna and to make land more inhabitable. Clark suggests that "As an alternative to both linear, progressivist narratives and flash-bang apocalypticism, attentiveness to long-term dwelling viewed in tandem with dynamic environmental history puts the stress on enduring, surviving, living on through whatever challenges the world delivers."[58] Although only some elements of the *Paraná Ra'anga* project involve the direct study of indigenous communities today, many of the works developed bring into view the question of how humans have negotiated—or might in the future negotiate—a more reciprocal relationship with a dynamic wetland environment. These visions provide a crucial alternative to the "flash-bang apocalypticism" that Clark deplores in contemporary environmentalist discourses.

Clark's call for an attentiveness to "long-term dwelling" in the context of a "dynamic environmental history" might also help us think differently about the relationship between colonialism and

---

56 Clark, "Aboriginal Cosmopolitanism," 739.
57 Clark, 740.
58 Clark, 740.

ecological change. In many ways, colonialism did produce a clear rupture in the evolutionary history of the Americas. But the language of rupture, tipping points, reversibility and irreversibility, which marks the globalist discourses of the Anthropocene, cannot account for the different temporalities that come into view when we consider the encounters between different cultures in a multispecies world. To think of ecological change in the region only or primarily as a form of rupture is to impose a linear movement from the authentic to the unnatural, the native to the colonized, from untouched wilderness to landscapes that have been thoroughly modified by human activity. These are also forms of colonial and Romantic myth. These landscapes had already been shaped in multiple ways by communities living in the region for thousands of years before the arrival of the Europeans. Their mode of inhabiting a territory was often based on migration, and they deployed methods of slash-and-burn agriculture. Silvestri reminds us that "la aspiración de autoctonía—plantas, paisaje y humanos—está demasiado cerca del ideal europeo de sedentarismo, y muy lejos de la concepción de territorio de los pueblos 'nómades' de las tierras bajas" (the dream of autochthony—plants, landscapes and humans—is too close to the European ideal of sedentary living, and very far from the conception of territory held by the 'nomadic' peoples of the lowlands).[59] To think in terms of rupture also fails to account for the agency of the natural world itself, which traces its own histories of migration and recolonization, with the dispersion of seeds propelled by river flows and floods. What the observers on Glusman's video saw is not an untouched Nature that has persisted through millennia, but a remarkable mobility, resilience, and capacity for regeneration that is characteristic of many plant colonizations.

Paraná Ra'anga demonstrates that understanding the relationship between human history and environmental change does not simply impel us to "zoom out" to imagine the vast scales of deep time, as challenging as that already is. It requires us to understand how dominant discourses of anthropogenic environmental change may, in their calls for united global action to save the future of humanity, obscure the colonial violence already wreaked on peoples and landscapes and justify the continued subjugation of the world to Western technology and universalism. It

---

59   Silvestri, *Las tierras desubicadas*, 36.

also leads us to grasp the disjunctions between the linear temporality of Western technomodernity and the periodic rhythms and turbulence of hydrological and other natural systems; to ask how we might navigate these tensions differently and to find new—or rediscover old—modes of dwelling in landscapes that may become even more challenging to inhabit in the future.

5. Albums, Atlases, and their Afterlives

The great expeditions of the eighteenth and nineteenth centuries to Latin America provided European monarchs and (after Independence) the leaders of new Latin American republics with vital information about the resources—present and potential—that they possessed within the frontiers of their lands. The lavish albums and atlases that brought together these expeditions' findings created a wealth of views of cities, coasts, and other landscapes, alongside ethnographic scenes and illustrations of a botanical or zoological nature. These volumes were commissioned to meet the needs of those defending those lands and governing its peoples. But their texts and images have had an enduring impact, well beyond their original readers and viewers. Constituting some of the first detailed depictions of the landscapes and customs of the region's peoples, these representations were to define many of the images and imaginaries on which regional and national identities were founded. Recent years have seen a renewed attention on the part of Latin American artists to the diaries, sketchbooks, catalogues, albums, and atlases produced by travelling European and *criollo* naturalists of the later colonial period.

Atlases and similar works were designed to provide a definitive account that would remain an obligatory reference for several generations: to "set the standards of a science in word, image, and deed—how to describe, how to depict, how to see."[1] This chapter explores artistic interventions that point to the continued influence of these works' Eurocentric perspectives on visions of Latin American nature (and cultures) well beyond the nineteenth century, or reflect more

---

1 Daston and Galison, *Objectivity*, 22.

broadly on the use of the medium of the printed book in the production and circulation of knowledge in this period. The first part discusses art projects that intervene directly into the books and other documents published by these travellers. Rodrigo Arteaga (Chile) and Tiago Sant'Ana (Brazil) work with the material forms—printed images, texts, and whole books—of the monumental atlases, albums, and catalogues that recorded the findings of scientific expeditions. Arteaga explores the transformation of the natural world into atlases and textbooks in a way that casts light on the role of books and other devices in the construction and circulation of knowledge; his works also demonstrate that this knowledge, seemingly extracted from its environment, is not separate from the natural world but subject to decline and succession in ways that are akin to organic processes of decay and recolonization. Sant'Ana explores the lasting power of the images created of enslaved workers in Brazil through a series of performances that produce re-readings of the racist legacies of these illustrations. Claudia Coca (Peru) and Donjo León (Argentina) turn their attention to the *National Geographic* magazine, founded in the late nineteenth century, which in many ways reproduces the imperialist, classifying gaze of the texts and images produced for earlier surveys carried out in Latin America. I argue that both artists attempt to subvert this gaze by emphasising the force of nonhuman agency.

The second part of the chapter focuses on artistic projects that have been inspired by the texts and images produced by Humboldt in his journey through the Americas (1799–1804). Antonio Bermúdez (Colombia) explores the scientific, commercial, and artistic afterlives of the iconic images produced by Humboldt, such as his famous cross-sectional study of the Chimborazo, demonstrating how scientific representations of nature, once published, are caught up in iterative processes of cultural mediation and commercial accumulation. The relationship between Humboldt's global science and colonial extractivism is suggested by Oscar Santillán (Ecuador); this is a theme I explore in greater depth in a reading of the decolonial perspectives developed in the extensive *Archivo Humboldt* (2011–) created by Fabiano Kueva (Ecuador).

The albums, atlases, and other works that are the subject of these more recent artistic projects span a period that takes us from the late colonial era to the first decades of the independent Latin American republics, formed in the early part of the nineteenth century. The fact that these new states also commissioned surveys of this kind, or gave permission for European expeditions to map out their geography, points to some important continuities in the extractive policies adopted by colonial powers and modern nation states in the region, as well as the enduring legacy of European and Eurocentric philosophies of nature in Latin America. It is precisely this ongoing legacy that becomes the central concern of the artistic projects analysed in this chapter.

In the 1980s and 1990s, Latin American artists were already exploring ways to rework the narratives and images created by the scientific expeditions of the eighteenth and nineteenth centuries. Each part of this chapter is introduced with a brief discussion of relevant works by Luis Fernando Benedit (Argentina, 1937–2011) and José Alejandro Restrepo (Colombia, 1959–), respectively, whose works can be read as precursors to the more recent ones that provide the main focus of this chapter. Benedit and Restrepo acknowledge the iconic value of the hegemonic texts and images created by travelling European naturalists while seeking ways to unweave and rework them. Their experiments bring into focus the more explicitly post-anthropocentric and decolonial aims of the later works explored in this chapter.

I. From Decolonization to Decomposition: Interventions into the Archive

Luis Fernando Benedit is most famous for the experimental habitats and labyrinths he designed for animals and plants, works that became emblematic of the "systems art" developed in Argentina and elsewhere in the 1970s. In several of his later works, he reflected on the narratives and images created by Europeans travelling to Argentina and Latin America on scientific expeditions, including Alessandro Malaspina (1789–1794) and Charles Darwin (1831–1836). For Benedit, the work he started to produce from 1978 onwards in relation to the Argentine countryside was a reflection on how "el campo [...] pasa de ser silvestre a ser cultural" (the countryside [...] moves from being wild to being cultural).[2] In many ways, Benedit's series on the expeditions of Malaspina and Darwin show a similar fascination with that passage from nature

---

2   Molina and Glusberg, *Luis Fernando Benedit*, 118.

to culture, returning to what were effectively the region's first archives, which introduced some of its most powerful and influential narratives and images. Darwin held a particular interest for Benedit because he provided "la primera descripción científica y realista del país" (the first scientific and realist description of the country), depicting it with the cold, distanced eye of a naturalist.[3] In Benedit's work, however, it is the impact of Darwin's work on the cultural imaginaries of the nation that is brought most often to the fore.

In his series *Del viaje del Beagle* (From the Voyage of the *Beagle*, 1987), Benedit superimposes cut-outs and even three-dimensional objects (twigs, animal and human figurines) onto his paintings of mountains and seascapes and their frames. This collage effect gives material form to the layering of citations that shapes the works. The inclusion of moulded forms of flora and fauna suggests the extent to which the texts and illustrations of natural historians such as Darwin have shaped imaginaries of Patagonia and the other places he visited. But this act of moulding also expresses the availability of those visions for acts of re-construction in the present. The figurines, standing out from the frames, create a series of reflexive gazes. In *Darwin observa una calandria en Maldonado* (Darwin Observes a Calandra Lark in Maldonado, 1987), the addition of a diminutive, three-dimensional epoxy figure of Darwin expressly thematizes the gaze. Wearing a frock coat and holding a walking stick, Darwin looks toward the large mockingbird depicted within the frame. The work suggests the extent to which Latin American flora, fauna, and landscapes (not to mention its original inhabitants) would always be framed by a European gaze.

Interestingly, though, in other works it is animals or insects that look onto the framed painting. In *Del viaje del Beagle—Los Andes—Villavicencio* (1987), a typical Andean landscape is surveyed by two imposing *vinchuca* beetles, of the kind popularly supposed to have caused Darwin's death from Chagas disease. As David Elliott writes, the *Beagle* expedition "fue el momento simbólico en el que la ciencia occidental enfrentó e intentó organizar la 'naturaleza salvaje' en toda su complejidad" (was the symbolic moment at which Western science confronted and attempted to organize 'wild nature' in all its complexity). But he also notes the

---

3   Molina and Glusberg, 119.

irony that Darwin's life was brought to an end by a tiny Andean insect.[4] Benedit's *Beagle* series thus not only draws attention to the power of the European archives and narratives that have shaped the natural and cultural history of Latin America, but also suggests a potential undoing of the human domination of the natural world. This is a theme that more contemporary artists have pursued, using a range of artistic resources to restore agency to the nonhuman world and to gesture toward a post-anthropocentric future.

Recombinations and Recolonizations: Nature and Print Culture in the Work of Rodrigo Arteaga

The French naturalist Claudio Gay (1800–1873) was contracted by the Chilean Government in 1830 to carry out a detailed survey of the history and geography of the new republic. The results of Gay's exhaustive research, undertaken between 1834 and 1842, were compiled in a monumental, multi-volume work entitled *Historia física y política de Chile* (Physical and Political History of Chile, 1854). Among the aspects studied were the nation's political history, the customs of its indigenous communities, its plants, animals, and landscapes, and the state of its agricultural industry. Two of these volumes, entitled *Atlas de la historia física y política de Chile* (Atlas of the Physical and Political History of Chile), contain maps of the country that were significantly more reliable than any others produced to date, along with illustrations of native flora and fauna. As Rafael Sagredo Baeza affirms, Gay's work was as important politically as it was scientifically: it consolidated and legitimated the new state, tracing its history and extending its knowledge of—and power over—the furthest reaches of its lands.[5]

Rodrigo Arteaga borrows the title of Gay's masterpiece for his own version of the *Atlas de la historia física y política de Chile* (2015–2016), for which he cut out hundreds of the illustrations of shells, insects, plants, birds, and fish that feature in Gay's atlas.[6] He folded wings, legs, and feelers to bring the images into three dimensions and then arranged

---

4   Elliott, "Luis F. Benedit en el Museo Nacional de Bellas Artes," 169.
5   Sagredo Baeza, "Ciencia, historia y arte como política," 183–84.
6   The work was shown as part of a solo exhibition entitled *Just as the Daylight was Fading*, held at the Sobering Galerie, Paris, in 2016.

them for display as if there were the objects themselves. The beetles and butterflies are pinned to the back of a specimen display case, the fish and other sea creatures are immersed in formaldehyde jars, and birds are arranged in a small wetlands diorama, while the plants and flowers have been gathered together as if to suggest the profusion of a wild garden (see Fig. 5.1). In creating these sculptures and installations, Arteaga draws attention to the transformations that have already taken place to register the natural world in texts and images. In particular, he brings to the fore the use of paper as a means of recording and transporting knowledge about the natural world. Bruno Latour affirms that "scientists master the world, but only if it comes to them in the form of two dimensional, superposable, combinable inscriptions."[7]

The *trompe l'oeil* effect of Arteaga's recombinations suggest the ease with which illustrations on paper are able to substitute for the real thing. More broadly, his *Atlas de la historia física y política de Chile* reflects on the processes we have developed to order, display, and circulate knowledge about nature. In restoring volume to two-dimensional images and re-ordering them in cabinets and other display units, Arteaga effectively studies how we study the natural world, and how we have rendered it in forms that allow it to be assembled, ordered, and classified in different ways. His aim was to "Hacer un atlas de otro atlas, una forma de organizar otras formas de organizar" (make an atlas of another atlas, a way of organizing ways of organization).[8] Rather than diminishing the integrity or the iconicity of Gay's epic by cutting it up into tiny pieces, Arteaga's installation could be understood to suggest that its power lies precisely in the simultaneously durable, mobile, and recombinable nature of its images, which have remained a key point of reference for scientists ever since.[9]

Yet this vision of durability and longevity—of the "immutable mobiles" constituted by flat images and documents, according to Latour[10]—should be balanced with the rather different fate suffered by books in another installation by Arteaga, *Botánica sistemática* (Systematic

---

7   Latour, *Pandora's Hope*, 29.
8   Gilardoni, "De biología, botánica y cosmología [interview with Rodrigo Arteaga]."
9   Sagredo Baeza, "El Atlas de Claude Gay y la representación de Chile," 132, 139.
10 Latour, "Visualisation and Cognition," 7.

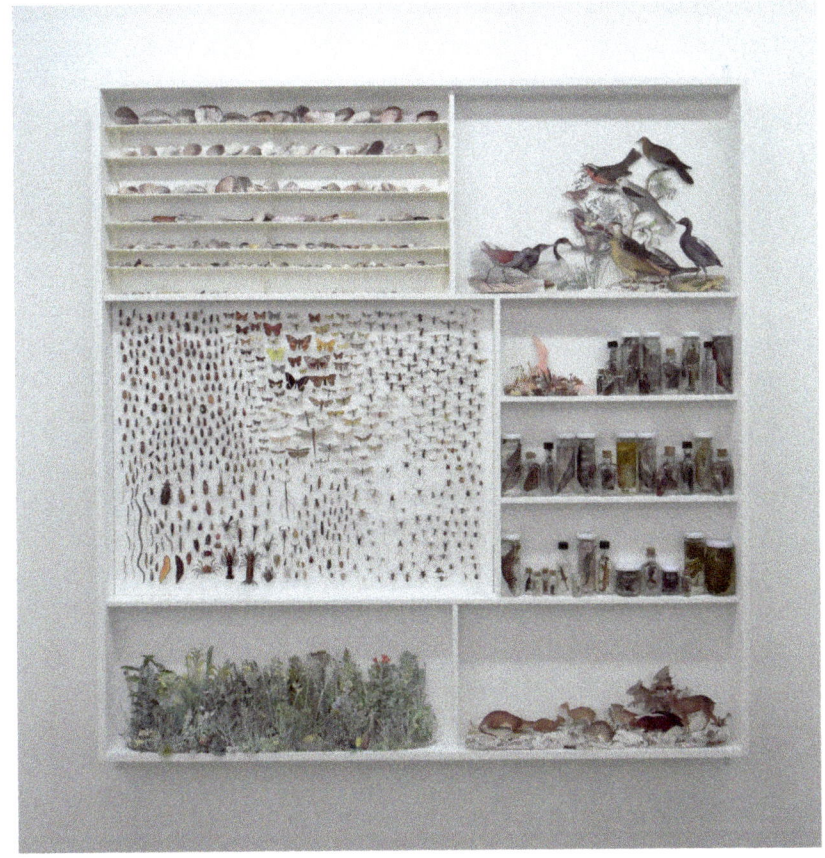

Fig. 5.1 Rodrigo Arteaga, *Atlas de la historia física y política de Chile* (2015–2016). Intervened cut-out illustrations, wooden structure, 140 x 120 x 8 cm. Sobering Galerie, Paris (photograph by the artist).

Botany, 2015).[11] For this installation, a series of botany textbooks were placed on a white table. From them sprout plants and flowers, either as cut-out illustrations or as real plants, cultivated in soil and added to the spines and pages of the books (see Fig. 5.2). The books are old editions that are no longer authoritative: a faded version of *Cours Complet d'Histoire Naturelle* by Gaston Bonnier (originally published in 1892), a worn copy of *La vida de las plantas* produced by *Revista Occidente* in 1959,

---

11 The work was first shown at the Carmen Araujo Arte gallery in Caracas, Venezuela, in 2015. Images may be viewed at http://www.rodrigoarteaga.com/Botanica-sistematica

and a coursebook on *Botánica sistemática* published by the Universidad de Concepción in 1954, its pages browned and its corners dog-eared.

Fig. 5.2 Rodrigo Arteaga, from *Botánica sistemática* (2015). Book intervened with plants and earth. Carmen Araujo Arte, Caracas (photograph by the artist).

With their utility confined to providing a substrate for the plants that are bursting forth from them, Arteaga's books seem to suggest the limits of human knowledge and the ultimate futility of attempts to control and manage the natural world through atlases and encyclopaedias. Arteaga's own reflections on the work do not emphasize a divide between (ordering) culture and (defiant) nature in this way, however. Instead, he wanted to convey the idea that knowledge is subject to the same processes of decomposition as everything else in the organic world. If encyclopaedias are born of the ambition to bring together the newest and most accurate information about the world, they nevertheless end up "obsoletas y olvidadas en viejas librerías" (obsolete and forgotten in old bookshops); they demonstrate the "fragility" of knowledge, or rather its "aspecto dinámico y orgánico" (dynamic, organic quality).[12] In the same way that the material repositories of our knowledge—books and other printed papers—are subject to decay over time, being

---

12   Gilardoni, "De biología, botánica y cosmología [interview with Rodrigo Arteaga]."

(re)colonized by fungi and plants, that knowledge itself is caught up in cycles of growth, dissemination, and decline.

Both *Atlas de la historia física y política de Chile* and *Botánica sistemática* are reflexive projects, then, that question the nature of our knowledge of nature. Arteaga explains that he wished to explore the relationship between images and the plants they represent, collapsing the conventional distinction between object and representation:

> Me interesa cómo y cuánto estas imágenes se distancian del objeto de estudio, en qué medida dejan de parecer naturales, o quizás son en sí mismas otra naturaleza. El gesto de recortar las ilustraciones de plantas para combinarlas es un intento obstinado por devolverlas a su origen. Imitando el crecimiento natural y orgánico.[13]

> (I am interested in how and to what extent these images become separated from the object of study, the degree to which they stop appearing natural, or perhaps they are themselves another kind of nature. The gesture of cutting out the illustrations of the plants to recombine them is a stubborn attempt to return them to their origin. Imitating natural and organic growth.)

In the arrangements of cut-out flowers for his *Atlas de la historia física y política de Chile: Herbario*, then, as well as in the plants sprouting from the books of *Botánica sistemática*, Arteaga suggests that these illustrations on paper cannot be understood as representations that are ontologically distinct from the objects they stand in for, but are themselves part of a dynamic, material world. They are not representations so much as transformations. The processes of inscription and conscription by which the natural world becomes an object of knowledge give rise to new meanings according the different affordances of the multiple systems, devices, repositories, archives with which we record, shape, and transmit knowledge. But those processes do not remove knowledge from the world: it is subject to the same organic processes that transform the biophysical sphere. Arteaga suggests that the ideas about nature that they encode should be—and are—exposed to similar operations of decline and recolonization.

In her analysis of Gay's atlas, Camila Ramírez Maldonado examines its power—which is common to all maps and atlases—to synthesize time

---

13   Gilardoni.

and space, unifying national territory in the illusion of a history and geography shared by all citizens.[14] Arteaga's works literally deconstruct this process, reintroducing the dimension of time to convey the mutability of the knowledge condensed in atlases and other encyclopaedic works. This returns knowledge to the natural world whose processes of decay and recomposition it might seem to transcend, in the relative durability of print culture.

Labour and Repetition: Images of Slavery in Tiago Sant'Ana's Performances

Tiago Sant'Ana's works of performance art reflect on Afro-Brazilian identities and the particular socioeconomic inequalities that have persisted in Brazil since slavery began in the sixteenth century. Many of his performances involve the use of sugar, an item of everyday consumption that he re-embeds within Brazil's violent history of colonization and slavery. In his works, sugar denotes the "violence, extermination, genocide" of forced migration and the experience of slaves on plantations, but also "a naturalization of whiteness as an acceptable parameter for life and of social organization."[15] It points to past wounds that have not yet been fully recognized, as well as the persistence of racial inequalities in Brazil long after the abolition of slavery, in part through the country's continued role as a producer of raw materials (Brazil is the world's largest exporter of sugar). The abundance of sugar used in the works alludes to the fact that sugar is no longer the luxury product that it was before enslaved labour dramatically reduced the cost of production. The back-breaking work of growing and refining sugar only became economically viable as a result of slavery.

Sant'Ana's *Refino* series (Refining, 2017) takes place in the ruins of an old sugar mill in Cachoeira, Bahia, which was built in 1812. Central to two of the pieces is a book containing the complete works of the French artist Jean-Baptiste Debret (1768–1848) in Brazil. Debret is best known for the extensive images he produced while living and travelling

---

14 Ramírez Maldonado, "Fragmentando la unidad," 173.
15 Lavigne, "The Naturalization of Whiteness as a Life Parameter [Interview with Tiago Sant'Ana]."

in Brazil between 1816 and 1831. Many of these were published on his return to France in a three-volume work with the title *Voyage pittoresque et historique au Brésil* (1834–1839), which contained no fewer than 232 lithographic prints. As Marcus Wood observes, images in works by Debret—as well as by Thomas Ender and João Maurizio Rugendas, who also published richly illustrated albums of their journeys in Brazil— have been repeatedly and uncritically reproduced, even in recent years, as if they represented "documentary truth."[16] Sant'Ana's performances insist on the need to interrogate those images and discourses created by Debret and other European travellers that have become part of the nation's canon of self-representations.

In *Refino #3*, a volume of the complete works of Debret in Brazil lies open at a page featuring a watercolour of a sugar cane press being operated by black slaves.[17] The book's pages are gradually sprinkled with sugar, which starts to form a heap, obscuring the text and images beneath it and eventually almost entirely burying the whole book under a cascading mound of white crystals (see Fig. 5.3).[18] *Refino #4* reverses the process. Sant'Ana painstakingly removes the sugar, one spoonful at a time, revealing the pages hidden beneath, before smoothing off the last granules with the palm of his hand (see Fig. 5.4).[19] The covering-over of these images of black men with white sugar gestures toward to the racist ideology of *branqueamiento* (whitening) in Brazil, which became prevalent around the turn of the twentieth century, according to which the "inferior" black "race" would gradually make progress over several generations of breeding with "superior" white people. In its play of veiling and unveiling, the performance also expresses the work, the labour, needed to make these images newly visible. These are images that had, in their time, granted only a limited visibility to black bodies, highlighting their labour at the service of Brazil's modernization but obscuring the lives that had been truncated through the violence of slavery and naturalizing their subordinate position within a racial hierarchy.

---

16   Wood, *Black Milk*, 37. Also see https://tiagosantanaarte.com/2017/10/19/refino-3-e-4/
17   Bandeira and Corrêa do Lago, *Debret e o Brasil: Obra completa 1816–1831*, 229.
18   A video of the *Refino #3* performance may be viewed at https://vimeo.com/498087531
19   A video of the *Refino #4* performance may be viewed at https://vimeo.com/498088172

Fig. 5.3 Still from video of performance by Tiago Sant'Ana, *Refino #3* (2017) (image provided by the artist).

Fig. 5.4 Still from video of performance by Tiago Sant'Ana, *Refino #4* (2017) (image provided by the artist).

Although in Debret's image the bodies of four black workers are prominent, the accompanying text centres almost entirely on a description of how the sugar cane press functions mechanically. In the longer version of the text published in *Viagem pitoresca e histórica ao Brasil*, he explains that in a larger, more industrial version of the process he has depicted, the slave required to feed the flattened sugar cane back through the press to crush it again is made redundant with the addition of a couple more rollers.[20] Debret's observation rather tellingly points to the slaves' integration into a techoeconomic system in which their bodies are reduced to labour, becoming fully expendable if they can be more efficiently replaced by a machine.

The four slaves are locked into a circular choreography in Debret's illustration, with two of them pushing a long wooden handle in circles and the other two passing canes to and fro through the rollers. This circularity is evoked in Sant'Ana's action, which covers only to uncover, adding only to remove. Together, these actions set up a contrast with the organization of Debret's *Viagem pitoresca* itself, which was consciously intended to reflect the "marcha progressiva da civilização no Brasil" (progressive march of civilization in Brazil).[21] While the first volume focused on the "primitive" Indian and the natural environment, the second centred on the industrial development of Brazil, and the third on the political, religious, and artistic characteristics of the modern, civilized colony. Debret's work is thus squarely founded on Enlightenment principles of progress and civilization, inscribing other cultures within a Eurocentric understanding of the evolution of society toward modernity. In this vision, slaves were simply a motor for economic progress and modernization, not beneficiaries of the wealth and freedom that could follow. Sant'Ana's performances, like the slaves' labour itself, are governed by a temporality that is based on monotonous repetition and circularity rather than linear progress. In this way, his work deconstructs the promise of modernity, in which advancement was granted to a few at the cost of the many.

Claudia Coca and Donjo León: Revisions and Recolonizations

The widespread circulation and avid readership of eighteenth- and nineteenth-century travellers' narratives and albums is perhaps matched most closely in our own era by the *National Geographic* (1888–). Famous

---

20 Debret, *Viagem pitoresca e histórica ao Brasil*, 250.
21 Debret, 149.

for its spectacular photojournalism, the *National Geographic* is one of the most-read magazines of all time within the US and beyond, with local editions published across the world in over thirty different languages.[22] Since the early 1960s, each iconic, yellow-bordered cover has boasted a vivid full-page image from one of the articles inside, often depicting people in traditional ethnic dress or rare and colourful species at risk. The magazine has been criticized both for its "blatant exoticization of the Other" and for an equally insidious erasure of cultural difference, appealing to essential human values in a way that "allows colonialism to grace the coffee table."[23]

Claudia Coca (Peru) has produced several series of mock cover designs for the *National Geographic*, developing a critique of the images and discourses it has so powerfully sold across the world.[24] Although she finds much of value in the *National Geographic* as a publication, Coca objects to the way that it perpetuates an idea of the marginal and the peripheral as an object of anthropological study: of the Other as "lejano, exótico y bárbaro" (distant, exotic and barbaric), counterposing the native and the savage to Western civilization.[25] In the *National Geographic*, Coca reads the violence of a modernity that is built on the exclusion of what it casts as primitive and barbaric. She replaces the high-colour, glossy covers of the *National Geographic* with humbler, more provisional, pencil drawings in black and white, erasing the brash colours and high definition of its photojournalistic realism and reminding us that the images it creates have no greater claim to truth than any other form of art.

Many of the *National Geographic* covers that Coca created early on in her *Tempestades* series (Tempests, 2015–) showed tumultuous seas and impenetrable forests that belonged to no specific region: together they epitomize the exuberant savagery of remote geographies as imagined by the modernizing West. In 2019, she produced another series of covers on the theme of the Ruta del Comercio de Indias (Americas Trade Route), this time designed to reverse the imperial gaze. These covers show recognizable landmarks in Seville, Madrid, and the southwest coast of

---

22 See https://nationalgeographicpartners.com/2021/02/february-magazine-covers-from-around-the-world/
23 Neuhaus, "Colonizing The Coffee Table," 2.
24 The works may be viewed at https://claudiacoca.com/cuentos
25 Claudia Coca, 'La tempestad" (2019), https://claudiacoca.com/cuentos

Spain that are associated with the imperial ventures of conquest, trade, and the comprehensive documentation of the New World, including the Archivo General de Indias, which contains the archives of the Spanish Empire. These iconic sites associated with the study and administration of the New World are overcome with raging waters and colossal palm trees, as she imagines the legendary ferocity of the furthest corners of the empire visited upon the metropolitan centre, toppling its institutions and endangering its archives.

One of the series produced for the *Tempestades* project contains images of the botanical gardens that were founded in Spain and other European countries to study and display the riches of New World flora. Coca's illustrations reproduce the rectangular format of the magazine's cover and its recognizable title. They focus on a single plant in the foreground, with the structures of a greenhouse visible above and behind (see Fig. 5.5). Often drawn from a very low angle, the plants take on predatory dimensions: one spreads its flame-red fronds toward the glass roof, another spirals upwards with long bristles, and another seems to advance toward the viewer, stretching its sharp, spiny leaves in our direction. We see nothing here of the ordered, classifying power of the botanical garden: the close-ups instead convey the rapacious, invading force of the plants themselves, which resist the conquest of nature celebrated in European botanical gardens and practise their own forms of colonization. The plants appear to outgrow the enclosures to which they have been confined. In most cases, they also obscure part of the "National Geographic" lettering, its staid font overwhelmed by the luxuriance of the plants and the bright sunlight streaming through the roof of the glass house. As the title fades against the light, overtaken by the plants it represents, we seem to witness the waning of an institution that has been so influential in shaping the Western imagination of distant lands and peoples.

A similar interest in challenging the classifying, exoticizing gaze of the *National Geographic* through an emphasis on nonhuman agency can be seen in Donjo León's *Revistas NG en descomposición* (Decomposing NG Magazines, Argentina, 2020).[26] Framed *National Geographic* covers

---

26 The work was shown as part of the *Simbiologías: Prácticas Artísticas en un Planeta en Emergencia* exhibition at the Centro Cultural Kirchner, Buenos Aires, Argentina, in 2021–2022. Images of the work may be viewed at https://simbiologia.cck.gob.ar/hashtags/hongo-fungii/

Fig. 5.5 Claudia Coca, four drawings from *Joyas remotas* (2020) from the *Tempestades* series (2015–2023). Charcoal and pastel on linen, 50 × 35 cm (photograph by the artist).

are displayed in varying states of decay, with bacteria and fungi feeding on the cellulose that is the major component of paper and card. Like Coca, León suggests the indifference of nature to our inscriptions of it, and the vulnerability of our archives to the natural cycles of decay and rebirth. In decomposing materials, fungi make their nutrients more available for other species. Ironically, therefore, the pristine pages of the *National Geographic* have finally become hosts for the biodiversity the magazine champions. *Revistas NG en descomposición* also raises questions about the role of the gallery that houses this decaying piece of art: if the function of the gallery or museum is normally to preserve cultural heritage against fungal invasions, here it frames the very decomposition of those archives. In this way, León suggests a new possible role for the museum in a postcolonial era: to exhibit the decline and effacement of (neo)colonial visions of nature.

Counter-Archives

The close relationship between science and print culture in Europe contributed to a false universalism, permitting the wide dissemination of Eurocentric visions of Latin America (and other regions of the world) under the guise of scientific empiricism. Nineteenth-century atlases and albums, together with more recent magazines like the *National Geographic*, are richly illustrated, collectible items. Arteaga, Sant'Ana, Coca, and León dissect the ways in which those texts and their images have so thoroughly shaped imaginaries of Latin America; they also intervene in the images they created to pronounce their obsolescence, producing their material effacement or decay. In the process, they create counter-archives in the form of new combinations and assemblages.

While Arteaga's interest lies in interrogating the role of books, display devices, and other forms of organization in the creation of knowledge about the natural world, Sant'Ana develops a more explicit critique of the power of images to naturalize slavery and the lasting forms of inequality that still govern Brazilian society. The continued prevalence in recent decades of images of exoticism and primitivism in the *National Geographic* demonstrates the persistence of colonial imaginaries in Western media, which Coca challenges through a reversal of the imperial gaze. León's work calls on cultural institutions to break their collusion with that gaze and to preside instead over the decomposition of the archive, in order to allow new and diverse forms of life to proliferate. The acts of revealing, concealing, decomposing, and recomposing to which these atlases, albums, and magazines are submitted become utopian gestures that show how their images may be reframed for decolonial and post-anthropocentric purposes.

II. Humboldt Remediated

The many texts and images produced by travelling naturalists in the eighteenth and nineteenth centuries were often a series of rediscoveries and remediations. Humboldt saw the Americas through the eyes of the French geographer and explorer Charles Marie de La Condamine (1701–1774), while his own narratives and images would influence travellers who followed in his footsteps, including Darwin and Ernst Haeckel (among other naturalists) and painters such as Johann Moritz Rugendas and Frederic Edwin Church. Even the individual images produced by naturalists and artists were usually composite views, combining features from sketches of different sites and co-composed by several different artists: sketch makers, painters, engravers, and colourers.

In more recent times, artists have highlighted the disparities and discontinuities that have emerged in these processes as a way of deconstructing the iconicity of images produced by travellers to Latin America and the authority of their narratives. They have also focused on the artistic and commercial afterlives of these images, which are still among the most prevalent depictions of Latin American landscapes to be found. By exploring how such texts and images have multiplied, circulated, and gained value, artists have developed critiques of the relationships between scientific knowledge, colonial power, and commerce, which have continued to be profitable to the present day. They have also sought to repurpose these images, however, in ways that move beyond deconstruction to indicate possible acts of repossession.

José Alejandro Restrepo's work has explored the powerful images produced of Latin America by Humboldt and other travelling scientists, such as the French botanist and physician Charles Saffray. *Paso del Quindío I* (The Quindío Pass I, 1992) has its origin in Restrepo's reading of Humboldt's diaries and his decision to retrace some of the voyages Humboldt made through Colombia, focusing particularly on his journey along the Paso del Quindío, an extremely perilous and often impassable mountain trail.[27] The work is an installation that comprises several television monitors arranged on steps to form a pyramid shape. Looped videos playing on each monitor show sequences of landscapes that have been made unfamiliar through abstraction, close-ups, rapid camera movements, and editing, before giving way to more sedate framings of palm trees and mountain slopes. They suggest a multiplicity of dephased, subjective gazes that refuse to coalesce to form a coherent, stable image, directly undermining the surveying, classifying gaze of the European scientist.

When the piece was first exhibited, a large woodcut of an engraving of the Paso del Quindío published by Humboldt was displayed behind the monitors. The work epitomized, for Restrepo, the multiple layers of mediation and interpretation that characterize any image supposed to convey a scientific or historical truth. As Restrepo explains, the sketch Humboldt had made *in situ* in 1801 was handed almost ten years later to Joseph Anton Koch in Rome, who produced the final drawing; that was then turned into a print by Christian Friedrich Traugott Duttenhofer in Stuttgart. The final version, published in *Vues des cordillères et monuments des peuples indigènes de l'Amérique* (1810) is, as Restrepo points out, "un palimpsesto, un bricolaje, un asunto de montaje" (a palimpsest, a bricolage, a thing of montage).[28] In the installation itself, this idea emerges clearly in the four quotations that are presented on the wall next to the monitors, each of which casts doubt on the accuracy of the historical descriptions and pictorial representations of the Quindío Pass, accusing travellers, illustrators, and printmakers of making too great a use of their imagination.[29] In one citation, for example, Humboldt complains that Koch did not follow his sketches properly in his painting of the Quindío Pass; in another, Koch himself accuses Duttenhofer of "excessive stylization" in his production of an engraving based on Koch's painting. As a whole, then, Restrepo's work reminds us that "la visión racionalista del mundo y de la historia no está exenta de errores

---

27 Gutiérrez, "Anexo 1: entrevista con José Alejandro Restrepo," 94.
28 Murphy Turner, "Historias del paisaje durante la colonización de América."
29 Wellen, "José Alejandro Restrepo," 178.

y prejuicios" (the rationalist vision of the world and of history is not exempt from errors and prejudices).[30]

The theme of the proliferation of the images sketched by Humboldt and the inconsistencies that emerge between their versions is taken up in Antonio Bermúdez's *De vuelta al centro del mundo* (2017), discussed below, which traces the commercial afterlives of these illustrations. In a more poetic register, Oscar Santillán's *Lost Star* (2013) expresses the relationship between Humboldt's universalizing science and Europe's extractive activities in Latin America. The *Archivo Humboldt* (2011–), a major project developed by Fabiano Kueva, makes this relationship fully explicit, drawing on decolonial theory to show how Humboldt's pursuit of a global science becomes central to European universalism and its continued hegemony. These projects move beyond Restrepo's critique, which was principally directed toward the inaccuracy of European representations of Latin America, to explore the broader relationship between knowledge, coloniality, and the global economy.

Antonio Bermúdez: The Global Economy of Humboldt's Images

In *De vuelta al centro del mundo* (Back to the Centre of the Earth, 2017), Antonio Bermúdez (Colombia) demonstrates the transnational commerciability of Humboldt's images.[31] The exhibition gathers together prints of the same famous engraving, produced for Humboldt's *Vues des Cordillères, et monumens des peuples indigènes de l'Amerique* (1810–1813), which shows a view of the Chimborazo volcano in Ecuador (see Fig. 5.6). The prints were sold and shipped to Bermúdez by galleries, bookshops, antique shops, and other sellers based in different countries, including France, Italy, Germany, Croatia. The labelling of the prints in a range of languages—one carries titles in German, French, and Russian—bears witness to the global reach of Humboldt's images. Their commercial value and circulation are also apparent in the display, alongside many of the prints, of receipts for their purchase and the packaging in which they were sent: envelopes, parcels made of cardboard, jiffy bags, and

---

30 Restrepo, *Musa paradisíaca*, 14.
31 The installation was first exhibited in Espacio El Dorado in Bogotá in 2017. Images may be viewed at https://antoniobermudez.com/Back-to-The-Center-of-The-World

a reused packing box from an Italian cured meats company, with the customs declarations labels still attached.

Fig. 5.6 Alexander von Humboldt, *The Chimborazo seen from the Plateau of Tapia*. Plate from *Vues des Cordillères et monumens des peuples indigènes de l'Amérique* (1810). Wellcome Collection. Attribution 4.0 International (CC BY 4.0).

Seeing the prints exhibited together highlights the variations between one engraving and another, and between different colourations of the same engraving. It also draws attention to the inconsistencies and errors that have crept in during the history of the image's reproductions: some situate the Chimborazo in Colombia, for example, while others correctly identify it as Ecuadorian. The curator Halim Badawi points out that the agave plant that features in the foreground is rarely to be found in the Andes; these and other clichés, such as palm trees, were often included to conjure up an exotic vision of the New World tropics that met viewers' expectations.[32]

Indeed, given what we know of the production of this image in particular—and of many images published by European travellers to Latin America in the nineteenth century—there is in fact no single or

---

32 See the curatorial text for the exhibition in Espacio El Dorado, reproduced at https://www.espacioeldorado.com/de-vuelta-al-centro-del-mundo

original image that could be identified as authentically Humboldt's own. Although Humboldt insists in his accompanying text that "The mountain has been drawn exactly as it is seen from the arid plain of Tapia" and that the llamas in the foreground are "drawn from life," he also admits that "The sketch that I had made on site served no other purpose than to give an exact indication of the contours of Chimborazo."[33] Like many images of the New World avidly consumed by Europeans, this one was designed, coloured, and engraved by artists who had never set foot in the Americas. In this case, Humboldt reveals, the drawing was executed by Jean-Thomas Thibault, who has "enlivened the scene with figures that are grouped very intelligently."[34] Since the production of this image, the large number of other versions produced by other engravers and colourers demonstrates the thorough dissemination of Humboldt's vision of Chimborazo across the world and to the present day. Bermúdez's installation asks us to consider how such images—often created, copied, and circulated far from Latin America, by artists with little or no direct knowledge of the region—have continued to shape imaginaries of the New World, despite their fabrications and falsities. It also points to the commercial opportunities seized by image-makers that have turned such illustrations into objects of consumption. The images produced by Humboldt and other scientists were not disconnected from this commercial enterprise but central to it.

Oscar Santillán: *Cosmos* and Extractivism

A stately tome stands upright in a glass case, its leather edges worn but its pages completely blank. Next to the book rests a tiny, pea-sized, black sphere (see Fig. 5.7). For his work *Lost Star* (2013), Oscar Santillán (Ecuador/Netherlands) took a nineteenth-century edition of Humboldt's epic work *Cosmos: Sketch of a Physical Description of the Universe*, published in five volumes between 1845 and 1862. He subjected its pages to a chemical process that allowed him to extract the ink, which he then formed into a miniature globe. Humboldt's *Cosmos* was his magnum opus, bringing together the knowledge he had acquired

---

33 Humboldt, *Views of the Cordilleras and Monuments of the Indigenous Peoples of the Americas*, 224, 226, 227.
34 Humboldt, 227. The drawing was engraved and coloured by Louis Bouquet.

in his many travels, but particularly his journey through the Americas. It combined insights from many different scientific fields to produce a unified vision of the natural world, tracing "those mutual relations which link together the various forces of nature," in Humboldt's words.[35] *Cosmos* was instantly popular; it was translated into most European languages and became "nada menos que la Biblia de la burguesía culta" (nothing less than the Bible of the educated bourgeoisie).[36]

Fig. 5.7 Oscar Santillán, *Lost Star* (2012–2013). 18 x 13 x 3 cm (photograph by Jhoeko). Courtesy of Jhoeko, Nest (The Hague) and the artist.

Santillán's work denudes Humboldt's masterwork of its content, reducing its vast enterprise to a miniscule sphere in a way that seems to mock its global aspirations and influence. At the same time, the tiny black globe, rather like a gemstone in appearance, suggests a different kind of value. *Lost Star* alludes to the relationship between scientific knowledge and the commercial exploitation of America's natural riches, including precious metals. It also encourages us to view Humboldt's magisterial volume itself as a work of extraction, mining the Americas for data that would serve the political and commercial interests of Europe,

---

35 Von Humboldt, *Cosmos*, 2:4.
36 Ette, "El Cosmos de la vida," 335.

in its quest for global domination. In its attempt to provide a physical description of the entire planet, Humboldt's enterprise was—as Mary Louise Pratt observes—"by no means independent of the great projects of commercial and political expansion that Europe was articulating simultaneously on a global scale."[37] Humboldt was not ignorant of the commercial potential of the knowledge he sought. Although he exalts the study of nature primarily for its capacity to enlarge the intellect, he finds that "science thus followed for her own sake will pour forth abundant, overflowing streams, to enrich and fertilise that industrial prosperity, which is a conquest of the intelligence of man over matter."[38]

That "industrial prosperity" was largely reserved for Europe, however, and it was fuelled by the extraction of raw materials from Latin America, just as the growth in European scientific knowledge was significantly propelled by the raw data generated by Humboldt and other travelling naturalists. Fabiano Kueva's project *Archivo Humboldt*, discussed below, uncovers in more explicit detail the imperial power relations that led to the development of Humboldt's "universal science" and the (European) mercantile interests that it served.

Fabiano Kueva: Humboldt, Universal Science, and Epistemicide

The *Archivo Humboldt* (Humboldt Archive, 2011–), devised by the Ecuadorian artist Fabiano Kueva, explores the voyage of Humboldt and Aimé Bonpland between 1799 to 1804 through territories now owned by Venezuela, Cuba, Colombia, Ecuador, Peru, and Mexico. The project has involved fieldwork, archival research, performances, the creation of videos, and the staging of public debates. In his exhibitions, Kueva has assembled some of the many texts and images produced by Humboldt, including maps, illustrations, letters, and inventories. To these are added excerpts from Kueva's own diaries, composed as he revisited places Humboldt sketched or wrote about, and herbaria, collected by Kueva but presented as if they were part of Humboldt's own archive.[39]

---

37 Pratt, "Alexander von Humboldt and the Reinvention of America," 243.
38 Von Humboldt, *Cosmos*, 2:39.
39 Exhibitions have been held in several cities, including Lisbon, Mexico City, and Quito. Two significant presentations of the project were made in the Humboldt

In re-performing that iconic journey, Kueva draws attention to the continuities and differences that separate Humboldt's time from the present, as a way of uncovering the enduring legacies—ideological and material—of his work on a continent that he would never visit again. Kueva's performances also reveal the performative dimensions of the original journey: how it creates certain repertoires and rituals, for example, and how the journey itself takes on an epistemological function that subtends and transcends Humboldt's many specimens, data, and insights. In the context of a renewed interest in Humboldt around the 250th anniversary of his birth, Kueva's work brings a critical perspective to celebrations on both sides of the Atlantic of the achievements of this pioneering scientist.

Humboldt's integrative, relational approach to studying organisms and environments has often been hailed as a significant precursor in the development of modern ecological thought. "Rather than discovering new, isolated facts," Humboldt wrote, "I preferred linking already known ones together."[40] His focus on the interconnections between living and non-living phenomena at local, regional, and global scales has gained even greater relevance in recent decades. Kueva's aim, however, was to draw out the consequences for Latin America of the European pursuit of a universal discourse of science, in which Humboldt played a key role. Recent scholarship on Humboldt has attempted to find, in the comparative perspectives he took to the study of botany and geology, the basis of an "intercultural" vision and of a project of modernity that was "plural" and "multipolar."[41] Kueva's project develops a more convincing decolonial perspective on Humboldt's quest for a global science. Drawing on the work of Santiago Castro-Gómez, Boaventura de Sousa Santos and others on cognitive justice, he shows how European "universalism" was an act of epistemicide, erasing indigenous knowledges and shoring up Western hegemony within a global order that is still dominant in the present day.

Forum, Berlin as part of *250 Jahre jung* (250 Years Young), a series of events to mark the 250th birthday of Humboldt, on 13 and 14 September 2019, and at the Bienal de Cuenca, Ecuador, between 10 December 2021 and 28 February 2022.

40 Humboldt, *Personal Narrative of a Journey to the Equinoctial Regions of the New Continent*, 72.
41 Ette, *Alexander von Humboldt y la globalización*, 11, 16, 9.

Humboldt emerges in Kueva's work as a central figure in the European exercise of knowledge-by-accumulation, a tactic that involved the removal of thousands of specimens, samples, and artefacts from Latin America to Europe, where they were classified and studied, and where they largely remain in closely guarded museums and depositories. With differing degrees of success, Kueva has attempted to access archives and sites relating to Humboldt in multiple countries across Europe and Latin America. For the most part, he filmed and photographed these archives illicitly, having signed documents committing himself to the "ethical" use of images in line with copyright laws. He decided not to respect these laws. "¿Por qué mejor no abordar la dimensión ética de las colecciones? ¿Por qué no retomar su posible retorno a los lugares y comunidades de origen?" (Why not address the ethical dimension of the collections instead? Why not focus on their possible return to the places and communities they came from?).[42] The *Archivo Humboldt* is fundamentally a project about dispossession, reflecting on how a continent came to be treated as a repository of resources for the global economy and what makes it possible for many of its most valuable artefacts to continue to be held in European museums. Kueva asks: "¿A quién pertenece lo que se ve, se nombra o se colecciona? ¿Qué hace legítimo lo que el científico viajero o el artista viajero toman, extraen o trasladan?" (To whom belongs that which is seen, named and collected? What makes it legitimate for the travelling scientist or artist to take, extract, move to another place?).[43]

To address these questions, Kueva develops a practice he calls "desarchivar" (dearchiving), which he defines as "hacer un archivo crítico o hacer que un archivo dado o encontrado se torne 'crítico' y hacer posible su uso/giro/quiebre hacia la ficción" (creating a critical archive, or transforming a given or found archive into one that is "critical" and using/twisting/breaking it down for the purposes of fiction).[44] Following in Humboldt's footsteps, Kueva takes samples from the plants he discovers, preserves them using a traditional flower press, and then ties them to a sheet of paper that has been made to look aged

---

42 Kueva, "Archivo Alexander von Humboldt: Interferencias sobre un canon," 50.
43 See https://www.archivohumboldt.org/preludio
44 See https://www.archivohumboldt.org/proyectos-1

by soaking it in tea (see Fig. 5.8).[45] With the addition of labels identical to those affixed to Humboldt's herbarium in the Jardin des Plantes in Paris, they might very well pass for Humboldt's own botanical plates. Indeed, even Andrea Wulf, Humboldt's award-winning biographer, was taken in when she visited the Berlin exhibition in 2019.[46] For his herbarium, Kueva chose those parts of a plant that had fallen to the ground or already dried up, opting to work with these "residuos vegetales" (vegetable residues) as an act of anti-extractivism.[47] His aim was to play with the fetishization of plants and their conversion into cultural objects, which take place as even the most unattractive or worthless specimens are labelled and displayed in a museum.

Fig. 5.8 Herbarium created by Fabiano Kueva. Installation view of *Archivo Alexander von Humboldt, 250 Jahre Jung: Celebrating Alexander von Humboldt's Birthday*, Humboldt Forum, Berlin, 13–14 September 2019 (photograph by David von Becker).

---

45 Kueva's project encodes several levels of meaning that are not immediately apparent to his exhibition visitors. For example, the paper he uses is made from the residues of sugarcane, creating a link with the theme of slavery (conversation with the author, 11 February 2022).

46 See Andrea Wulf, Twitter post, 13 September 2019, https://twitter.com/andrea_wulf/status/1172464727894757376

47 Conversation with the author, 11 February 2022.

Visitors might realize that all is not what it seems when they view the other elements displayed alongside the herbarium: the similarly yellowed pages from a travel diary dated 2015, for example, or the video-essay, in which Kueva's decolonial critique is made much more explicit. In the first video produced for the project, *Humboldt 2.0* (2011–2012), Kueva uses a multi-channel format to present images of walking feet, rivers, and mountains, together with close-ups of plants and flowers. In some of the sequences, Kueva appears as a travelling botanist in eighteenth-century apparel, examining a cactus, striding into the distance, or posing as if for a portrait (see Fig. 5.9). In a voiceover, he recites passages from Humboldt's texts alongside ideas developed by Latin American decolonial scholars, including Enrique Dussel, Santiago Castro-Gómez, and Silvia Rivera Cusicanqui. Over images of an abundance of tropical vegetation, Kueva intones: "Medir, recolectar, calcular, catalogar, archivar, relatar, naturalizar América" (measure, collect, calculate, catalogue, archive, narrate, naturalize America). These are the operations through which science has established an authoritative account of the region, and through which it cast America as an object of study rather than a producer of knowledge: a place of nature, for Humboldt, and not of history.[48]

As Castro-Gómez argues, imperial power is established through the imposition of "una sola forma única y verdadera de conocer el mundo: la suministrada por la racionalidad científico-técnica de la modernidad" (one single and reliable way of knowing the world: that which is supplied by the techno-scientific rationality of modernity).[49] In this endeavour, the role of botanists and other scientists was crucial in forging the Enlightened ideal of the "punto cero" (zero point): a neutral position from which the natural world could be described in a universal language that was valid for all times and all places.[50] *Humboldt 2.0* exposes the relationship between universal science, the discourses of progress and modernity it has underpinned, and the colonial distribution of power that often continues to structure Latin America's relations with the rest of the world. It makes explicit the relationships

---

48 Humboldt, *Personal Narrative of a Journey to the Equinoctial Regions of the New Continent*, 78.
49 Castro-Gómez, *La hybris del punto cero*, 14.
50 Castro-Gómez, 278.

5. Albums, Atlases, and their Afterlives 191

Fig. 5.9 Still from Fabiano Kueva, *Humboldt 2.0* (2011–2012). Video (image provided by the artist).

that bind Enlightenment science, coloniality, and what Boaventura de Sousa Santos has called "epistemicide": the destruction of the knowledge and cultures of indigenous societies.[51] "Ciencia universal, hegemonía cognitiva, superioridad de unos conocimientos sobre otros, control económico, social y simbólico, del mundo" (universal science, cognitive hegemony, superiority of some knowledges over others, economic and social control of the world and its representations): Kueva's enunciation of these terms in a list suggests a kind of inexorability that connects one logically to the next, moving from the quest for a universal science, founded on European principles, to the erasure of other forms of knowledge and to a global order that cements the power of the self-defined centre.

Eoin Bourke is one of several scholars who have sought to emphasize Humboldt's critical engagement with slavery and the Spaniards' mistreatment of the indigenous population; he even points to some comments that voice a general disapproval of Christianization and colonization.[52] Humboldt certainly expresses disgust at the brutality of the Spanish and their "insatiable greed" that leads to "acts of inhumanity" toward Indians and Africans alike.[53] Kueva's selections from Humboldt's writings focus less on his defences of liberty and equality, however, and more on his collusion with colonial authorities and the racial prejudice revealed in his texts. In his video *Ensayo geopoético* (2011–2019), Humboldt is presented as rather satisfied with the favour and support he has won from the Spanish crown and its imperial institutions. He lists "indígenas semi-salvajes" (half-savage natives) among the continent's natural marvels, along with tigers and armadillos. The contradiction embedded in Humboldt's phrase "Mi primer viaje lo hice solo, con un indio" (my first expedition I undertook alone, with an Indian), which Kueva borrows for the *Ensayo geopolítico*, speaks volumes about Humboldt's construction of a land without science, as he effectively erases the importance of his native guide, who not only shared his expertise with him but—by Humboldt's own account—also risked his own life in assisting his attempt to climb the Chimborazo.[54]

---

51 See, for example, De Sousa Santos, *Epistemologies of the South*, 92.
52 Bourke, "'The Second Columbus?,'" 259, 261–62, 267–68.
53 Humboldt, *Personal Narrative of a Journey to the Equinoctial Regions of the New Continent*, 142.
54 Humboldt, *Mi viaje por el camino del Inca (1801–1802)*, 184.

Mary Louise Pratt denounces the evocations of Columbus in passages from Humboldt's accounts that clearly echo the conquistador's first encounter with an undiscovered New World.[55] If Humboldt is frequently hailed as the "rediscoverer" of America, Pratt insists that "one must inquire what it means to relive Columbus's primal gesture after three centuries of Spanish colonial rule."[56] Kueva's *Archivo Humboldt* focuses, in turn, on the question of what it means to re-enact Humboldt's journey over two hundred years later. The superimposition of visual and audio tracks in the *Ensayo geopolítico* often suggests historical continuities between Humboldt's work and the extractive industries that are responsible for many social and environmental problems in twenty-first-century Latin America. As Kueva surveys the River Magdalena, the most important river in Colombia and a key trading route linking the interior of the region to European ports in colonial times, we hear words from Humboldt's *Cosmos*: "De la zona boreal, los gérmenes de la civilización han sido importados a la zona tropical" (From the northern zone, the seeds of civilization have been imported into the tropical zone).[57] This "civilization" is clearly represented at this point in the video in the forms of a railway track and a huge tanker.

In a similar vein, Kueva is filmed walking across the longest bridge in Colombia, the Viaducto Balseadero—completed in 2015 as part of the El Quimbo hydroelectric plant—and observing the largest oil refinery in the country, a site of immense proportions in the city of Barrancabermeja. As he stands motionless before its tanks and stacks (see Fig. 5.10), the monstruous evidence of the impact of industrial-scale extractivism and engineering projects on Latin America lends a brutal irony to the question we hear: "Cuál es la huella del viajero? Dónde encontrar sus efectos?" (What trace does the traveller leave behind? Where are his effects to be found?). In the *Ensayo geopoético* we witness a New World remade in the image of the Old, a New World rebuilt to supply the needs of the Old: indeed, as the video shifts between locations, the tight framing of baroque statues or modernist buildings often makes us unsure whether we are in Europe or Latin America.

---

55 Pratt, "Alexander von Humboldt and the Reinvention of America," 246.
56 Pratt, 247.
57 The quotation paraphrases von Humboldt, *Cosmos*, 2:15.

Fig. 5.10 Still from Fabiano Kueva, *Ensayo geopoético* (2011–2019). Video (image provided by the artist).

What Pratt finds to be missing from Humboldt's narratives is a study of colonial society and, more broadly, historicity, both of which are largely passed over in his "project of reinvention."[58] She asserts that "Humboldt's eye depopulates and dehistoricizes the American landscape even as it celebrates its grandeur and variety."[59] If Kueva's landscapes are also largely depopulated, we are led to understand that this emptiness is, in part, the result of colonial violence and dispossession. The rich material culture of the regions Humboldt visited is highly visible in Kueva's videos, but almost exclusively in the form of the many hundreds of precious artefacts that we see under careful lock and key in European museums and depositories. Back in Latin America, the ancient sites of pre-Hispanic civilizations have long since been abandoned by their original inhabitants and secured for the use of tourists. Indeed, tourists comprise most of the people we see in the *Ensayo geopoético*. In one sequence, Kueva restages an encounter between Humboldt and Leandro Sepla y Oro, an Andean chief. As the two look across to Ingapirca, the largest Inca site in Ecuador, they survey the hundreds of tourists milling around its empty structures (see Fig. 5.11). In this way, the image acquires a historical density, laying bare a fundamental logic that binds

---

58 Pratt, "Alexander von Humboldt and the Reinvention of America," 247.
59 Pratt, 246.

scientific exploration then and global tourism now, both made possible by the dispossession of precolonial societies.

Fig. 5.11 Still from Fabiano Kueva, *Ensayo geopoético* (2011–2019). Video (image provided by the artist).

Kueva's performative encounters with nineteenth-century paintings of the New World also provide a way of historicizing the landscapes he visits. The views sketched by Humboldt were quintessentially Romantic in their idealization and timelessness. Humboldt's iconic image of the Chimborazo volcano, *Le Chimborazo, vu depuis le plateau de Tapia*, is a majestic vision, rising steeply from the plateau, its white flanks sharply traced against the deep blue sky (see Fig. 5.6 above). Kueva's version, by contrast, is shrouded in mist, and seemingly dwarfed by his own person, standing proud against the distant summit and enlarged by a low camera angle (see Fig. 5.12). The perspective speaks to the mythification of Humboldt, who seems to acquire gigantic dimensions as the iconic Chimborazo—whose nobility had enhanced Humboldt's own heroic reputation—recedes into the background. Kueva draws attention to the atemporality of Humboldt's tableaux in filmed sequences in which he poses, immobile, for minutes on end. In his version of Humboldt's Chimborazo, Kueva and a llama exchange gazes for an unconsciously long time during a sequence of rapid playback.

Fig. 5.12 Still from Fabiano Kueva, *Humboldt 2.0* (2011–2012). Video (image provided by the artist).

The act of restaging specific poses and perspectives draws attention to the palimpsestic quality of such landscape views, which are always already mediated by their Romantic-era precursors. The shot of Chimborazo that Kueva composes bears a strong resemblance to the framing of the portrait of Humboldt and Bonpland at Chimborazo painted in 1806 by Friedrich Georg Weitsch (see Fig. 5.13), one of many landscape artists who were deeply influenced by Humboldt's depictions of the New World. Kueva objects to the ease with which such picturesque views "se convertirán en los paisajes nacionales, versión estética y simplificada de nuestra complejidad" (would turn into the national tradition of landscapes, an aestheticized and simplified version of our complexity).[60] His own vision is decidedly more opaque. Symbolically, as he turns to watch, the snow-covered peak of the Chimborazo disappears entirely behind the clouds.

Although Ottmar Ette concedes that Humboldt's account of indigenous communities is sometimes guided by European colonial prejudices, he asserts that "se opone fuerte y constantemente a una modernidad adaptada sólo a los intereses de Europa o de su población" (he was strongly and consistently opposed to a modernity that conformed

---

60 Kueva, "Archivo Alexander von Humboldt," 141.

5. *Albums, Atlases, and their Afterlives*   197

Fig. 5.13 Friedrich Georg Weitsch, *Alexander von Humboldt und Aimé Bonpland am Fuß des Vulkans Chimborazo* (1806). Public Domain, via Wikimedia Commons, https://commons.wikimedia.org/wiki/File:Humboldt-Bonpland_Chimborazo.jpg

only to the interests of Europe or its people).[61] It would be difficult to ascribe a consistent position of this kind to Humboldt on the basis of his writings. Any attempt to rehabilitate him for a contemporary era would have to start by acknowledging, as Kueva asks us to, the ways in which his work both forged a new global imaginary and, simultaneously, cemented a global order built on dispossession and epistemicide. In his silent transit through the many museums, observatories, monuments, libraries, and other sites that are dedicated to the memory of Humboldt, Kueva starts to unpick the laudatory narratives that have developed around his achievements, in Latin America as much as in Europe. His objective is to "provocar dudas, sospechas que **desnaturalicen los colonialismos** que nos atraviesan día con día" (provoke doubts, suspicions that **denaturalize the colonialisms** that pierce us every day).[62] His critique is not directed toward Humboldt so much as to the

---

61 Ette, *Alexander von Humboldt y la globalización*, 158.
62 See https://www.archivohumboldt.org/preludio (original emphasis).

unquestioning embrace of science and positivism by Latin American nations, which have celebrated the heroic achievements of European scientists without counting the cost of the imperialist ventures their science supported.

Despite its dearchival, deauthorizing poetics, Kueva recognizes that his project "no ha logrado desmarcarse de las prácticas oficiales regionales y globales que insisten en 'contemporaneizar' a Humboldt" (has not succeeded in disassociating itself from those official regional and global practices that insist on "contemporanizing" Humboldt), and that, like every artistic work, it is ultimately caught up in the same confluence of capital, power, and knowledge that it denounces.[63] One of the challenges Kueva faces is how to make present, in a museum setting, "un saber distinto" (a different knowledge): the kind of knowledge that has been erased in the pursuit of a universal science.[64] Indigenous knowledges in Latin America are not based on the same logic of classification and display. Kueva considers that the objects he exhibits do call us to encounter them in a different way: that they possess "una entidad" (an essence) that cannot be reduced to texts that label them.[65] For some of his exhibitions, he has created cabinets in which he has placed a miscellany of crafted objects—jewellery, pottery, taxidermy—alongside his natural specimens (see Fig. 5.14). The absence of labels, the diversity of these items and their placement alongside each other, without order or hierarchy, invites the viewer to create alternative meanings and logics. These may include the kind of uses to which these objects are put in a non-Western setting: in everyday domestic rituals, or in those of a shamanic nature. As part of his artistic process, Kueva has sought to understand the relationship between such objects and knowledge in indigenous communities in Ecuador. One of the most important things he has learned is to "dejar que las cosas digan" (let things speak for themselves): this, he believes, is where epistemic difference lies.[66]

In a future exhibition, Kueva plans to replace the cabinets altogether with a replica of an indigenous reserve, in which visitors would be able to touch objects and encounter them in ways that are not usually permitted

---

63 Kueva, "Archivo Alexander von Humboldt: Interferencias sobre un canon," 51.
64 Conversation with the author, 11 February 2022.
65 Conversation with the author, 11 February 2022.
66 Conversation with the author, 11 February 2022.

Fig. 5.14 Cabinet created by Fabiano Kueva. Installation view of *Archivo Alexander von Humboldt, 250 Jahre Jung: Celebrating Alexander von Humboldt's Birthday*, Humboldt Forum, Berlin, 13–14 September 2019 (photograph by David von Becker).

in a museum.[67] In many senses, this would be an extension of the *Archivo Humboldt* project, which seeks to question how archives and institutions accord economic, historical, and cultural values to certain objects. Through the repetitions, substitutions, supplements, and fabrications that are at the heart of his performative gestures, Kueva's work exposes the imperial logic that allowed Latin America to be exoticized and exploited, both in Humboldt's time and in our own, but also traces a path for a kind of repossession, by circumventing the exhibition practices that have accompanied the rise of the modern museum.

Conclusion

By multiplying and remediating the images created by Humboldt and other European travellers to Latin America, the artists presented in this chapter explore their possible recuperation for decolonizing purposes. This recuperation often takes the form of displacing the ocularcentrism

---

67 Conversation with the author, 11 February 2022.

and logocentrism of Western modernity through the exploration of other senses, embodied experiences, and material processes: the emphasis on walking and other kinds of material embodiment in Kueva's *Archivo Humboldt*, for example; the becoming-sculpture of two-dimensional images in Arteaga and the becoming-substrate of his books; the processes of decay deployed by León; the use of performance by Sant'Ana, whose other works in the *Refino* series involve the artist's bodily immersion in sugar. As José Alejandro Restrepo reflects, "El caminar y el narrar son formas de crear espacios que en su esencia no pueden reducirse a trazos gráficos. Son geografías fuera de las totalizaciones imaginarias del ojo" (Walking and narrating are ways of creating spaces that cannot, by their nature, be reduced to lines of a drawing. They are geographies that exist beyond the totalizing imaginaries of the eye).[68]

These acts also reintroduce the crucial dimension of time to images and texts that have been fixed in print and that, in turn, have attempted to represent a natural world that is timeless, or even a continent without history. Arteaga, Sant'Ana, Coca, León, Bermúdez, Santillán, and Kueva examine the afterlives of those foundational images and texts that have purported to encompass the diversity of a region's natural and social history. They imagine or perform acts of counter-invasion and recolonization on the part of the natural world; they subject books and other printed materials to accelerated processes of decay and decomposition; they overwrite narratives and images with their own representations. They do so not only to assert the provisionality of all knowledge, but to return these texts and images to their proper place in the context of colonial violence and epistemicide, to trace the continued impact of coloniality in Latin America today, and to construct alternative futures for those images that might express new political and ecological relationships.

---

68 Murphy Turner, "Historias del paisaje durante la colonización de América."

6. Taxidermy and Natural History Dioramas

Many writers of late-nineteenth-century taxidermy manuals traced their art back to ancient times, while taking pride in more recent techniques that allowed them to preserve animals in ever more life-like attitudes.[1] Such manuals were much in demand, as William Temple Hornaday noted in his own contribution to the genre, both by "eager young naturalists" pursuing zoology as a hobby and by professional collectors supplying a raft of new science museums.[2] For Hornaday, a pioneering member of the wildlife conservation movement in the United States, the imperative to build up zoological collections stemmed from "the rapid and alarming destruction of all forms of wild animal life which is now going on furiously throughout the entire world."[3] The spectacular and costly habitat dioramas that were commissioned for museums in North America and Europe between 1880 and 1930 exhibited groups of taxidermied animals in theatrical scenes that evoked, as faithfully as possible, the appearance of savannas, jungles, or other natural environments. They were designed to give the urban public a rudimentary understanding of ecosystems and to instill in them "a deep respect for nature, or what might be described more accurately as a deep longing for a wilderness at the edge of existence."[4] These displays thus combined naturalist precision with a Romantic nostalgia for the primitive, for what might lie beyond the limits of culture.

With time, taxidermy came to embody a more contradictory and questionable set of meanings. It became impossible to ignore the

1 See, for example, Maynard, *Manual of Taxidermy*; Browne, *Practical Taxidermy*.
2 Hornaday and Holland, *Taxidermy and Zoological Collecting*, vii.
3 Hornaday and Holland, vii.
4 Poliquin, *The Breathless Zoo*, 104.

imperialist discourses and practices that underpinned the hunting, collecting, and ordering of animal life from other regions of the world. The fact that early conservationists were often also major advocates of big-game hunting meant that the preservation of wild nature for which they campaigned was also a defence of the kind of masculinist values associated with sporting prowess. Donna Haraway's influential account of early-twentieth-century dioramas in New York's American Museum of Natural History locates taxidermy at the heart of the museum's attempts to arrest the decay of (patriarchal) civilization and to preserve "imperialist, capitalist, and white culture" against the threat of decadence.[5] Objections to taxidermy have also highlighted the cruelty to animals often involved in its practices. As a highly ambiguous object, the taxidermied animal presents us both with the simulation of life and the materiality of death. Zoe Hughes draws attention to the processes of disavowal at work as taxidermy "is encountered as animal material, harkens back to the animal, but erases the violence in between—the death, skinning, stretching, and sewing."[6]

More recently, artists have sought to reclaim the practice of taxidermy, either to confront its role in a history of animal objectification or to repurpose it for other aims. Their more critical or creative approaches have been described as "botched taxidermy,"[7] "rogue taxidermy"[8] or "speculative taxidermy."[9] While some animal studies scholars reject outright the use of animal skins in art on the basis that they represent a gesture of human supremacy over animals, others have found, as Giovanni Aloi suggests, that "the new and often uncanny presence of this medium in contemporary art can propose critically productive opportunities to rethink human/animal relations."[10] In the work of Antonio Becerro (Chile), Vitor Mizael (Brazil), and Berenice Olmedo (Mexico), for example, taxidermy has been used to draw attention to the neglect, abuse, and slaughter of stray dogs in urban centres. Contemporary approaches to taxidermy may also facilitate a

---

5   Haraway, "Teddy Bear Patriarchy," 57.
6   Hughes, "Performing Taxidermy or the De- and Reconstruction of Animal Faces in Service of Animal Futures," 172.
7   Baker, *The Postmodern Animal*, 54–76.
8   Marbury, *Taxidermy Art*, 12–15.
9   Aloi, *Speculative Taxidermy*.
10   Aloi, 16.

(reflexive) questioning of the exhibition practices of natural history museums, while promoting alternative narratives about ecology and the environment. One or both of these aims are central to the works presented in this chapter by Daniel Malva (Brazil), Adriana Bustos (Argentina), Pablo La Padula (Argentina), Rodrigo Arteaga (Chile), and Walmor Corrêa (Brazil).

Of these artists, only Corrêa deploys taxidermy techniques directly, although he chooses to work with specimens that have already been preserved. Malva photographs taxidermy animals and insects; Bustos intrudes into a diorama in a performance captured on video; La Padula and Arteaga create interventions with taxidermied animals in natural history collections and dioramas in museum settings. All five artists deconstruct the illusions of realism that devices of display so carefully generate and demonstrate how taxidermy objects and practices can be repurposed to create a critical dialogue with Eurocentric conceptions of the natural world or, more specifically, the role played by natural history in the formation of national and global imaginaries. These artists create "afterlives" for taxidermy animals that invite us to consider shifting entanglements between nature and culture or between science and popular myth; they also explore how taxidermy may be used to restore animal agency or to create alternative narratives for a post-anthropocentric era.

Animal Spectrality in Daniel Malva's *Natural History Museum*

In the resurgence of taxidermy that has become evident in art over recent decades, epitomized in the work of Damien Hirst and Polly Morgan, Amanda Boetzkes finds an interest in communicating the "existential pathos of animal lives" lived in subordination. This is combined, however, with an attempt "to expose the particularity of those animal bodies and overturn the predominant aesthetic regime by which humans conceal animals in anthropocentric systems of signification."[11] This dual emphasis—registering a loss of animal agency while seeking, in part, to return it—is also evident in Daniel Malva's *Natural History*

---

11 Boetzkes, "Art," 65.

Museum (2009–2014).[12] The series comprises ninety-six photographs of exhibits from small and lesser-known museums and other collections in the state of São Paulo, Brazil, including insects, taxidermied animals, skeletons, and specimens in jars of formaldehyde. Boasting an elephant foetus, a severed human hand, and a tarantula, Malva's collection yields a frisson of the macabre. His inclusion of preserved human organs and tissues points to the mortality that we share with nonhuman animals as a result of our (often disavowed) animality. It also sets into relief the (often arbitrary) divisions that Western societies have erected between humans and other animals, which have justified—and continue to justify—the capture and killing of animals and the preservation of their skins and organs.

Most of Malva's photographs are not post-processed in any way, although they are scaled to reproduce the dimensions of the original organs and organisms. Malva hacked into his digital camera to insert a software programme that prevented the camera from making its usual corrections to the image's exposure or colour. In other respects, however, the images depart from naturalism. As part of ongoing experiments with the construction of homemade lenses, Malva created a lens for this series from the lid of a shampoo bottle, which—in addition to the software hack—gives the images a cloudy, faded appearance. These ghostly apparitions give the exhibition an elegiac tone, as if it were a memorial to a series of extinct species, living only in our dreams or memories, or confined to the archives that have so exhaustively collected and classified them. Indeed, some of the specimens photographed here, together with the museums that housed them, no longer exist.[13] Photography is perhaps the medium that most evocatively connects loss with the desire to preserve, serving as a memento or memorial that fixes the dead in its living past. For both Barthes and Sontag the photograph is always an "emanation" of a past reality, a trace of a material existence, a vestige of something now absent.[14] In the uncertain outlines and the vaporous textures of Malva's images, this "emanation" acquires

---

12   Some pieces were shown at the Galeria Mezanino, São Paulo, Brazil, in 2009. More complete exhibitions of the series were held in 2014 with the title *Gabinete de curiosidades* (Cabinet of Curiosities) at the Kristin Hjellegjerde Gallery in London and the Shoot Gallery in Oslo.
13   Correspondence with the author, 19 January 2022.
14   Barthes, *Camera Lucida: Reflections on Photography*, 88; Sontag, *On Photography*, 154.

a mystical character, taking on something of the viscous, luminous quality of ectoplasm, or the eerie transparency of spirits "captured" in nineteenth-century photographs.

Malva's choice of lens suggests the extent to which we view the natural world through the prism of industrialization and mass production, while simultaneously allowing him to reject the naturalism of digital photography and the hypervisibility of contemporary nature documentaries. These animals are doubly removed from their original habitat, having been captured once for inclusion in a scientific collection and again in photographs for display in an art gallery. Their representation here draws attention to the processes of drying, stuffing, embalming, mounting, and pinning through which they have already been preserved and displayed (see Figs 6.1 and 6.2). For Malva, "era bem importante mostrar que essas peças não eram vivas" (it was very important to show that these exhibits were not alive).[15] For this reason, many of the photographs show the labels, display stands, and glass jars that contain and explain the objects in a museum context. Malva's images also demonstrate that the various techniques and compounds used to "fix" tissues and animals in a life-like state only slow down the process of decay rather than halting it altogether. The caiman's heart (see Fig. 6.3, far left) is not naturally a different colour from those of the mammals with which it is displayed, but over time it has lost its pinkness. The photographs capture the decomposition of some of the tissues suspended in formaldehyde. Human handling of the objects has also caused damage: some of the taxidermied animals and insects have parts that are broken, twisted, or scratched.

Boetzkes argues that "the persistent appearance of dead animal bodies in contemporary art's revival of taxidermy nevertheless signals a disruption of the way in which humans imagine animals in a fundamental state of quiescence."[16] Malva's photographs testify to the subordination of nonhuman animals, made perpetually available to our gaze through taxidermy, but they also undermine it through the use of portraiture, a genre usually reserved for human subjects. In many of his photographs it is possible to see the creases of a white sheet held up behind the animal, in order to separate it from the other taxidermy

---

15   Conversation with the author, 2 February 2022.
16   Boetzkes, "Art," 68.

206   *Decolonial Ecologies*

Fig. 6.1 Daniel Malva, *Mandrillus Sphinx*, photograph from *Natural History Museum* (2013). 80 x 53.3 cm.

6. Taxidermy and Natural History Dioramas

Fig. 6.2 Daniel Malva, *Elephas maximus: fetus*, photograph from *Natural History Museum* (2009). 30 x 20 cm.

Fig. 6.3 Daniel Malva, series of photographs of hearts, from *Natural History Museum* (from left to right): Caiman Latirostris, Equus Caballus, Homo Sapiens, Chrysocyon Brachyurus, Canis Lupus-Familiaris, Panthera Leo. 30 x 20 cm. As exhibited in a solo show entitled *OJardim*, Galeria Mezanino, São Paulo, Brazil, 2017 (photograph by the artist).

objects on display in the museum. This isolation, against a plain background, emphasizes the loss of the habitat from which the animal has been torn. But by photographing animals in this way, Malva returns to them an individuality that is lost in the natural history museum, in which they serve as exemplars of different species.

In many ways, however, the *Natural History Museum* encourages us to perceive characteristics that are shared across all species. The distancing effect achieved in Malva's images reduces the differences between one specimen and the next, making their particularities less distinct.

In a series of photographs of preserved hearts, for example, exhibited alongside each other, the resemblances are much more striking than the disparities. Malva includes a human heart alongside those of a caiman, horse, a maned wolf, a dog, and a lion (see Fig. 6.3 above). The human specimen is slightly smaller, but otherwise very similar in its shape, its colour, and the distribution of its pale pink coronary arteries, branching across the surface of the heart. Even the image of a whale heart usually exhibited near the series—an impressive 80x80 cm in size—bears a striking morphological resemblance to the others. These arresting correlations remind us that "on a biological level, we are all one and the same, the same material, the same mortal flesh."[17]

Malva considers that what unites his many different photographic projects—which include studies based on dental x-rays, skulls, teeth, and body parts in formaldehyde from a human anatomy collection—is "o tema da morte, porque eu acho que a gente fecha os olhos para ela" (the theme of death, because I find that people close their eyes to it).[18] Akira Mizuta Lippit claims that "No longer a sign of nature's abundance, animals now inspire a sense of panic for the earth's dwindling resources." They take on a spectral form, never entirely vanishing but existing in "a state of *perpetual vanishing.*"[19] In photographing taxidermied animals, Malva's *Natural History Museum* captures this liminal existence, this extinction-in-progress. If the great European natural history collections were built on possession, Malva's signifies loss and decay. Far from representing humanity's subordination of the natural world, Malva's photographed taxidermy speaks to us, not only of the silent extinctions of animals all around us, but of our own inevitable subjection to the most basic law of nature, death; perhaps even of our own extinction to come.

Paisajes del alma and the Diorama as a Regime of Visibility and Possession

Paisajes del alma (Landscapes of the Soul, 2011) is a collaboration between the Argentine artist Adriana Bustos and the German writer Sabine Küchler. It is a video of a performance that took place in a diorama

---

17 See https://www.meer.com/en/8974-daniel-malva-gabinete-de-curiosidades
18 Conversation with the author, 2 February 2022.
19 Lippit, *Electric Animal*, 1 (original emphasis).

constructed in 1990 by the Museo de Ciencias Naturales in Salta, in the north of Argentina.[20] Before visiting the museum, both Küchler and Bustos had taken part in a two-month expedition to the Yungas forest near Salta, funded by the Goethe Institute. The video begins with still close-ups of some of the taxidermied animals that form part of the museum's Yungas diorama, before opening out to a view of the whole scene. The images are overlaid with Küchler's voice reading a passage from her book *Was ich im Wald in Argentinien sah* (2010), in which she relates her journey through the forest and a visit to the museum itself. Bustos enters the diorama to sit on a stool amid the ferns (Fig. 6.4), reading aloud from the book, although the voice we continue to hear is, at first, still Küchler's. As Küchler's text concludes, the final shot cuts to a view of the diorama with an empty stool.

Fig. 6.4 Still from video produced by Adriana Bustos, *Paisajes del alma* (2011). Video available at https://vimeo.com/688169765

The use of three languages in *Paisajes del alma*—the German voice-over, the Spanish translation read by Bustos that occasionally intrudes only to cede again to the German, together with the obligatory English subtitles, the *lingua franca* of science today—alludes to the (neo)colonial dynamics that have shaped natural history in Argentina. As Bustos explains, the nineteenth-century nation imagined and constructed

---

20 The video may be viewed at http://www.adrianabustos.com.ar/portfolio/recursos-2014/

by Sarmiento required the employment of a considerable number of German naturalists, who came to organize the nation's knowledge of its flora and fauna, with little or no reference to local knowledges.[21]

Paisajes del alma contrasts the wildness of the Yungas with its domesticated, fictionalized version in the museum and reflects on the relationship, real and imagined, of humans with a forest that is so thick with vegetation that it is practically impenetrable. Küchler's jungle is a chaotic battle scene, in which trees are described as wounded, twisted, and disfigured, ravaged by wind and fire. They are "desperate" and "exhausted" by the struggle to climb through a tangled mess of rotting branches to reach the light. With every attempt she and her companions make to open up a path, the jungle closes back around them: no trace of their presence would remain by the following day. In the circumstances, Bustos – who was the photographer on the expedition – suggested a trip to the Museo de Ciencias Naturales in Salta. There, Küchler writes, the animals were gathered, as if awaiting their visit. Her depiction of the Yungas forest contrasts with the sedate, manicured arrangement of the diorama, in which trees and plants give way courteously to render the animals fully available to our view and to allow us to appreciate the horizon vanishing into the distance on the customary painted backdrop. As Haraway writes of the African Hall dioramas in the American Museum of Natural History, "No visitor to a merely physical Africa could see these animals. This is a spiritual vision made possible only by their death and literal re-presentation. Only then could the essence of their life be present."[22] The diorama is thus a counter-jungle, a representation of animals that humans could never access in reality: an encounter only made possible through the death of those animals.

Aloi observes that the dioramas that became popular in natural history museums toward the end of the nineteenth century "excluded man from the unspoiled, deep nature" they depicted.[23] Haraway also argues that the technology of the diorama both reproduces the innocence and purity of nature, "imagined to be without technology, to be the object of vision," and, at the same time, the separation of man from nature: "Man is not in nature partly because he is not seen, is not the

---

21 Correspondence with the author, 21 October 2022.
22 Haraway, "Teddy Bear Patriarchy," 25.
23 Aloi, *Speculative Taxidermy*, 105.

spectacle."²⁴ In *Paisajes del alma*, the incongruous presence of Bustos in the carefully arranged scene exposes the inherently performative nature of the natural history diorama, transforming it from a window onto the natural world into a theatrical stage. Her entrance onstage disrupts the false vision of an untouched nature, and turns the animals and plants into mere props or minor characters of a drama that is ultimately a projection of human interests and desires. Indeed, in the final line of Küchler's text, the photographer explains that she loves the museum because "it tells us so much about the human being."

Paisajes del alma also exposes another fiction often encoded in dioramas, that of the timelessness of nature. Exhibition, as Haraway reminds us, is "a practice to produce permanence, to arrest decay."²⁵ The emphasis in *Paisajes del alma* on the gradual decay of the diorama acts to historicize the vision of nature it conveys and to attenuate its effects of realism. In Küchler's description, the diorama's preservation of a timeless nature had already begun to show its age. She explains that, with time, the bright colours of the painted backdrop had dulled, fading to the pastel shades of a little girl's bedroom and lending an agreeable tone to the scene. She notes that the taxidermied animals' fur was thinning and that dust had settled like ash on the birds' feathers. Like the diorama itself, the vibrant ecosystem it depicts is also in decline, as a result of uncontrolled deforestation. The *yaguareté* (jaguar) shown in the video's first shot is a critically endangered species whose population in Argentina has drastically reduced since the beginning of the twentieth century, largely due to the destruction of its habitat and to hunting, in order to protect grazing cattle. In recent years, it has been estimated that fewer than 250 jaguars are in existence in the country, and that ninety-five percent of their habitat has been destroyed.²⁶ If the Yungas diorama showcases the region's diversity, the many animals it includes either remain difficult for humans to access or are fast disappearing as a result of the human exploitation of the forest. Although many dioramas are intended to convey the importance of conserving wild nature, the idyllic vision presented here of a healthy, biodiverse biome

---

24 Haraway, "Teddy Bear Patriarchy," 52.
25 Haraway, 57.
26 Jara, "Situación crítica del yaguareté." The yaguareté has in recent years been the target of several successful conservation initiatives in Argentina, including the Proyecto Yaguareté and the Fundación Rewilding Argentina.

arguably perpetuates the fiction that the natural world is readily visible and available for human observation and ignores the reality of our destruction of it.

Paisajes del alma thus brings to the forefront how animal bodies have been expended in order to tell human stories. Both taxidermy and the diorama are illusions that conceal the killing that brought them into being and the everyday destruction that continues to threaten animals and their habitats. Küchler's words and Bustos's performance undermine the effect of permanence created by these technologies of preservation and exhibition, reinserting them in a broader history of habitat loss and extinction.

Expanded Dioramas in the Work of Rodrigo Arteaga

For the exhibition *This Path, One Time, Long Ago* (2018), Rodrigo Arteaga made a series of interventions in dioramas created for The Potteries Museum and Art Gallery in Stoke-on-Trent, UK.[27] Although these dioramas are simpler in execution than some of those created for the great science museums in the early twentieth century, they share several of their features. Animal mounts in life-like poses are set among three-dimensional reproductions of rocks, reeds, and ponds in the foreground that appear to merge into a broader landscape, painted on the back wall using techniques that create an illusion of depth and continuity. Despite their commitment to scientific accuracy and naturalism, dioramas make extensive use of elements appropriated from the theatrical arts, such as an enclosed stage, complex lighting designs, and the use of (frozen) gestures and the spatial arrangement of figures to suggest relationships and evolving narratives. While appearing to present a mere window onto the natural world, such dioramas effectively cast animals as "actors in a morality play on the stage of nature," as Haraway puts it.[28]

What dioramas of the early twentieth century usually portrayed was an Edenic scene of ecological balance and "an immaculate vision of nature uncontaminated by human presence."[29] Arteaga's interventions

---

27 The exhibition was a collaboration with AirSpace Gallery, Stoke-on-Trent, where Arteaga completed a residency in 2017. Further images may be viewed at http://www.rodrigoarteaga.com/This-path-one-time-long-time-ago
28 Haraway, "Teddy Bear Patriarchy," 24.
29 Poliquin, *The Breathless Zoo*, 104.

into the Potteries Museum dioramas were to disrupt these narratives entirely, by introducing artefacts of human craftmanship into natural scenes and shattering any illusion of realism in staging. In *Wetland*, painted ceramic ducks are placed next to taxidermied ones, while in *Moorland*, the overhead lights have become dramatically detached from the ceiling, hanging down amid stray cables (Fig. 6.5). Arteaga defies an important convention of diorama design, according to which the animals featured should show no awareness of human activity, much less be seen to respond to the violence of their hunters. Here, instead, the stag in *Moorland* appears to be startled by the falling lights; in *Wetland*, a taxidermied duck and its ceramic counterpart gaze at each other with mutual curiosity.

Fig. 6.5 Installation view of Rodrigo Arteaga, *Moorland from This Path, One Time, Long Ago* (2018). Potteries Museum & Art Gallery PMAG, Stoke-on-Trent, United Kingdom (photograph by the artist).

In exposing the artifice of diorama design and inserting objects of human culture, Arteaga deconstructs the illusion of a pure, untouched nature. He reminds us that the "resurrection" of animals through taxidermy is always a rebirth into a *cultural* world in which they will be recast and resignified according to human values, conscripted to serve a particular vision of nature. Here, there can be no release from that imposition of human meaning but there can be a making-multiple of meanings that might oppose or complicate human purposes. If a taxidermy animal is rendered fully available for shaping and arranging by human artists and collectors, Arteaga's animals seem to retain a possible agency and a capacity to participate in encounters that were not initially planned by the diorama designer. At the very least, the ambiguity of the taxidermy object is greatly amplified by these intrusions and the enmeshing of truth and fiction.

This Path, One Time, Long Ago proposes a "cross-pollination" of different sections within the museum that have conventionally been kept separate.[30] The pottery ducks are intruders from the museum's vast ceramics collection, infiltrating into the Natural Sciences dioramas, while animal mounts from the dioramas become interlopers in the Local History tableaux. In one of these, *The Victorian House* (Fig. 6.6), a hare sits on its haunches on the kitchen table while an owl presides over the room from a high shelf; the worn interior of *The Pub* has been overrun with birds and foxes. These mutual intrusions challenge distinctions between nature and culture, wildness and civilization, and animal and human. It is these distinctions that have underpinned efforts in both conservation and eugenics, two closely related philosophies that Haraway identifies as powerful forces shaping both research and exhibition at the American Museum of Natural History between 1890 and 1930. Arteaga's work illustrates something of the contradictory practices that Bruno Latour finds to be constitutive of modernity: on the one hand, a "work of purification" that separates humans from nonhumans, and on the other, the proliferating creation of "hybrids of nature and culture."[31] As Arteaga explains, the intervention was designed to capture the radical "instability" of our perceived relations with the nonhuman world.[32]

This idea is also very effectively explored in the "expanded diorama" Arteaga had created for his residency at the AirSpace Gallery the year before.[33] The diorama was presented as if it were still under construction, or perhaps in the process of being dismantled, and there was no division between exhibition space and viewing space. Museum visitors could

---

30 See https://www.stokemuseums.org.uk/pmag/this-path-one-time-long-time-ago
31 Latour, *We Have Never Been Modern*, 20.
32 Arteaga, "A Natural Selection—Residency by Rodrigo Arteaga—#4."
33 Images from the exhibition may be viewed at http://rodrigoarteaga.com/Natural-selection-AirSpace

Fig. 6.6 Installation view of Rodrigo Arteaga, *The Victorian House* from *This Path, One Time, Long Ago* (2018). Potteries Museum & Art Gallery PMAG, Stoke-on-Trent, United Kingdom (photograph by the artist).

wander at will between a half-unrolled strip of plastic turf, a swan still wrapped in protective polythene, and numerous animal mounts with their storage identification labels attached (see Fig. 6.7). As well as thoroughly deconstructing the artifices central to diorama design, which sought to create a seamless vision of a single landscape, Arteaga's expanded diorama thus created the possibility of a mutual invasion of spaces. Gallerygoers were able to enter the traditionally bound space of the diorama, and—conversely—taxidermy animals were placed in spaces of the museum that are normally reserved for humans. If the panoptic spatial relations of the conventional diorama tend to reinforce a sense of visual mastery and superiority, here viewers had to navigate a shared space in which they were the apparent object of multiple gazes, as birds stared down from the gallery's ceiling lights and mice peered over high ledges. The original habitat dioramas embodied the "community concept" developed by Karl Möbius, whose emphasis on the relationships between animals, and between animals and their environment, was extremely influential in shaping late-nineteenth-century approaches to biology and ecology.[34] By expanding the diorama

---

34 Rader and Cain, *Life on Display*, 54.

beyond its usual spatial boundaries, Arteaga alludes to the complexity of relations in more-than-human communities, a subject of growing urgency in the twenty-first century.

Fig. 6.7 Installation view of Rodrigo Arteaga, *Natural Selection* (2017). AirSpace Gallery, Stoke-on-Trent, United Kingdom (photograph by the artist).

Arteaga's works also challenge the qualities of stasis, permanence, and transcendence that are quintessential to the diorama's aesthetic and its narratives about nature. *Natural Selection* does this by extending the temporality of the diorama to include scenes of the preparation and storage that precede or follow an exhibition. Similarly, with its deliberately collapsed lighting systems, *This Path, One Time, Long Ago* suggests the decay of the museum's fabric over time. Such techniques emerge from Arteaga's understanding that "the tradition of the diorama is a place of contingency,"[35] and that it may, in artistic remakings, chart the perceptual and conceptual reorganizations of our relationship with nature. The many different works and objects that make up the *Natural Selection* exhibition include mobile sculptures, in which a taxidermy mannequin is joined by organic and inorganic objects found on a brownfield site near the museum, all of which were suspended together

---

35   Arteaga, "A Natural Selection—Residency by Rodrigo Arteaga—#4."

in an ever-shifting spatial relationship. These continually moving constellations capture both our contemporary sense of the fragile balance of ecosystems and the fact that "our ways of thinking about ecology are also constantly changing, or ecology is constantly changing while we keep trying to understand it."[36]

In *Diorama en expansión*, exhibited in 2001 in Santiago (Chile), Arteaga brought an understanding of these dynamic interactions into a more explicit dialogue with Chile's ecological crisis.[37] The diorama he created again invited viewers to move around the space; the addition of sound art and hanging mobile constructions that circled slowly also had an immersive effect. Prominent place was given to species that play an important role in regulating ecosystems, such as fungi and bats. Arteaga also included in the exhibition some pieces he had originally developed for the 2018 Slade School of Fine Art Degree Show (London), entitled *Monocultivos (pinus radiata)* and *Monocultivos (eucalyptus globulus)*.[38] These consisted of large sheets of paper from which the forms of leaves, seeds, and branches had been burned, leaving silhouettes. As Arteaga explains, they were intended to draw attention to the excessive monocultures of Monterey pines and fast-growing eucalyptus trees in Chile, and the relationship between these plantations and the recent increase in droughts and forest fires.[39] In Arteaga's hands, dioramas are rather more than "mausoleums of a vanishing heritage";[40] instead, they represent dynamic encounters that encourage an awareness of the continual transformations that characterize both the natural world and our constructions of it.

Pablo La Padula: *Museo liberado* and the Violence of the Modern State

A mischievous intent animates Pablo La Padula's *Museo liberado* (Liberated Museum, 2021), which stages the "release" of taxidermy

---

36 https://www.stokemuseums.org.uk/pmag/this-path-one-time-long-time-ago/
37 *Diorama en expansión* was exhibited at the Museo de Artes Visuales (MAVI) in Santiago, between 25 September and 28 November 2021. Images of the exhibition may be viewed at https://www.rodrigoarteaga.com/ES/Diorama-en-expansion
38 The series were created in collaboration with the illustrator Marcela Mella.
39 Correspondence with the author, 21 October 2022.
40 Wonders, "Habitat Dioramas as Ecological Theatre," 285.

animals from their usual homes in the glass display cases and basement storage rooms of the Museo Nacional de Historia Natural (MNHN) in Montevideo, Uruguay. La Padula's concept involved a collaboration between the museum and the neighbouring Espacio de Arte Contemporáneo (EAC), with which it shares a building. The museum's taxidermied animals were brought into the art gallery and positioned as if they were making a break for freedom: crawling, prowling, strutting, waddling, and swooping their way to the exit (see Fig. 6.8). The two interconnected rooms of the EAC's Sala Miguelete have their architectural counterparts in two other rooms, situated across the corridor, which house dioramas curated by the MNHN. The mirroring of these two spaces allowed La Padula to reflect on the different ways in which art and science have sought to capture, interpret, and display the natural world. The theme of captivity acquires broader resonances given the history of the larger building that now accommodates both the MNHN and the EAC. This operated between 1888 and 1986 as Uruguay's first and most important prison, and the first in Latin America to have been built according to the panopticon design; it also functioned as a detention centre for political prisoners during the military regime of 1973–1985.

Entrance to the *Museo liberado* is through the "Sala de Captura" (Capture Hall). Working entirely with material borrowed from the MNHN, La Padula laid out in this space some of the techniques and devices used to capture and order the natural world, including illustrations, microscopes, and encyclopaedias (see Fig. 6.9). Many of these items, such as an old wooden card index cabinet and sepia portraits of the museum's founder and a major patron, return us to the museum's nineteenth-century past (it opened in 1838). Most of the yellowing notebooks, the insectariums and the specimens preserved in jars of formaldehyde relate to two expeditions organized by the Museum: to the Mato Grosso, Brazil (1955) and the Orinoco, Venezuela (1957) (see Fig. 6.10). Some of the room's objects, such as the fossils and butterfly cabinets, were intended for public display, while many of them have remained in museum basements, store cupboards, and laboratories. Their presence draws attention to the customary division of the modern museum's spaces into ones for professional use and others for public use. Antiquated museum pieces themselves, these artefacts also point to the gradual shift, since the nineteenth century, of the locus of scientific

Fig. 6.8 Installation view of Pablo La Padula, *Sala de Escape* from *Museo liberado* (2021). Museo Nacional de Historia Natural, Montevideo, Uruguay (photograph by Elena Téliz and Maite Silva, Espacio de Arte Contemporáneo).

activity from the museum to the controlled conditions of laboratories based elsewhere.

6. *Taxidermy and Natural History Dioramas* 221

Fig. 6.9 Installation view of Pablo La Padula, *Sala de Captura* from *Museo liberado* (2021). Museo Nacional de Historia Natural, Montevideo, Uruguay (photograph by Elena Téliz and Maite Silva, Espacio de Arte Contemporáneo).

Fig. 6.10 Installation view of Pablo La Padula, *Sala de Captura* from *Museo liberado* (2021). Museo Nacional de Historia Natural, Montevideo, Uruguay (photograph by Elena Téliz and Maite Silva, Espacio de Arte Contemporáneo).

The direct comparisons suggested by the architectural relationship between the *Museo liberado* and the MNHN galleries sharpen the institutional and decolonial critiques developed in La Padula's installation. On the other side of the corridor, in the MNHN's recently modernized dioramas, the fossils and taxidermied animals that have been recruited to showcase the major eras of the Earth's pre-history are organized along a thick red timeline. As in many scientific collections and displays, these objects are categorized and made legible within a linear narrative of evolution that rests on (Western) ideas of time and progress. Their confinement in glass cases clearly demarcates a divide between viewing subject and object to be viewed. Across the way, in the *Museo liberado*'s "Sala de Captura," there is no fixed path through the exhibition, no narrative, no timeline, and its objects are fully available to be touched, picked up and rearranged. No labels define them within expert taxonomies: La Padula firmly resisted the museum staff's desire to identify the date and provenance of each item, wishing visitors to move freely around the room and to construct their own narratives in relation to the material they viewed.

This technique encourages a reflection on how the "meaning" of a specimen changes or is lost altogether when it is removed from its context within a thematic or narrative display. *Museo liberado* demonstrates that knowledge is not simply constructed through the observation of objects themselves; it emerges from a complex interplay between objects and their emplacement in particular spaces, as well as their insertion in regimes of visuality and their relationship with the texts that accompany them, in the form of labels, notes, and guides. As objects are moved from one space to another, as their labels are changed or removed, and as the circumscribed gaze of spectatorship becomes an opportunity for different kinds of interaction, the values that had seemed to be inherent in those objects become subject to change.

In presenting his proposal to redeploy objects from the MNHN, La Padula needed to reassure staff there that his intention was not to undermine the authority of science but to expand its perspectives. Reflecting on his own use of materials from natural history museums, Mark Dion finds that artists engaged in institutional critique fall into two camps: those who see the museum as "an irredeemable reservoir of class ideology" and those who adopt a critical stance toward the museum "because they want to make it a more interesting and effective cultural institution."[41] La Padula's approach certainly falls into the latter category. *Museo liberado* encourages us to reflect on the historical relationship between the rise of the natural history museum and the consolidation of state power in Latin America, expressed in its capacity to extract, expropriate, and preserve life. The significant boom in scientific activity that took place in the region in the last part of the nineteenth century and the first three decades of the twentieth was driven by the faith that the political elites placed in science as a means of making the economy more productive, mapping out territories that had not yet been fully explored, Europeanizing local cultures, and educating, disciplining, and controlling large populations.[42] La Padula's critique is directed toward the powerful legacy of positivism that is still evident in the organization of many of Latin America's museums; he considers that among the general public, "la ciencia sigue siendo un espejo de la naturaleza y maneja una verdad única e irrevocable" (science remains a mirror of nature and administers a unique and irrevocable truth).[43]

Positivism played a significant role, not only in the founding and shaping of museums in Latin America, but in the application of a rather reductive scientific logic to an understanding of the evolution of human society. For Auguste Comte, the French philosopher who first developed the doctrine of Positivism, humanity—rather than God or nature—was the horizon of positivist thought. The "diverse branches" of knowledge Comte describes are unified in a single science of which "our existence is at once the source and the end."[44] The two permanent dioramas presented by the MNHN, fittingly named "Nuestro Pasado" (Our Past) and "Nuestro Presente" (Our Present), communicate a clear vision of the role of science in society that accords with this positivist and humanist agenda. Printed on the glass through which the visitor views taxidermied animals and fossilized remains is the reminder that "conocer el pasado es un ejercicio fundamental para entender el presente y proyectar el futuro" (knowing the past is essential in understanding the present and projecting the future). Pointing to the importance of

---

41 Corrin, Miwon, and Bryson, "Miwon Kwon in Conversation with Mark Dion," 16.
42 Carreras and Carrillo Zeiter, "Las ciencias en la formación de las naciones americanas: Una introducción," 16.
43 Conversation with the author, 22 April 2021.
44 Comte, *A Discourse on the Positive Spirit*, 39.

natural history in explaining the processes that underpin climate change, the Museum glosses over its own role, past and present, in the crises it now narrates: its collusion in colonial and capitalist expansion and the extinctions aided by its own collecting practices.

An allusion to this role is made in *Museo liberado* in the screening of *Una aldea Makiritare* (A Makiritare Village, 1958), a short documentary directed by Roberto Gardiol Armand'Ugon during the Orinoco Expedition, on a television in the corner.[45] The film suggests a broader relationship between the zeal to collect and categorize natural specimens and the appropriative, exoticizing, imperialist gaze of mid-twentieth-century anthropology. In it, the camera lingers as it describes the pronounced muscular development of the thoracic cage in male members of the Makiritare tribe, objectifying them even as the narrator admires their primitive skills in canoe-building. The inclusion of the film in La Padula's exhibition makes explicit the connection between collecting and conquering, reminding us that even in the new Latin American republics, the state's assumption of the role of collection-building "contiene un acto de violencia estatal: la conquista de un territorio, la dominación de un grupo, la muerte de los individuos vivos, la internalización por coerción o consenso de determinadas reglas sociales" (contains an act of state violence: the conquest of a territory, the domination of a group, the death of living individuals, the internalization—by coercion or consensus—of certain social rules).[46]

The objects placed in the "Sala de Captura" thus emphasize the function of the Museum, not primarily as a space of displays to serve the aim of public education, but as the leader and sponsor of scientific expeditions and the curator of collections intended for research. These roles have been shaped by political, economic, and cultural objectives as much as scientific ones. *Museo liberado* insists on an essential point of equivalence between the natural history dioramas and the art gallery installations. It is not that one is more "natural" and the other more "cultural": in their approach to the natural world, both are profoundly shaped by (Western) cultural paradigms, from colonialism to conservationism.[47]

---

45 The film may be viewed at https://vimeo.com/160761571
46 Podgorny and Lopes, *El desierto en una vitrina*, 20.
47 The insertion in the "Sala de Captura" of works by two invited Uruguayan artists, Magela Ferrero (*El libro de las migas*) and Brian Mackern (*Frecuencias de resonancia*),

In the "Sala de Escape" (Escape Hall), the taxidermied animals positioned as if they were heading for the exit include many species that are native to Uruguay, such as the rhea, the coati, the armadillo, and the carpincho. Their presence reminds us of the particular importance of natural history in the decades following Independence for many Latin American states. Given the absence of significant linguistic or cultural differences between *criollo* elites and their former colonizing power, natural history collections made a crucial contribution to the search for a national identity, while allowing the state to extend its power over its territory and to measure the economic value of its natural resources.[48] While the taxidermied animals in the "Nuestro Presente" exhibition across the corridor are neatly segregated in dioramas to represent Uruguay's major ecosystems (including native forests, wetlands, farmland, and coastal regions), in the "Sala de Escape" they are torn from their ecological niches and made, improbably, to share the same space. This uprooting is only a pale reflection, of course, of the much more violent extraction that brought them to the museum in the first place. These animals' collective bid for freedom points to the cost—in animal, plant, and human life—of the consolidation of nations as political, economic, and cultural systems, both in Latin America and elsewhere.

The "Sala de Escape" was the subject of intense negotiations with the MNHN. The Museum had wanted all the taxidermy specimens to be carefully protected, placed on platforms and in glass cases, despite the fact that the animals loaned to La Padula were some of the museum's most neglected and deteriorated objects, many of which had been piled up between cupboards in the basement.[49] The opening of the exhibition was in fact delayed by several weeks while MNHN staff cleaned and restored some of the specimens to ready them for public viewing. In the end, after much discussion, no platforms were used but some of the animals were shown in glass cases. La Padula was content with the outcome, as it demonstrated the challenges of negotiating with an institution with its own rationales of preservation and exhibition,

---

also pointed to the considerable convergence between scientists' modes of capturing nature and those of artists.

48 Carreras and Carrillo Zeiter, "Las ciencias en la formación de las naciones americanas: Una introducción," 13.
49 Conversation with the author, 6 October 2021.

often very different from those of a contemporary art gallery. It also gestured toward the deliberately partial, compromised "freedom" that the animals had been granted. The taxidermied animals are arguably "freed" from serving as types or examples in of particular ecosystems or stages of evolution. But their expropriation for the purposes of an art installation does not, of course, liberate them: it simply subjects them to another kind of capture. As La Padula suggests, once these animals have become enmeshed in human culture, there can be no return for them to the wild.[50] Their stiffened heads, many turned unnaturally away from their direction of travel, remind us that they were originally designed for another context and that their co-option into this exodus simply inscribes them into another fiction of human making.

In a context in which—as La Padula believes—"el común de la población tiende a pensar que el científico tiene una voz más veraz que la del campo de las artes visuales, la cultura" (the general population tends to think that the scientist's voice is more truthful than those of the fields of visual arts or culture),[51] *Museo liberado* relocates and recombines exhibits to highlight the illusory coherence of the natural history museum's narratives and to construct a role for art in presenting a different kind of truth: one that reflects on the practices and the values that have produced the knowledge accumulated in the museum's dioramas. Many natural history museums have been resignifying their exhibits to create new narratives on the current crises of biodiversity loss and climate change. Yet these themes may be no less deterministic or human-centred than older, positivist narratives of progress, order, and civilization.

Museo liberado reminds us of the many and varied ways in which animals have been, and continue to be, conscripted for human purposes, whether in science or in art. It reflects on the systems of capture through which the (animal and human) other is disciplined, but also those through which viewers become subject themselves to the disciplining power of the state. It is in this sense that Jens Andermann observes that the modern museum "looks forward to the camp,"[52] a chilling alliance

---

50 See https://pablolapa.wordpress.com/museo-liberado-eac-mnhn-montevideo-uy-2021-2022/
51 Conversation with the author, 22 April 2021.
52 Andermann, *The Optic of the State*, 17.

that is underscored in this case by the installation of *Museo liberado* in Montevideo's ex-prison. As we contemplate the modern museum's "collection of corpses," Andermann suggests, "the silent threat implied in the museum's visual pedagogy" is that we, too, might become exposed to the violence contained in the gaze.[53] La Padula demonstrates that nature, once captured, cannot be freed from the self-regarding fantasies of human culture; likewise, in *Museo liberado* both humans and animals are ultimately caught up in the thanatopolitics of the liberal Latin American state.

Walmor Corrêa's Animal Recompositions and Repatriations

Among the various maps, drawings, photographs and paintings included in Walmor Corrêa's *Sporophila Beltoni* exhibition (2018) are two forged documents proving Brazilian citizenship (an identity card and a passport) and a fake pilot's licence issued by the national civil aviation authority (see Fig. 6.11).[54] The creation of these forgeries would have been a crime, but for the fact that the putative owner of the documents is a Brazilian finch, a small, stubby-beaked bird staring squarely and solemnly at us in the identifying photograph.

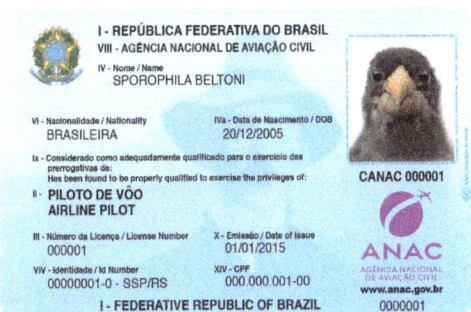

Fig. 6.11 Walmor Corrêa, forged pilot's licence, *Sporophila Beltoni* (2018). Instituto Ling, Porto Alegre, Brazil (photograph by artist).

---

53   Andermann, 57.
54   *Walmor Corrêa e Sporophila Beltoni* was held in the Instituto Ling in Porto Alegre, Brazil, in 2018.

The bird has remained still enough to photograph because it is a taxidermy specimen. Abandoned and incorrectly labelled, it was discovered by Corrêa at the back of a drawer in the National Museum of Natural History in Washington, D.C. The journey that took him there had involved extensive research and correspondence with museum curators and Brazilian specialists, in the hope of finding a *Sporophila beltoni*, a bird formally identified only in 2013 by ornithologists from the Rio Grande do Sul. The specimen had been misclassified when it arrived in the museum in 1820, and had languished there since then, undiscovered. Corrêa's research reconstructs the history of the bird's death and its subsequent travels, hypothesizing—on the basis of the date on its identification tag and the signature tilt given to its head— that it was captured by the Austrian naturalist and taxidermist Johann Natterer. At a meeting with the Brazilian Ambassador to the US, Corrêa formally petitioned for the recognition of the bird's Brazilian citizenship in the form of a passport. The many documents Corrêa commissions for the specimen, which include birth and death certificates, are a playful way of creating an identity for a bird that died for the sake of scientific knowledge but lay forgotten and wrongly catalogued for nearly two centuries. The project as a whole draws attention to the ways in which birds and other animals have been—and continue to be—killed and expatriated in the name of science, and how those specimens (and the knowledge they make possible) became concentrated in wealthy museums in Europe and North America.

Corrêa traces a cultural afterlife for the taxidermy bird, resituating it within the geopolitics of scientific exploration in the past and creating resonances with the barriers to human migration and citizenship that divide our "global" world in the present. Aloi suggests that an emphasis on the afterlives of taxidermied objects may return to the animal "a kind of individuality" through "the mapping of specific events that shaped its material existence."[55] Most importantly, it demonstrates that "the biological death of the animal does not equate to the end of animal agency."[56] Even in death, he argues, material animal bodies are "capable of affecting, and reflexively shaping, human/animal

---

55 Aloi, *Speculative Taxidermy*, 54.
56 Aloi, 54.

relations."⁵⁷ Corrêa's *Sporophila beltoni* does not only tell the expected story of science's collusion with power in the forms of colonialism and capitalism, but also points to the omissions, the mistakes, and the missing links that interrupt the construction and global circulation of knowledge. These chinks and ruptures in our systematization of nature allow us to imagine—if only playfully and temporarily—the overturning of the authority that justified imperial acts of dispossession on the part of museums in Europe and North America.

Other works by Corrêa create fictional afterlives for animals by intervening directly in taxidermy objects themselves. These are always bought from specialists or received via donations and resignified for artistic purposes. In *Para onde vão os pássaros quando morrem?* (Where Do Birds Go When They Die?, 2012), he constructs miniature dioramas of the kind commonly to be found as ornaments in nineteenth-century homes, with small taxidermy animals arranged under a glass dome. Typically, as Pat Morris points out, such displays were more decorative than scientifically accurate: species of birds from different continents were mixed together, adopting poses that were often unnatural but designed to show off their colourful plumage in the most favourable way.⁵⁸ Brightly coloured hummingbirds were particularly popular in such displays, caught by professional bird trappers in Central and South America and sent to markets in London and Paris.⁵⁹ Corrêa's own dioramas often feature hummingbirds, modelled with precision to create beautiful, delicate specimens. They are perched elegantly on twisted twigs against a background of vivid green foliage, combining ferns, firs, grasses, and cacti in a deliberate disregard for ecological verisimilitude. The hummingbirds themselves are also a work of fiction. Their beaks are curled gracefully into a spiral, rendering them completely useless as a means for feeding. Other taxidermy animals recreated by Corrêa unexpectedly combine feathered bodies with heads of small rodents, joined so neatly at the neck that they seem entirely natural.

In part, Corrêa's fictional creatures point to the artifice at the heart of taxidermy's naturalism. The shock of the real in the taxidermic object—this is an animal that has lived and stands before us—is always

---

57   Aloi, 56.
58   Morris, *A History of Taxidermy*, 56.
59   Morris, 56–57.

created through a series of fabrications, which produce the effect of a living, breathing animal. Through animal re-creation, Mark Simpson suggests, taxidermy claims itself to be "an *artless* art—an art *for* nature and *against* artifice, a mode of mediation beyond mediation itself."[60] However, the "truth-value" of taxidermy specimens in a museum display, their usefulness as a pedagogic tool, depends not only on the painstaking creation of casts and models on the basis of careful measurements but also on multiple "small frauds."[61] "Composites" were often constructed, for example, to supply a single, unblemished specimen, as these were rarely to be found in nature (and much less, as Michael Rossi points out, when the subjects were whales killed by exploding harpoons).[62] Corrêa's work alludes to the fabrications and idealizations that guarantee the taxidermic reproduction of lifelikeness. Unlike the deliberately incongruous taxidermy hybrids produced by the German sculptor Thomas Grünfeld for his *Misfits* series (1989–), Corrêa's exquisite recreations trick the eye, seeming so natural that we only notice their falsities on closer inspection.

These highly decorative ensembles of reinvented animals also seem to comment on the anatomical and ecological absurdities that resulted from taxidermy's slippage in the nineteenth century from an object of scientific study to one of fashion and lucrative marketability. Yet Corrêa's hybrids are also inspired by the particular fabrications and errors that are to be found in early Jesuit accounts of the wonders of Brazilian nature. Padre José de Anchieta describes an insect that may metamorphose into a rat or into a butterfly, and tiny hummingbirds that "alimentam-se só de orvalho" (feed only on dew).[63] Anchieta also writes that one species of hummingbird is believed by all to derive from the butterfly, echoing a belief that was widespread at the time.[64] As if to provide a poetic illustration of this heterogenesis, one of Corrêa's dioramas depicts a tower of tropical butterflies, with two hummingbirds placed at the apex (see Fig. 6.12).

---

60 Simpson, "Powers of Liveness," 60.
61 Rossi, "Fabricating Authenticity," 353.
62 Rossi, 353.
63 Anchieta, *Carta de São Vicente 1560*, 27, 30, 46n58. This would of course be a biological impossibility, and in fact hummingbirds feed mainly on small insects and spiders.
64 Anchieta, 30, 46n58.

6. Taxidermy and Natural History Dioramas   231

Fig. 6.12 Walmor Corrêa, diorama from *Para onde vão os pássaros quando morrem?* (2012). Plastic, taxidermy, paint, resin, paper and glass, 60 × 20 cm (photograph by Letícia Remião).

In many of his domes, Corrêa adds a tiny trace of human consumption in the form of a cigarette butt, a piece of chewed gum, or the crumpled top of a Coca-Cola bottle, shattering the myth of an untouched nature that was so often depicted in natural history museum dioramas. The careless intrusion of trash in an otherwise perfected nature also points to the increasing incursion of human waste into natural environments. The themes of waste and disposability are developed more fully in the installation *Voçê que faz versos* (*You Who Write Poetry*, 2010), for which Corrêa assembled a scene of wooden crates and trash cans and introduced a number of his rodent-headed birds as scavengers, feeding on discarded cookies and other detritus (see Fig. 6.13).[65] As in Arteaga's

---

65 *Voçê que faz versos* was shown in 2010 at the Instituto Goethe in Porto Alegre and the Galeria Laura Marsiaj in Rio de Janeiro, Brazil. The exhibition's title is taken from "José" (1942), a well-known poem by the Brazilian writer Carlos Drummond de Andrade (1902–1987) that is often read as an expression of uncertainty and anguish, composed at a time of war on the international stage and political repression at home.

Diorama en expansión, animals are not simply there to be looked at, confined within a remote wilderness and brought to us via the devices of museum displays. Instead, they are thoroughly interpolated in our own urban habitat in ways that confront and discomfort us.

The freezing in time and space of this scene seems to give it a noble quality that is belied by its prosaic subject matter. Aloi argues that the stasis of diorama displays bestows a quality of transcendence through an association with classical sculpture and painting.[66] In classical art, "sculptural stillness constitutes the representational element signifying a moral dimension imbued with a meditative sense, suggesting the solemnity of an event and the ethical elevation of a subject matter."[67] In its own sculptural stasis, taxidermy also takes on the values of classical art and particularly its ennobling of nature, lending itself to the "ventriloquization of decorum" as a value expressed both in moral virtue and aesthetic elegance.[68] Mark Dion's taxidermy diorama *Landfill* (1999–2000) refuses to comply with this convention; as Aloi affirms, the scavengers picking over mounds of human-generated waste are a far cry from the heroic animals of classical art and cannot easily be inscribed with the attributes and values to which humans aspire.[69] In a similar way, Corrêa's *Voçê que faz versos* provokes a sense of deep incongruity in appearing to ennoble animals that we would normally overlook or exterminate without compunction.

The animal virtues that *Voçê que faz versos* seems to uphold in its aesthetic debt to classical sculpture are not ones of beauty or dignity, but those of adaptability and the capacity to recycle and repurpose. These are skills that are often found in synanthropic species, which have adapted their behaviour to urban living and benefit from the warmth, increased food supplies, and nesting opportunities they derive from a proximity to humans. In a similar way to Mark Dion in his *Concrete Jungle (Mammalia)* (1993), in which taxidermied rats, cats, and raccoons feed off human refuse, Corrêa points to the extent to which nature is reworked in culture. But in Corrêa's *Voçê que faz versos* those skills of adaptation and recycling are also expressed in the artist's own refashioning of taxidermy objects.

---

66 Aloi, *Speculative Taxidermy*, 114.
67 Aloi, 122.
68 Aloi, 127.
69 Aloi, 108.

6. *Taxidermy and Natural History Dioramas* 233

Fig. 6.13 Walmor Corrêa, scene from *Você que faz versos* (2010). Instituto Goethe de Porto Alegre, Porto Alegre, Brazil (photograph by Letícia Remião).

To recompose the disposable, to make new creations from waste, are certainly skills that twenty-first-century humans are learning to respect and admire. If *Concrete Jungle* (*Mammalia*) reveals how human culture has thoroughly shaped the habitats and practices of other animals, *Voçê que faz versos* draws equal attention to what we may learn ourselves from the animals that cohabit with us: their adaptability, their resilience, their ingenious use of available sources of energy. Corrêa's taxidermy hybrids are a celebration of the inventiveness, the diversity, and the resilience of life, which persists despite our continual depredations of it.

Conclusion

In 2015, the Natural History Museum, a project created by an activist artist collective based in the US, restaged a diorama that had formed part of an exhibition on climate change a few years earlier at the American Museum of Natural History (AMNH) in New York.[70] The original diorama had featured a polar bear clambering over a pile of garbage. In its recreation, the Natural History Museum inserted a Koch Industries oil pipeline into the pile as a protest against the entanglement of the interests of fossil fuel industries with those of AMNH, where David H. Koch was a board member and exhibition sponsor. Another activist art collective based in Argentina, the Grupo Etcétera, created its own diorama in 2021 as a protest against neo-extractivist practices in the region (see Fig. 6.14).[71] Instead of taxidermied animals, it featured round, pink piggybanks set against a black-and-white backdrop of an entirely industrialized countryside. A video showing a cartoon version of *The Three Little Pigs* warns viewers to be wary of how one might build for the future. Entitled *Diorama, Museo del Neo Extractivismo* (Diorama, Museum of Neo-Extractivism), the installation also questioned how the museum as an institution might be implicated in constructing and disseminating fables about nature and our interventions in it, situating it squarely within a capitalist system that commodifies and exploits the natural world.

---

70 The diorama, entitled *Our Climate, Whose Politics?*, was shown at the American Alliance of Museums Annual Convention in Atlanta in 2015.

71 Diorama, Museo del Neo Extractivismo was shown as part of an exhibition entitled *Simbiología: Prácticas artísticas en un planeta en emergencia* at the Centro Cultural Kirchner, Buenos Aires, Argentina, in 2021–2022.

6. *Taxidermy and Natural History Dioramas*　　　235

Fig. 6.14 Installation view of Grupo Etcétera, *Diorama, Museo del Neo Extractivismo* (2021). Centro Cultural Kirchner, Buenos Aires, Argentina (photograph by the author).

In their own remediations of, or interventions into, natural history museums and taxidermy animals, Arteaga, Bustos, Corrêa, La Padula, and Malva may be understood as engaging in forms of institutional critique. This critique is often of a different kind, however, to that pursued by the Natural History Museum, the MTL Collective, Grupo Etcétera, and other activist-artists who have sought to decolonize the (Western) museum, denouncing its role in operations of colonial exploitation, extraction, and erasure, as well as its fantasies of possession, its continued Eurocentrism, and its collusion with carbon-intensive industries or corporations with low ethical standards. The works explored in this chapter are more philosophical than overtly political in their critique. They interrogate the epistemological divisions between human and animal, nature and culture, subject and object, on which Western modernity has been founded, and which have driven its universalizing, imperialist, anthropocentric expansion across the world. This expansion was not checked by the transition to independence in Latin America:

the new republics often engaged in even more brutal acts of subjugation in order to extend their governance over heterogeneous populations and profit from the natural resources available within the borders of their nations. The deconstructions, reconstructions, displacements, and remediations carried out by Arteaga, Bustos, Corrêa, La Padula, and Malva reconnect natural history with social history, showing how the modern museum in Latin America is implicated in a violence that includes both human and nonhuman animals. If there can be no return to nature for animals caught up in human culture, these artists do trace ways in which the use of taxidermy in art may return agency to animals, and even express values that are less anthropocentric.

Conclusion

This conclusion reframes some of the central arguments I have pursued in this book in two principal ways. Firstly, I explore how many of the artworks discussed could be read as instances of a *decolonial neobaroque*. I tease out what this might add to our understanding of their critical approach to modernity and the Enlightenment, as well as their gestures toward the existence of alternative modernities. In the second part of the conclusion, I discuss the relationship forged in these artworks between humans and the rest of the natural world in the light of Enrique Leff's concept of *environmental democracy*, finding in the correlation between biodiversity and cultural diversity the basis of an argument for local responses to environmental change, in place of the West's typical search for "one-world" solutions. In the context of Latin America today, as Maristella Svampa and Enrique Viale argue, this provides an opportunity to counter the paralysing catastrophism of Western discourses of the Anthropocene.

The Politics of the Decolonial Neobaroque

The artworks presented in this book produce clear critiques of forms of knowledge and practice that are associated with Enlightenment philosophy and science. They compose alternative discourses of modernity that are less exclusionary, although they are (for the most part) still forged in dialogue with the scientific, literary, and visual traditions that have characterized the evolution of natural history in Europe and the Anglophone world. One way in which they do this is to create baroque imaginaries, firstly to invoke the baroque's historical co-option in Latin America as an instrument for anticolonial and anti-institutional expression, and secondly, to access a storehouse of techniques that may be turned to decolonial and post-anthropocentric ends.

I suggested in Chapter Three that Baraya's absurd quest to collect and identify every type of artificial plant in the world should be read as a parody of the exhaustive encyclopaedism of the Enlightenment. Replacing this ambition with a playful theatricality, which extends to the use of *trompe l'oeil* and reflexive techniques, aligns his *Herbario de plantas artificiales* with the ludic repetitions and illusionism of the (neo) baroque. A similar reading could be proposed of Kueva's painstaking re-enactments of Humboldt's journeys and the extensive false herbarium he assembles, Corrêa's mock seed collection and the intricate forgeries he creates for his *Sporophila Beltoni* project, and the plants that sprout from Arteaga's *Botánica sistemática*. Romo himself identifies his portrayal of nature as "baroque" in its excess and exuberance: he represents the natural world "como un carnaval en permanente despliegue" (as a continually unfolding carnival).[1] The baroque folding-in of the stage and the world is the principal strategy used in Arteaga's diorama works, such as *This Path One Time Long Ago*, as it is in La Padula's *Museo liberado*. A baroque sensuality and excess define many works by Cardoso and Coca, while the great baroque theme of mortality and the transience of life is amply explored in taxidermy works by Corrêa, Malva, and others. In the symbiotic, co-evolutionary relationships depicted by Cardoso and Rodríguez, we might even find strong echoes of ways in which baroque art typically troubled the distinction between subject and object, multiplying perspectives and confounding hierarchies, as "in a co-evolutionary relationship every subject is also an object, every object a subject."[2]

What might profitably be read as instances of a decolonial neobaroque, I will argue, must be carefully positioned in relation both to the historical baroque and to the postmodern neobaroque in Latin America. A significant body of scholarship has traced indigenous and *criollo* counter-appropriations of the baroque in seventeenth- and eighteenth-century Latin American art and architecture. Many writers and researchers have attempted to locate a nascent American cultural identity in such subversions. In an influential essay published in 1957,

---
1   Farías, "'El álbum de la flora imprudente,'" 23.
2   Pollan, *The Botany of Desire*, xx.

José Lezama Lima identified the baroque as "an art of counterconquest" in the New World, as the cultural hybridization evident in the work of sculptors such as Aleijadinho and El Indio Kondori disrupts the imposition of colonial authority, relativizing it through the inclusion of indigenous figures and myths.³ Overly simplistic accounts that pit a hybrid baroque against a conservative one have been usefully nuanced in more recent years, allowing a more heterogeneous and fluid understanding of the Latin American baroque to emerge, as a phenomenon that cannot be characterized as largely derivative or wholly revolutionary.⁴ In a similar way, the art projects explored in this book simultaneously borrow from and reject traditions of the European Enlightenment, creating paradoxical constellations that reflect complex histories of intellectual and cultural exchange.

The "wayward, rich afterlife" of the baroque has inspired many "neobaroques."⁵ Drawing on seminal essays by Lezama Lima, Severo Sarduy, and Alejo Carpentier, critics have identified traits of the neobaroque in the fictional texts of many twentieth-century Latin American writers that bridge elite and popular cultures, modernity, and the non-rational.⁶ For Sarduy, for example, the baroque is the epitome of artifice. His emphasis on linguistic play makes of the baroque an "espacio de dialogismo, de la polifonía, de la carnavalización, de la parodia y la intertextualidad" (space of dialogism, polyphony, carnivalization, parody and intertextuality).⁷ His analysis strongly concurs with many Anglophone and European studies of the techniques developed in postmodernist texts to subvert authority and any kind of ontological certainty, defining the neobaroque as an "arte del destronamiento" (art of dethronement).⁸

Redefining the baroque too broadly may lessen its analytical value, however, by stripping it of its historicity and its capacity for social and cultural critique. Mabel Moraña finds that the postmodern pluralities

---

3   Lezama Lima, "Baroque Curiosity," 213.
4   See, for example, Gruzinski, *The Mestizo Mind*, 198; Cacho Casal, "Introduction: Locating Early Modern Spanish American Poetry," 1–5.
5   Kaup, *Neobaroque in the Americas*, 2.
6   See, for example, Arriarán, *Barroco y neobarroco en América Latina*. The seminal essays most often cited are those by Lezama Lima, *La expresión americana*; Sarduy, "El barroco y el neobarroco"; Carpentier, "El barroco y lo real maravilloso."
7   Sarduy, "El barroco y el neobarroco," 175.
8   Sarduy, 183.

and polyphonies of Sarduy's baroque "existen fuera de la historia y más allá de la especificidad de la cultura, es decir, más allá de toda referencialidad y de todo proyecto social organizado" (exist outside of history and beyond cultural specificity, that is to say, beyond all referentiality and any organized social project).[9] Likewise, she objects to the dehistoricized version of the baroque offered by Omar Calabrese, arguing that his readings rest on a series of abstract, universalized features that he considers to be inherent in baroque culture everywhere.[10]

The baroque has thus variously referred to a specific historical period, a movement in the history of art and architecture, an expression of anticolonial resistance, and a postmodern poetic strategy. I wish to recuperate the term here in a way that connects all of these, but focuses principally on its critique of Enlightenment philosophy and European (and Eurocentric) modernity. In using the term "neobaroque" to describe the reinventions of natural history by recent Latin American artists, I acknowledge the specific continuities they suggest with the historical baroque, namely, the rearticulation of aesthetic strategies that pluralize European narratives of modernity. On the other hand, I wish to drive a wedge between a "postmodern" neobaroque, which—in much literary criticism, at least—celebrates excess and performance in order to subvert authority, linear histories, and essentialized identities, and a "decolonial" neobaroque, which, in the work of these artists, involves acts of historical re-embedding as much as ones of disembedding. Here, the excesses and the hybridizing effects of the neobaroque become important means of rehistoricization, as they return to specific moments in the history of art and scientific illustration, both pre- and post-Enlightenment, in order to incorporate a critique of modernity within some of its most paradigmatic genres.

This approach aligns them with a decolonial project that, for Dussel, does not share postmodernism's critique of reason *per se*, but certainly concurs with its critique of the "violent, coercive, genocidal reason" that is generated by the Eurocentric myth of modernity.[11] My argument is closely aligned here with that of Irlemar Chiampi, who argues that the baroque reappears in the twentieth century in Latin

---
9   Moraña, *La escritura del límite*, 77.
10 Moraña, 64; see Calabrese, Neo-Baroque.
11 Dussel, "Eurocentrism and Modernity," 75.

America "to bear witness to the crisis or end of modernity and to the very condition of a continent that could not be assimilated by the project of the Enlightenment."¹² In this way, the neobaroque becomes "an archaeology of the modern" that reveals something of the character of Latin America's "dissonant modernity."¹³

These artists amply demonstrate how the neobaroque may serve a decolonial critique of modernity in the Latin American context. They do not invoke the baroque as an inherent and ahistorical trait, as Alejo Carpentier risks doing when he claims that Latin America is baroque because of "the unruly complexities of its nature and its vegetation [...] our nature is untamed, as is our history."¹⁴ Instead, they develop a specific critique of the colonial imposition of Enlightenment thought, which has become synonymous with the emergence of modernity and scientific rationalism in the European context. As a response to the abstractions and extractions of Enlightenment and colonial science, their work comprises a series of symbolic acts of *re*insertion and *re*connection. Their embrace of baroque concerns and aesthetics is therefore not primarily a postmodern, dehistoricizing bid to unseat the discourses of the metropolitan centre, but a decolonial, *re*historicizing venture that seeks to rebuild Latin American modernity in a way that excludes neither its pre-Enlightenment past nor the centuries of cross-fertilization between indigenous and European imaginaries. In the introduction, I suggested that the multiple temporalities convened in the artworks discussed in this book create a series of "folds." Deleuze identifies the creation of folds as the "operative function" of the Baroque.¹⁵ These folds do not subject historical references to an indiscriminate mash-up, however, but allow us to grasp the multiple temporalities of modernity that are often made invisible in Western accounts. The techniques of citation, repetition, and reenactment used in these art projects contest the linear, unified history of positivism and humanism in order to reveal its violence, but also to recover something of value for the present in what it has excluded in the past.

---

12 Chiampi, "Baroque at the Twilight of Modernity," 508.
13 Chiampi, 508.
14 Carpentier, "The Baroque and the Marvelous Real," 105.
15 Deleuze, *The Fold*, 3.

The connection between the neobaroque and decolonial thought in the Latin American context has been briefly proposed but not fully developed in recent scholarship. Both Aníbal Quijano and Walter Mignolo return to the scene of the historical baroque in America to give instances of the kind of critical appropriation and resignification of European culture that would provide the foundation for a new Latin American cultural identity born out of colonial difference.[16] Neither considers, however, how the particular aesthetic and conceptual modes of the baroque might be carried forward to create opportunities for a critical revision of European modernity in our own time. This possibility is suggested by Monika Kaup, who grasps the potential of the neobaroque for the construction of "a new kind of temporality."[17] Kaup proposes that we understand the baroque as an "alternative modernity" that rejects the Enlightenment's rupture with the past and with nonrationalist thought, affirming instead "the impure, hybrid coexistence of the disjunctive (modern and premodern, global and local, faith and reason, science and wonder)."[18]

César Augusto Salgado suspects that the deep interest in the baroque in Latin American cultural theory "may have no equivalent in current postcolonial thinking."[19] Bhabha, Spivak, and other postcolonial theorists who speak from other regions of the colonized world are of course centrally concerned with the contradictions that are inherent to colonial projects; for Bhabha, cultural hybridity marks out the "ambivalent space" of colonial power, where "other 'denied' knowledges enter upon the dominant discourse and estrange the basis of its authority."[20] But as the European colonization of the Americas *predates* the Enlightenment, its contestation also implies, as Salgado argues, "a response to the failure of enlightened ideals to transform and modernize Latin American society and culture."[21] In addition, I would argue, it involves a response to the epistemic and ecological violence involved in that project of transformation and modernization.

---

16 See Quijano, "Colonialidad del poder, cultura y conocimiento en América Latina," 142; Mignolo, *The Idea of Latin America*, 61–62.
17 Kaup, *Neobaroque in the Americas*, 21.
18 Kaup, 6.
19 Salgado, "Hybridity in New World Baroque Theory," 317.
20 Bhabha, *The Location of Culture*, 114, 112.
21 Salgado, "Hybridity in New World Baroque Theory," 326n4.

Although they are often irreverent in their articulation, these artistic projects also represent more serious endeavours to recover a cultural history that has often been supplanted or sidelined. When artists and sculptors from Mexico or Brazil inserted Amerindian or African deities among the Western gods and goddesses that were a mainstay of baroque art, Serge Gruzinski observes, they opened the way for "the recomposition and rescue" of non-European pasts.[22] Works by Toriz, Romo, Corrêa, Villavicencio and others reinscribe popular and indigenous myths and practices into cultural histories from which they have often been erased. Their palimpsestic, transhistorical techniques unfold alternative temporalities that yield us a glimpse, to borrow Kaup's phrase, of "a modernity without an irreversible break with the past."[23]

An aesthetics of reconnection and recomposition also allows these artists to explore how art expands our knowledge of the world, both for and beyond the purposes of modern science. If baroque art was a response to "the gathering regimentation of knowledge" in the Renaissance,[24] then the neobaroque techniques of these artists expose, from the perspective of the other "end of modernity," the gross insufficiency of Enlightenment systems of knowledge in the face of environmental crisis and the many forms of cultural and economic dispossession that have resulted from the historical collusion between European colonialism, capitalism, and modern science. Not content merely to show where Western science has fallen short, these works also demonstrate the potential in art to assemble and create plural epistemologies, promoting the kind of interaction between scientific and other forms of knowledge and practice that is essential to the decolonial project. As the "global" project of modernity careers into ever more grievous forms of social and environmental crisis, these works clearly demonstrate that the contemporary power of the baroque lies, as Bolívar Echeverría affirms, in the force with which it poses "la posibilidad y la urgencia de una modernidad alternativa" (the possibility and the urgency of an alternative modernity).[25]

---

22 Gruzinski, "The Baroque Planet," 120.
23 Kaup, *Neobaroque in the Americas*, 22.
24 Greene, "Baroque and Neobaroque," 150.
25 Echeverría, *La modernidad de lo barroco*, 15.

Environmental Democracy and the "Humanization" of Nature

Plural epistemologies and multiple modernities may, these works suggest, assemble a more effective response to global environmental crisis. In Chapter Three, I read the agroecological practices depicted in Rodríguez's illustrations alongside research on the relationship between biodiversity and cultural diversity. A similar correlation is also suggested in the works of Toriz, Corrêa, Romo, Baraya, and De Valdenebro. Against the globalizing pretensions of Western technomodernity, many political ecologists in Latin America have called for an "environmental democracy," which Leff defines not merely as the right for voices to be heard, but as "the right to inhabit the world through different cultural rationalities and territorial conditions."[26] "Environmental democracy" is in part a call to recognize that the value of nature "cannot be translated or reduced to market prices": that equity cannot be wrought by providing economic compensation to indigenous groups for the loss of natural resources, and that it is impossible to calculate the present or future value of biodiversity, which is "the result of centuries and millennia of ethno-ecological co-evolution."[27] In the context of the conflicts that have arisen between indigenous communities on the one hand, and transnational biotech companies, mining companies, state development agencies, and other actors on the other, Leff states unequivocally that "Equity can only be achieved by subverting and abolishing any and all barriers to the autonomy of peoples and by creating conditions for appropriating the ecological potential of each region through the cultural values and social interests of each community."[28]

The commitment of many artists discussed in this book to exploring perspectives on the natural world that are deliberately subjective, partial, or multiple may be read alongside the rejection of many Latin American political ecologists of "one-world" solutions to environmental problems that merely reinforce the power of the global capitalist order. This becomes both a political stance and an epistemological one. In her own search for a rational knowledge that is not tied to militarism,

---

26 Leff, "Power-Knowledge Relations in the Field of Political Ecology," 243.
27 Leff, "On the Social Reappropriation of Nature," 89, 102.
28 Leff, 100.

patriarchy, capitalism, and colonialism, Haraway wants to replace a "disembodied vision" and "the view from above" with "partial sight" and "objectivity as positioned rationality."[29] This partiality is to be understood as a recognition of the situated nature of all knowledge, but for Haraway it also opens up routes through which science might connect with subjugated knowledges. As she states, "We do not seek partiality for its own sake, but for the sake of the connections and unexpected openings situated knowledges make possible."[30] Leff similarly locates an "environmental rationality" in "a politics of difference," arguing that "the construction of an environmental rationality is achieved through the socialization of nature and community management of resources, founded on principles of ecological and cultural diversity."[31]

A focus on the partial, the plural, and the local combats the globalist approach to environmental crisis that has become dominant in the responses explored by Western governments and scientists since the 1980s. These have tended to favour planet-wide solutions—such as a global carbon tax or mega-scale geoengineering projects—that would only increase the power of "green" companies and the hegemony of technological modernity.[32] Focusing on the local also allows us to look beyond the catastrophism of many environmentalist discourses. Maristella Svampa and Enrique Viale observe that the dystopian global narrative of environmental apocalypse, which merely induces paralysis, may be contrasted with myriad initiatives at a local level across Latin America that are based on self-determination, sustainability, and social economy enterprises.[33] They lament that these sources of hope and innovation are difficult to translate into projects with a global reach. But the kind of pact they envision would not be one that negates the value of the local but draws its dynamism from it: if they dare to imagine "un gran pacto ecosocial y económico desde el Sur, en clave nacional y latinoamericana" (a great national and Latin American ecosocial and economic pact emerging from the South), this would be founded on

---

29 Haraway, *Simians, Cyborgs, and Women*, 196.
30 Haraway, 196.
31 Leff, "On the Social Reappropriation of Nature," 104.
32 For an excoriating critique of "Big Green" and the "magical thinking" of planetary-scale geoengineering projects to combat climate change, see Naomi Klein, *This Changes Everything: Capitalism vs. the Climate*.
33 Svampa and Viale, *El colapso ecológico ya llegó*, 261.

the existence of a plural politics shaped by diverse organizations and on the recognition that "las luchas en defensa del planeta adoptan una carnadura local y territorial polifacética cada vez más urgente y radical que ya no puede ser ignorada" (struggles to defend the planet are adopting a multifaceted local and territorial form that is increasingly urgent and radical, and that can no longer be disregarded).[34]

Leff's call for "the socialization of nature" pulls in a rather different direction from the purist views expressed by some First-World environmental thinkers, for whom "nature" should be entirely removed from human projections and values.[35] Rosi Braidotti objects to the anthropomorphism she finds at the heart of "deep ecology" approaches, such as those proposed by Arne Naess, which extend morality and rights to nonhumans. She identifies deep ecology's "full-scale humanization of the environment" as "sentimental" and "regressive."[36] Yet the artistic reinventions of natural history I have explored in this book suggest that the "humanization" of nature is not necessarily to be feared or denounced. If the root of ecological destruction is the ontological separation between humans and the rest of the natural world, which is at the core of the Enlightenment project, then finding ways of resocializing or even rehumanizing it becomes an important mode of contestation.

This might take the form of emphasizing the cultural and personal value of collections or acquisitions that are usually governed by exchange value (Baraya, La Padula), re-entangling animal lives with the myths and fantasies that arose from our past proximity with them (Romo, Toriz, Corrêa), exploring embodied forms of encountering the natural world that create relationships of horizontality and reciprocity (Villavicencio), creating exhibition spaces that break down distinctions between the natural and the cultural (Arteaga), exploring the symbiotic relationships between flowers and human desire (Cardoso), or highlighting practices that increase biodiversity through the selective

---

34 Svampa and Viale, 276.
35 Michael Soulé's influential work in conservation biology maintained that species have an intrinsic value, beyond human use (see Soulé, "What Is Conservation Biology?" (1985). This position has been challenged, for example by Peter Kareiva and Michelle Marvier in "What Is Conservation Science?" (2012), who argue that "ecological dynamics cannot be separated from human dynamics" (962) and that it is indefensible to protect biodiversity when the cost is mostly borne by the "poor and politically marginalized" (967).
36 Braidotti, *Transpositions*, 116.

cultivation of seeds and the practice of polyculture (De Valdenebro, Rodríguez). These artists' works sit alongside others that are critical of the precise ways in which nature has been "humanized" in Western technomodernity, through extractivism (Kueva), museum practices of killing and exhibiting animals in order to promote nationalist discourses or to domesticate other species (La Padula, Malva, Bustos), and the power of commercially circulated images of Latin American nature that are idealized or otherwise inaccurate (Sant'Ana, Bermúdez, Coca). In relation to the rest of my corpus, some of the works produced for the *Paraná-Ra'anga* expedition—such as the photographs by De Zuviría and a number of the views expressed in Glusman's video—appear anomalous in their representation of an apparently "untouched" nature, an idea that is roundly renounced by the expedition's ecologists. They demonstrate how difficult it remains for us in the West today to grasp the extent to which the natural world has already been reorganized as a result of human activity.

What emerges from this corpus as a whole is a recognition that there is little about the natural world that has not already been "humanized," and that the impact of anthropogenic activity on the environment may be, but is not necessarily, destructive. Indeed, these art projects call us to entwine our lives more closely than ever with the natural world, and to question the ontological divide between the human and the nonhuman on which Western modernity has been founded. Paying closer attention to the non-linear histories of ecological change allows us to understand the roles of imperialism and global capitalism in shaping the environmental crises of today, but also to glimpse alternative ways in which we might dwell in changing landscapes in the future.

Bibliography

Acosta, José de. *Historia natural y moral de las Indias*. Edited by Fermín del Pino-Díaz. Madrid: Consejo Superior de Investigaciones Científicas, 2008.

Aloi, Giovanni. *Speculative Taxidermy: Natural History, Animal Surfaces, and Art in the Anthropocene*. New York: Columbia University Press, 2018. https://doi.org/10.7312/aloi18070

Alzate y Ramírez, José Antonio de. "Carta satisfactoria dirigida a un literato por don José de Alzate, autor de la Gaceta Literaria, sobre lo contenido en el suplemento a la de México de 16 de mayo de 1788." In *Linneo en México. Las controversias sobre el sistema binario sexual 1788–1798*, by Roberto Moreno, 19–32. Mexico City: Universidad Nacional Autónoma de México, 1989. https://historicas.unam.mx/publicaciones/publicadigital/libros/251/linneo_mexico.html

Amoureux, Jack, and Varun Reddy. "Multiple Anthropocenes: Pluralizing Space-Time as a Response to 'the Anthropocene.'" *Globalizations* 18, no. 6 (August 18, 2021): 929–46. https://doi.org/10.1080/14747731.2020.1864178

Anchieta, Padre José de. *Carta de São Vicente 1560*. Edited by José Pedro de Oliveira Costa. São Paulo: Conselho Nacional da Reserva da Biosfera da Mata Atlântica, 1997. http://www.rbma.org.br/rbma/pdf/Caderno_07.pdf

Andermann, Jens. *The Optic of the State: Visuality and Power in Argentina and Brazil*. Pittsburgh: University of Pittsburgh Press, 2007. https://doi.org/10.2307/j.ctv10tq44x

Arriarán, Samuel. *Barroco y neobarroco en América Latina: Estudios sobre la otra modernidad*. Mexico, D.F.: Editorial Itaca, 2007.

Arteaga, Rodrigo. "A Natural Selection—Residency by Rodrigo Arteaga—#4." *AirSpace Gallery Blog* (blog), July 13, 2017. http://airspacegallery.blogspot.com/2017/07/a-natural-selection-residency-by_13.html

Auerbach, Jeffrey. "The Picturesque and the Homogenisation of Empire." *The British Art Journal* 5, no. 1 (2004): 47–54.

Baker, Steve. *The Postmodern Animal*. London: Reaktion, 2000.

Balee, William. "The Research Program of Historical Ecology." *Annual Review of Anthropology* 35 (2006): 75–98. https://doi.org/10.1146/annurev.anthro.35.081705.123231

Bandeira, Julio, and Pedro Corrêa do Lago, eds. *Debret e o Brasil: Obra completa 1816–1831*. Rio de Janeiro: Capivara, 2020.

Baraya, Alberto. "Leí El Río en el río." *Piedepágina: Revista de libros* 2 (March 2005). http://www.piedepagina.com/numero2/html/rio.htm

Barber, Richard, trans. *Bestiary [MS Bodley 764]*. Woodbridge: The Boydell Press, 1999.

Barrera-Osorio, Antonio. *Experiencing Nature: The Spanish American Empire and the Early Scientific Revolution*. 1st ed. Austin: University of Texas Press, 2006. https://doi.org/10.7560/709812

Barthes, Roland. *Camera Lucida: Reflections on Photography*. Translated by Richard Howard. London: Vintage, 2000.

Baudelaire, Charles. "The Salon of 1859." In *The Mirror of Art: Critical Studies*, translated by Jonathan Mayne, 217–99. London: Phaidon Press, 1955.

Beck, Ulrich. "Climate for Change, or How to Create a Green Modernity?" *Theory, Culture & Society* 27, no. 2–3 (March 1, 2010): 254–66. https://doi.org/10.1177/0263276409358729

Benjamin, Walter. *Origin of the German Trauerspiel*. Translated by Howard Eiland. Boston: Harvard University Press, 2019. https://doi.org/10.4159/9780674916357

Berger, John. *About Looking*. New York: Vintage, 1992.

Bergero, Patricia, Julio Calzada, Federico Di Yenno, and Emilce Terré. "El Gran Rosario es el nodo portuario agroexportador más importante del mundo." *Bolsa de Comercio de Rosario: Informativo Semanal* XXXVIII, no. 1964 (July 24, 2020). http://www.bcr.com.ar/es/mercados/investigacion-y-desarrollo/informativo-semanal/noticias-informativo-semanal/el-gran-0

Bertuzzi, María Laura. "La costa del río Paraná: cultura, naturaleza y territorio." *Apuntes: Revista de Estudios sobre Patrimonio Cultural* 22, no. 1 (June 2009): 68–81. http://ref.scielo.org/thyvx7

Bhabha, Homi K. *The Location of Culture*. London and New York: Routledge, 1994.

Bleichmar, Daniela. *Visible Empire: Botanical Expeditions and Visual Culture in the Hispanic Enlightenment*. Chicago: University of Chicago Press, 2012. https://doi.org/10.7208/chicago/9780226058559.001.0001

———. *Visual Voyages: Images of Latin American Nature from Columbus to Darwin*. New Haven and London: Yale University Press, 2017.

Boetzkes, Amanda. "Art." In *The Edinburgh Companion to Animal Studies*, edited by Lynn Turner, Undine Sellbach, and Ron Broglio, 65–79. Edinburgh Companions to Literature. Edinburgh, Scotland: Edinburgh University Press, 2018. https://doi.org/10.1515/9781474418423-008

Boivin, Nicole L., Melinda A. Zeder, Dorian Q. Fuller, Alison Crowther, Greger Larson, Jon M. Erlandson, Tim Denham, and Michael D. Petraglia. "Ecological Consequences of Human Niche Construction: Examining Long-Term Anthropogenic Shaping of Global Species Distributions." *Proceedings of the National Academy of Sciences* 113, no. 23 (June 7, 2016): 6388–96. https://doi.org/10.1073/pnas.1525200113

Borges, Jorge Luis, and Margarita Guerrero. *The Book of Imaginary Beings*. Translated by Norman Thomas di Giovanni. Harmondsworth: Penguin, 1974.

Bosteels, Bruno. "Hegel in America." In *Hegel and the Infinite: Religion, Politics, and Dialectic*, edited by Slavoj Žižek, Clayton Crockett, and Creston Davis, 67–90. New York: Columbia University Press, 2011.

Bourke, Eoin. "'The Second Columbus?'" In *Cosmos and Colonialism: Alexander von Humboldt in Cultural Criticism*, edited by Rex Clark and Oliver Lubrich, 258–70. New York and Oxford: Berghahn Books, 2012.

Bóveda, Agatha. "Lo que cambia y lo que permanece. Notas sobre la biodiversidad paranaense." In *Paraná Ra'anga: Un viaje filosófico*, edited by Graciela Silvestri, 241–51. Rosario, Argentina and Barcelona: Centro Cultural Parque de España (CCPE), Agencia Española de Cooperación Internacional y Desarrollo (AECID), Revista Altaïr S. A., 2011.

Braidotti, Rosi. *Transpositions: On Nomadic Ethics*. 1st ed. Oxford: Polity Press, 2006.

Brown, Carmen. "Bestiary Lessons on Pride and Lust." In *The Mark of the Beast: The Medieval Bestiary in Art, Life, and Literature*, edited by Debra Hassig, 53–70. New York and London: Garland Publishing, 1999.

Browne, Montagu. *Practical Taxidermy*. London: "The Bazaar" Office, 1878.

Cabarcas Antequera, Hernando. *Bestiario del Nuevo Reino de Granada: La imaginación animalística medieval y la descripción literaria de la naturaleza americana*. Bogotá: Colcultura, Biblioteca Nacional de Colombia, 1994.

Cacho Casal, Rodrigo. "Introduction: Locating Early Modern Spanish American Poetry." In *The Rise of Spanish American Poetry 1500–1700: Literary and Cultural Transmission in the New World*, edited by Rodrigo Cacho Casal and Imogen Choi, 1–27. Cambridge: Legenda, 2012. https://doi.org/10.2307/j.ctv16kkz3k.4

Calabrese, Omar. *Neo-Baroque: A Sign of the Times*. Translated by Charles Lambert. Princeton, N.J.: Princeton University Press, 1992.

Caldas, Francisco José de. "Del influjo del clima sobre los seres organizados." In *Obras completas de Francisco José de Caldas*, 79–120. Bogotá: Imprenta Nacional, 1966.

Cañizares-Esguerra, Jorge. *Nature, Empire, and Nation: Explorations of the History of Science in the Iberian World*. Stanford: Stanford University Press, 2006. https://doi.org/10.1515/9781503626324

Cardoso, María Fernanda. "Matrimonio entre ciencia y arte: La creación del Museo de Órganos Copulatorios." *Errata#: Revista de artes visuales* 8 (Inter/transdisciplinariedad) (August 2012): 179–83.

———. "The Aesthetics of Reproductive Morphologies." Doctoral thesis, Sydney College of the Arts, The University of Sydney, 2012. https://mariafernandacardoso.com/wp-content/uploads/2019/03/Cardoso.-Maria-Fernanda.-The-Aesthetics-Of-Reproductive-Morphologies.-University-of-Sydney.-2012.pdf

Carpentier, Alejo. "El barroco y lo real maravilloso." In *Razón de ser*, 38–65. Caracas: Universidad Central de Venezuela: Ediciones de Rectorado, 1976.

———. "The Baroque and the Marvelous Real." In *Magical Realism: Theory, History, Community*, edited by Wendy B. Faris and Lois Parkinson Zamora, 89–108. Durham and London: Duke University Press, 1995.

Carrasco González, Guadalupe, Alberto José Gullón Abao, and Arturo Jesús Morgado García. *Las expediciones científicas en los siglos XVII y XVIII*. Madrid: Editorial Síntesis, 2016.

Carreras, Sandra, and Katja Carrillo Zeiter, eds. "Las ciencias en la formación de las naciones americanas: Una introducción." In *Las ciencias en la formación de las naciones americanas*, 9–23. Madrid: Iberoamericana, 2014.

Castro-Gómez, Santiago. *La hybris del punto cero: Ciencia, raza e Ilustración en la Nueva Granada (1750–1816)*. Bogotá: Editorial Pontificia Universidad Javeriana, 2010. http://biblioteca.clacso.edu.ar/Colombia/pensar-puj/20180102042534/hybris.pdf

Cenzi, Ivan. "La natura del mostro." In *Bestiario mexicano*, by Claudio Andrés Salvador Francisco Romo Torres, translated by Federico Taibi, 3–5. Modena: Logosedizione, 2018.

Chakrabarty, Dipesh. "Anthropocene Time." *History and Theory* 57, no. 1 (March 1, 2018): 5–32. https://doi.org/10.1111/hith.12044

Chiampi, Irlemar. "Baroque at the Twilight of Modernity." In *Baroque New Worlds: Representation, Transculturation, Counterconquest*, edited by Lois Parkinson Zamora and Monika Kaup, translated by William Childers, 508–28. Durham and London: Duke University Press, 2010. https://doi.org/10.1215/9780822392521-025

Clark, Nigel. "Aboriginal Cosmopolitanism." *International Journal of Urban and Regional Research* 32, no. 3 (2008): 737–44. https://doi.org/10.1111/j.1468-2427.2008.00811.x

Clement, C. R., J. M. McCann, and N. J. H. Smith. "Agrobiodiversity in Amazônia and Its Relationship with Dark Earths." In *Amazonian Dark Earths: Origin Properties Management*, edited by Johannes Lehmann, Dirse C. Kern, Bruno Glaser, and William I. Woods, 159–78. Dordrecht: Springer, 2004. https://doi.org/10.1007/1-4020-2597-1_9

Coccia, Emanuele. *The Life of Plants: A Metaphysics of Mixture*. Translated by Dylan J. Montanari. Cambridge: Polity Press, 2019.

Cohen, Jeffrey Jerome. "Monster Culture (Seven Theses)." In *Monster Theory: Reading Culture*, edited by Jeffrey Jerome Cohen, 3–25. Minneapolis: University of Minnesota Press, 1996. https://doi.org/10.5749/j.ctttsq4d.4

Comte, Auguste. *A Discourse on the Positive Spirit*. Translated by Edward Spencer Beesly. London: William Reeves, 1903.

Corrin, Lisa Graziose, Kwon Miwon, and Norma Bryson, eds. "Miwon Kwon in Conversation with Mark Dion." In *Mark Dion*, 8–35. London: Phaidon Press, 1997.

Cortázar, Julio. "Polonia y El Salvador: Mayúsculas y minúsculas." In *Papeles inesperados*, edited by Aurora Bernárdez and Carles Álvarez Garriga, 331–35. Buenos Aires: Aguilar, Altea, Taurus, Alfaguara, 2009.

Crary, Jonathan. *Techniques of the Observer: On Vision and Modernity in the Nineteenth Century*. Cambridge, Mass.: MIT Press, 1990.

Crosby, Alfred. *The Columbian Exchange: Biological and Cultural Consequences of 1492*. 30th Anniversary Edition. Westport: Praeger, 2003.

Curley, Michael J. *Physiologus*. Chicago: University of Chicago Press, 2009. https://doi.org/10.7208/chicago/9780226128719.001.0001

Da Câmara Cascudo, Luís. *Geografia dos Mitos Brasileiros*. São Paulo: Global Editora, 2012.

Darwin, Charles. *The Variation of Animals and Plants under Domestication*. Vol. 2. Cambridge: Cambridge University Press, 2010. https://doi.org/10.1017/CBO9780511709517

Daston, Lorraine, and Peter Galison. *Objectivity*. New York: Zone Books, 2010.

Daston, Lorraine, and Katherine Park. *Wonders and the Order of Nature, 1150–1750*. New York: Zone Books, 1998.

Davies, Surekha. "Catalogical Encounters: Worldmaking in Early Modern Cabinets of Curiosities." In *Early Modern Things*, edited by Paula Findlen, 2nd ed., 227–54. London: Routledge, 2021. https://doi.org/10.4324/9781351055741-14

Davis, Wade. *El Río: exploraciones y descubrimientos en la selva amazónica*. Translated by Nicolás Suescún. Bogotá: El Áncora Editores; Fondo de Cultura Económica, 2004.

———. *One River: Explorations and Discoveries in the Amazon Rain Forest*. New York: Simon & Schuster, 1997.

De Assunção, Paulo. *A terra dos brasis: A natureza da América portuguesa vista pelos primeiros jesuítas (1549–1596)*. Kindle edition. São Paulo: Annablume, 2020.

De Asúa, Miguel, and Roger French. *A New World of Animals: Early Modern Europeans on the Creatures of Iberian America*. London and New York: Routledge, 2016.

De Sousa Santos, Boaventura. *Epistemologies of the South: Justice Against Epistemicide*. London and New York: Routledge, 2014.

De Valdenebro, Eulalia. "CUERPOPERMEABLE: Conocer el páramo en el cuerpo." In *Arte y naturaleza*, edited by Dilma Valderrama Gil, 134–42. Bogotá: Universidad Distrital Francisco José de Caldas, 2014.

Debret, J. B. *Viagem pitoresca e histórica ao Brasil*. Translated by Sérgio Milliet. São Paulo: Imprensa Oficial do Estado de São Paulo, 2016.

Deleuze, Gilles. *The Fold: Leibniz and the Baroque*. Translated by Tom Conley. London: The Athlone Press, 1993.

Dendle, Peter. "Cryptozoology in the Medieval and Modern Worlds." *Folklore* 117, no. 2 (August 1, 2006): 190–206. https://doi.org/10.1080/00155870600707888

Denevan, William M. "The Pristine Myth: The Landscape of the Americas in 1492." *Annals of the Association of American Geographers* 82, no. 3 (1992): 369–85. https://doi.org/10.1111/j.1467-8306.1992.tb01965.x

Derrida, Jacques. "The Animal That Therefore I Am (More to Follow)." Translated by David Wills. *Critical Inquiry* 28, no. 2 (Winter 2002): 369–418. https://doi.org/10.1086/449046

Diener, Pablo. "The Traveler Artist: The Construction of Landscape, the Picturesque, and the Sublime." In *Traveler Artists: Landscapes of Latin America from the Patricia Phelps de Cisneros Collection*, edited by Katherine Manthorne, 24–31. New York: Fundación Cisneros, 2015.

Dirección de Poblaciones del Ministerio de Cultura. "Estudios de la lengua Nonuya," 2011. https://www.mincultura.gov.co/areas/poblaciones/APP-de-lenguas-nativas/Paginas/default.aspx

Dussel, Enrique. "Eurocentrism and Modernity (Introduction to the Frankfurt Lectures)." *Boundary 2* 20, no. 3 (1993): 65–76.

Dyer, Katie, and Lizzie Muller. "Objects, Energies and Curating Resonance across Disciplines." In *Curating Lively Objects: Exhibitions Beyond Disciplines*, edited by Lizzie Muller and Caroline Seck Langill, 244–65. London: Routledge, 2022.

Echeverría, Bolívar. *La modernidad de lo barroco*. Mexico, D.F.: Ediciones Era, 2000.

Elliott, David. "Luis Benedit: Del viaje del Beagle." In *Luis F. Benedit en el Museo Nacional de Bellas Artes: obras 1960–1996*, translated by Norman Thomas di Giovanni, 167–70. Buenos Aires: Museo Nacional de Bellas Artes, 1996.

Enenkel, Karl A. E. "The Species and Beyond: Classification and the Place of Hybrids in Early Modern Zoology." In *Zoology in Early Modern Culture: Intersections of Science, Theology, Philology, and Political and Religious Education*, edited by Karl A. E. Enenkel and Paul J. Smith, 55–148. Leiden and Boston: Brill, 2014. https://doi.org/10.1163/9789004279179_004

Eriksson, Gunnar. "Linnaeus the Botanist." In *Linnaeus: The Man and His Work*, edited by Tore Frängsmyr, 63–109. Berkeley and Los Angeles: University of California Press, 1983.

Escobar, Arturo. *Pluriversal Politics: The Real and the Possible*. Translated by David Frye. Durham and London: Duke University Press, 2020. https://doi.org/10.1515/9781478012108

———. "Whose Knowledge, Whose nature? Biodiversity, Conservation, and the Political Ecology of Social Movements." *Journal of Political Ecology* 5, no. 1 (December 1, 1998): 53–82. https://doi.org/10.2458/v5i1.21397

Ette, Ottmar. *Alexander von Humboldt y la globalización. El saber en movimiento*. Mexico City: El Colegio de México, 2019. https://doi.org/10.2307/j.ctvkwnqnd

———. "El Cosmos de la vida: Alexander von Humboldt y su obra mayor." In *Ciencia-Mundo: Orden republicano, arte y nación en América*, edited by Rafael Sagredo Baeza, 321–38. Santiago: Universitaria, Centro de Investigaciones Diego Barros Arana de la DIBAM, 2010.

Fara, Patricia. *Sex, Botany, and Empire: The Story of Carl Linnaeus and Joseph Banks*. Duxford: Icon Books, 2003.

Farías, Claudia. "'El álbum de la flora imprudente': La fantasía botánica de Romo [interview]." *El Sur* [*Concepción, Chile*], February 8, 2008, sec. Espectáculos. http://www.bibliotecanacionaldigital.gob.cl/bnd/628/w3-article-564191.html

Flusser, Vilém. *Towards a Philosophy of Photography*. Translated by Anthony Mathews. London: Reaktion, 2000.

Foucault, Michel. *The Order of Things*. London and New York: Routledge, 1970. https://doi.org/10.4324/9780203996645

Gal, Ofer, and Raz Chen-Morris. "Baroque Modes and the Production of Knowledge." In *Science in the Age of the Baroque*, edited by Ofer Gal and Raz Chen-Morris, 1–9. Dordrecht: Springer Science+Business Media, 2013. https://doi.org/10.1007/978-94-007-4807-1_1

Gangui, Alejandro, Graciela Silvestri, and Pablo Vena. "La expedición Paraná Ra'anga." *Ciencia, Publico y Sociedad* 1 (2012): 100–07. https://docplayer.es/18018543-La-expedicion-parana-ra-anga.html

Gascoigne, John. "Crossing the Pillars of Hercules: Francis Bacon, the Scientific Revolution and the New World." In *Science in the Age of Baroque*, edited by Ofer Gal and Raz Chen-Morris, 217–37. Dordrecht: Springer Science+Business Media, 2013. https://doi.org/10.1007/978-94-007-4807-1_9

Gilardoni, Claudia. "De biología, botánica y cosmología [interview with Rodrigo Arteaga]." *De Libros, Artes y Ciencias*, February 18, 2016. Originally published at http://arteyciencia.leamosmas.com/2016/02/18/entrevista-rodrigo-arteaga but no longer available. Reproduced at http://www.rodrigoarteaga.com/TEXTOS

Gilpin, William. "On Picturesque Beauty." In *Three Essays: On Picturesque Beauty; on Picturesque Travel; and on Sketching Landscape: To Which Is Added a Poem, on Landscape Painting*, 3–33. London: R. Blamire, 1792. https://ota.bodleian.ox.ac.uk/repository/xmlui/bitstream/handle/20.500.12024/K079648.000/K079648.000.html

Gordon, Bob. "Elton John Concert at Chichen Itza Encounters Opposition." *Digital Journal*, April 3, 2010, sec. Entertainment. http://www.digitaljournal.com/article/289969

Greenblatt, Stephen. *Marvelous Possessions: The Wonder of the New World*. Chicago: University of Chicago Press, 1991.

Greene, Roland. "Baroque and Neobaroque: Making Thistory." *PMLA* 124, no. 1 (2009): 150–55. https://doi.org/10.1632/pmla.2009.124.1.150

Gretler, Corinne, and Angus Whitley. "Nestle Pulls Beso de Negra, Red Skins Candy in Racial Review." *Bloomberg.Com*, June 2, 2020. https://www.bloomberg.com/news/articles/2020-06-22/nestle-pulls-beso-de-negra-candy-reviews-portfolio-for-racism

Grupo de Investigación en Derechos Colectivos y Ambientales (GIDC), Colombia. "El despojo de la propiedad intelectual a través del Convenio UPOV 91." *Revista Semillas* 53/54 (January 28, 2014). https://www.semillas.org.co/es/el-despojo-de-la-propiedad-intelectual-a-trav

Gruzinski, Serge. "The Baroque Planet." In *Ultrabaroque: Aspects of Post-Latin American Art*, edited by Elizabeth Armstrong, translated by Susan M. Berkeley, 111–25. La Jolla, C.A.: Museum of Contemporary Art, San Diego, 2009.

———. *The Mestizo Mind: The Intellectual Dynamics of Colonization and Globalization*. Translated by Deke Dusinberre. Oxford and New York: Taylor & Francis Group, 2012. https://doi.org/10.4324/9781315023267

Gutiérrez, Natalia. "Anexo 1: entrevista con José Alejandro Restrepo." In *Cruces: una reflexión sobre la crítica de arte y la obra de José Alejandro Restrepo*, 80–111. Bogotá: Alcaldía Mayor de Bogotá, 2000. https://icaa.mfah.org/s/en/item/1091801

Haraway, Donna. *Simians, Cyborgs, and Women: The Reinvention of Nature*. New York: Routledge, 1990. https://doi.org/10.4324/9780203873106

———. "Teddy Bear Patriarchy: Taxidermy in the Garden of Eden, New York City, 1908–1936." *Social Text*, no. 11 (1984): 20–64. https://doi.org/10.2307/466593

Hegel, Georg Wilhelm Friedrich. *Lectures on the Philosophy of World History*. Translated by Hugh Barr Nisbet. Cambridge Studies in the History and Theory of Politics. Cambridge: Cambridge University Press, 1975. https://doi.org/10.1017/CBO9781139167567

Heise, Ursula K. *Imagining Extinction: The Cultural Meanings of Endangered Species*. Chicago: University of Chicago Press, 2016. https://doi.org/10.7208/chicago/9780226358338.001.0001

Henderson, Caspar. *The Book of Barely Imagined Beings: A 21st Century Bestiary*. Chicago: Chicago University Press, 2013. https://doi.org/10.7208/chicago/9780226044842.001.0001

Hooke, Robert. *Robert Hooke: The Posthumous Works*. Edited by Richard Waller and Bernhard Fabian. Vol. 3. Oxford and New York: Routledge, 2018.

Hornaday, William T., and W. J. Holland. *Taxidermy and Zoological Collecting: A Complete Handbook for the Amateur Taxidermist, Collector, Osteologist, Museum-Builder, Sportsman, and Traveller*. 4th ed. New York: Charles Scribner's Sons, 1894. https://www.biodiversitylibrary.org/item/20686

Hughes, Zoe. "Performing Taxidermy or the De- and Reconstruction of Animal Faces in Service of Animal Futures." *Configurations* 27, no. 2 (2019): 163–86. https://doi.org/10.1353/con.2019.0011

Hui, Yuk. *Art and Cosmotechnics*. Minneapolis: University of Minnesota Press, 2021. https://doi.org/10.5749/j.ctv1qgnq42

———. *The Question Concerning Technology in China: An Essay in Cosmotechnics*. Falmouth, UK: Urbanomic, 2016.

Humboldt, Alexander von. *Cosmos: Sketch of a Physical Description of the Universe*. Edited by Edward Sabine. Vol. 2. Cambridge: Cambridge University Press, 2010. https://doi.org/10.1017/CBO9780511708992

———. *Letters of Alexander Von Humboldt: Written between the Years 1827 and 1858, to Varnhagen Von Ense; Together with Extracts from Varnhagen's Diaries, and Letters from Varnhagen and Others to Humboldt*. Cambridge: Cambridge University Press, 2009. https://doi.org/10.1017/cbo9780511694035

Humboldt, Alexander von. *Mi viaje por el camino del Inca (1801–1802): Quito, Cuenca, Cajamarca, Trujillo, Lima. Antología*. Edited by David Yudilevich L. Santiago: Editorial Universitaria, 2006.

———. *Personal Narrative of a Journey to the Equinoctial Regions of the New Continent*. Translated by Jason Wilson. London: Penguin, 1995.

———. *Views of the Cordilleras and Monuments of the Indigenous Peoples of the Americas: A Critical Edition*. Edited by Vera M. Kutzinski and Ottmar Ette. Translated by J. Ryan Poynter. Chicago: University of Chicago Press, 2013. https://doi.org/10.7208/chicago/9780226865096.001.0001

Hume, David. *An Enquiry Concerning Human Understanding*. Edited by Peter Millican. Oxford: Oxford University Press, 2007. https://doi.org/10.1017/cbo9780511808432

Hurtado, Diego. *La ciencia argentina: Un proyecto inconcluso: 1930–2000*. Buenos Aires: Edhasa, 2010.

Impey, Oliver, and Arthur MacGregor. "Introduction." In *The Origins of Museums: The Cabinet of Curiosities in Sixteenth- and Seventeenth-Century Europe*, edited by Oliver Impey and Arthur MacGregor, xvii–xx. London: House of Stratus, 2001.

Ingold, Tim. *Being Alive: Essays on Movement, Knowledge and Description.* London: Taylor & Francis, 2011.

———. "Introduction." In *What Is an Animal?*, edited by Tim Ingold, 1–16. London and New York: Routledge, 1988.

Instituto Latinoamericano de Investigación en Artes. "Entrevista a Cristian Villavicencio," n.d. https://soundcloud.com/user-979859888/entrevista-a-cristian-villavicencio

Jara, Fernanda. "Situación crítica del yaguareté: en Argentina quedan menos de 250 y salvarlo parece una utopía." *infobae*, September 24, 2017. https://www.infobae.com/sociedad/2017/09/24/situacion-critica-del-yaguarete-en-argentina-quedan-menos-de-250-y-salvarlo-parece-una-utopia/

Kareiva, Peter, and Michelle Marvier. "What Is Conservation Science?" *Bioscience* 62, no. 11 (2012): 962–69.

Kaup, Monika. *Neobaroque in the Americas: Alternative Modernities in Literature, Visual Art, and Film.* Charlottesville and London: University of Virginia Press, 2012.

Klein, Naomi. *This Changes Everything: Capitalism vs. the Climate.* New York: Simon & Schuster, 2014.

Kreimer, Pablo. *Ciencia y periferia: Nacimiento, muerte y resurrección de la biología molecular en la Argentina.* Buenos Aires: Eudeba, 2010.

Kueva, Fabiano. "Archivo Alexander von Humboldt." In *Museología crítica: temas selectos. Reflexiones sobre la Cátedra William Bullock / Critical Museology: Selected Themes. Reflections from the William Bullock Lecture Series*, edited by Ekaterina Álvarez Romero, 137–53. Mexico City: Museo Universitario Arte Contemporáneo (MUAC), 2019. https://secureservercdn.net/50.62.89.111/8e9.cab.myftpupload.com/wp-content/uploads/2020/07/cuadernos_muac-catedra_bullock.pdf

———. "Archivo Alexander von Humboldt: Interferencias sobre un canon." In *Archivo Alexander von Humboldt* [*exhibition catalogue*], 16–51. Mexico City: Ex Teresa Arte Actual, 2019. https://issuu.com/exteresaarteactual/docs/archivo_alexander_von_humboldt

La Padula, Pablo. "La red de humo: Por una teoría gaseosa de la vida." *Blanco sobre blanco: Miradas y lecturas sobre artes visuales* 7 (May 2015): 57–65.

Lafuente, Antonio. "Enlightenment in an Imperial Context: Local Science in the Late-Eighteenth-Century Hispanic World." *Osiris* 15 (2000): 155–73. https://doi.org/10.1086/649324

Lafuente, Antonio, and Nuria Valverde. "Linnaean Botany and Spanish Imperial Biopolitics." In *Colonial Botany: Science, Commerce, and Politics in the Early Modern World*, edited by Londa Schiebinger and Claudia Swan, 134–47. Philadelphia: University of Pennsylvania Press, 2005.

Latour, Bruno. *Pandora's Hope: Essays on the Reality of Science Studies*. Cambridge, Mass. and London: Harvard University Press, 1999.

———. "Visualisation and Cognition: Drawing Things Together." In *Knowledge and Society: Studies in the Sociology of Culture Past and Present*, edited by H. Kuklick, Vol. 6. Greenwich, CT: Jai Press, 1986.

———. *We Have Never Been Modern*. Cambridge, Mass.: Harvard University Press, 1993.

Lavigne, Nathalia. "The Naturalization of Whiteness as a Life Parameter [Interview with Tiago Sant'Ana]." *C& América Latina*, March 18, 2019. https://amlatina.contemporaryand.com/editorial/a-naturalizacao-da-branquitude-como-parametro-de-vida-tiago-santana/

Leff, Enrique. *Discursos sustentables*. Mexico: Siglo XXI, 2008.

———. "On the Social Reappropriation of Nature." *Capitalism, Nature, Socialism* 10, no. 3 (1999): 89–104. https://doi.org/10.1080/10455759909358876

———. "Power-Knowledge Relations in the Field of Political Ecology." *Ambiente & Sociedade* 20, no. 3 (September 2017): 225–56. https://doi.org/10.1590/1809-4422asocex0004v2032017

Lewis, Simon L., and Mark A. Maslin. *The Human Planet: How We Created the Anthropocene*. London: Pelican, 2018.

Lezama Lima, José. "Baroque Curiosity." In *Baroque New Worlds: Representation, Transculturation, Counterconquest*, edited by Lois Parkinson Zamora and Monika Kaup, translated by William Childers, 212–40. Durham and London: Duke University Press, 2010. https://doi.org/10.1215/9780822392521-012

———. *La expresión americana*. La Habana: Inst. Nacional de Cultura, Ministerio de Educación, 1957.

Linnaeus, Carolus. *Systema Naturae. Facsimile of the First Edition*. Utrecht: HES & De Graaf Publishers, 2003.

Linné, Carl von. *Diaeta naturalis, 1733: Linnés tankar om ett naturenligt levnadssätt*. Edited by Arvid Hjalmar Uggla. Uppsala: Almqvist & Wiksell, 1958.

———. *Förspel till Växternas Bröllop = Prelude to the Betrothal of Plants: Faksimil Med Svensk Transkription Och Engelsk Översättning Av Praeludia Sponsaliorum Plantarum 1729 = Facsimile with a Swedish Transciption and an English Translation of Praeludia Sponsaliorum Plantarum 1729*. Edited by Xtina Wootz and Krister Östlund. Uppsala: Uppsala Universitetsbibliothek, 2007.

———. *Linnaeus' Philosophia Botanica*. Translated by Stephen Freer. Oxford: Oxford University Press, 2005.

Lippit, Akira Mizuta. *Electric Animal: Toward a Rhetoric of Wildlife*. Minneapolis: University of Minnesota Press, 2000.

Luna, Sergio. "La voz interrogada: Entrevista con Rafael Toriz." *Definitivamente Jueves* [*Revista de Literatura de El Columnista*] 0, no. 19 (April 23, 2009): 2–3. https://circulodepoesia.com/wp-content/uploads/2009/06/Definitivamente-Jueves-No.19.pdf

MacGregor, Arthur. *Curiosity and Enlightenment: Collectors and Collections from the Sixteenth to the Nineteenth Century*. New Haven and London: Yale University Press, 2007.

Maciel, Maria Esther. "Imagens zoológicas da América Latina." *Gragoatá* 6, no. 10 (June 30, 2001): 89–96. https://periodicos.uff.br/gragoata/article/view/49020

Maffi, Luisa, and Ellen Woodley. *Biocultural Diversity Conservation: A Global Sourcebook*. London: Taylor & Francis Group, 2010.

Marbury, Robert. *Taxidermy Art: A Rogue's Guide to the Work, the Culture, and How to Do It Yourself*. 1st edition. New York: Artisan, 2014.

Marcaida, José Ramón, and Juan Pimentel. "Green Treasures and Paper Floras: The Business of Mutis in New Granada (1783–1808)." *History of Science* 52, no. 3 (September 2014): 277–96. https://doi.org/10.1177/0073275314546967

Marcaida López, José Ramón. *Arte y ciencia en el barroco español: Historia natural, coleccionismo y cultural visual*. Seville and Madrid: Fundación Focus-Abengoa and Marcial Pons, 2014.

Marcaida López, José Ramón, and Juan Pimentel. "Dead Natures or Still Lives? Science, Art and Collecting in the Spanish Baroque." In *Collecting Across Cultures: Material Exchanges in the Early Modern Atlantic World*, edited by Daniela Bleichmar and Peter Mancall, 99–105. Philadelphia: University of Pennsylvania Press, 2011. https://doi.org/10.9783/9780812204964.99

Marks, Laura U. *The Skin of the Film: Intercultural Cinema, Embodiment, and the Senses*. Duke University Press, 2000. https://doi.org/10.1215/9780822381372

Mauriès, Patrick. *Cabinets of Curiosities*. London: Thames and Hudson, 2002.

Maynard, Charles Johnson. *Manual of Taxidermy: A Complete Guide in Collecting and Preserving Birds and Mammals*. Boston: S.E. Cassino and Co, 1883.

Melville, Elinor G. K. *A Plague of Sheep: Environmental Consequences of the Conquest of Mexico*. Studies in Environment and History. Cambridge: Cambridge University Press, 1994. https://doi.org/10.1017/CBO9780511571091

Mendoza, Diego. *Expedición botánica de José Celestino Mutis al Nuevo Reino de Granada y memorias inéditas de Francisco José de Caldas*. Madrid: Libreria General de Victoriano Suarez, 1909.

Mergler, Agata, and Cristian Villavicencio. "Collaboration, Media, Praxis: Haptic/Visual Identities Project." *Post(s)* 3, no. 1 (2017): 188–208. https://doi.org/10.18272/posts.v3i1.1006

Mignolo, Walter D. *The Idea of Latin America*. Oxford: Blackwell, 2005.

Minguet, Carlos. "La obra de Humboldt." In *Carlos III y la ciencia de la Ilustración*, edited by Manuel Sellés, José Luis Peset, and Antonio Lafuente, 387–402. Madrid: Alianza, 1988.

Molina, Enrique, and Jorge Glusberg. *Luis Fernando Benedit: Memorias australes desde el Río de la Plata hasta el Canal del Beagle*. Buenos Aires: Ediciones Philippe Daverio, 1990.

Moraña, Mabel. *La escritura del límite*. Madrid and Frankfurt: Iberoamericana and Vervuert, 2010. https://doi.org/10.31819/9783964566355

Morris, P. A. *A History of Taxidermy: Art, Science and Bad Taste*. Ascot, UK: MPM, 2010.

Müller-Wille, Staffan. "Linnaeus and the Love Lives of Plants." In *Reproduction: Antiquity to the Present Day*, edited by Lauren Kassell, Nick Hopwood, and Rebecca Flemming, 305–18. Cambridge: Cambridge University Press, 2018. https://doi.org/10.1017/9781107705647.028

Murphy Turner, Madeline. "Historias del paisaje durante la colonización de América [interview with José Alejandro Restrepo]." *MOMA Magazine*, October 6, 2020. https://www.moma.org/magazine/articles/430

Narro, Itziar. "El artista Alberto Baraya se inventa herbarios con flores artificiales [interview with Alberto Baraya]." *Architectural Digest España*, September 8, 2020. https://www.revistaad.es/decoracion/jardines-y-plantas/articulos/artista-alberto-baraya-inventa-herbarios-flores-artificiales/27139

Nettle, Daniel, and Suzanne Romaine. *Vanishing Voices: The Extinction of the World's Languages*. Oxford: Oxford University Press, 2000.

Neuhaus, Jessamyn. "Colonizing The Coffee Table: 'National Geographic' Magazine and Erasure of Difference in the Representation of Women." *American Periodicals* 7 (1997): 1–26.

Nieto Olarte, Mauricio. *Remedios para el imperio: historia natural y la apropiación del nuevo mundo*. Bogotá: Ediciones Uniandes, 2006. https://journals.openedition.org/revestudsoc/28712

Orbigny, Alcide Dessalines d'. *Voyage dans l'Amérique méridionale*. Vol. 1. Paris: Chez Pitois-Levrault et ce., 1835. https://www.biodiversitylibrary.org/item/163116#page/7/mode/1up

Pacheco, José Emilio. *El reposo del fuego*. Mexico City: Ediciones Era, 1999.

Padrón, Juan Nicolás, and Claudio Romo. *Bestiario: Animales reales fantásticos*. Santiago: Ediciones LOM, 2008.

Page, Sophie. "Good Creation and Demonic Illusions: The Medieval Universe of Creatures." In *A Cultural History of Animals in the Medieval Age*, edited by Brigitte Resl, 2:27–58. London: Berg, 2007. https://doi.org/10.5040/9781350049512-ch-001

Pimentel, Juan. "Baroque Natures: Juan E. Nieremberg, American Wonders, and Preterimperial Natural History." In *Science in the Spanish and Portuguese Empires, 1500–1800*, edited by Daniela Bleichmar, Paula De Vos, Kristin Huffine, and Kevin Sheehan, 93–111. Stanford: Stanford University Press, 2009. https://doi.org/10.1515/9780804776332-011

———. *Testigos del mundo: ciencia, literatura y viajes en la ilustración*. Madrid: Marcial Pons Historia, 2003.

Plato. *Cratylus*. Translated by B. Jowett. Project Gutenberg EBook, n.d. https://www.gutenberg.org/files/1616/1616-h/1616-h.htm

Podgorny, Irina, and Maria Margaret Lopes. *El desierto en una vitrina: Museos e historia natural en la Argentina, 1810–1890*. Mexico: Editorial Limusa, 2008.

Poliquin, Rachel. *The Breathless Zoo: Taxidermy and the Cultures of Longing*. Pennsylvania: Pennsylvania State University Press, 2012. https://doi.org/10.1515/9780271059617

Pollan, Michael. *The Botany of Desire: A Plant's-Eye View of the World*. London: Bloomsbury, 2001.

Pratt, Mary Louise. "Alexander von Humboldt and the Reinvention of America." In *Cosmos and Colonialism: Alexander von Humboldt in Cultural Criticism*, edited by Rex Clark and Oliver Lubrich, 240–57. New York and Oxford: Berghahn Books, 2012.

———. *Imperial Eyes: Travel Writing and Transculturation*. 2nd ed. London and New York: Routledge, 2008.

Purugganan, Michael D., and Dorian Q. Fuller. "The Nature of Selection during Plant Domestication." *Nature* 457, no. 7231 (February 2009): 843–48. https://doi.org/10.1038/nature07895

Quijano, Aníbal. "Colonialidad del poder, cultura y conocimiento en América Latina." *Dispositio* 24, no. 51 (1999): 137–48.

———. "Colonialidad del poder, eurocentrismo y América Latina." In *La colonialidad del saber: Eurocentrismo y ciencias sociales. Perspectivas latinoamericanas*, edited by E. Lander, 201–46. Buenos Aires: CLACSO, 2000.

Quijano, Aníbal, and Immanuel Wallerstein. "Americanity as a Concept, or the Americas in the Modern World-System." *International Journal of Social Sciences* 134 (1992): 549–57.

Rader, Karen R., and Victoria E. M. Cain. *Life on Display: Revolutionizing U.S. Museums of Science and Natural History in the Twentieth Century*. Chicago and London: University of Chicago Press, 2014. https://doi.org/10.7208/chicago/9780226079837.001.0001

Ramírez Maldonado, Camila. "Fragmentando la unidad: análisis de la representación territorial chilena en el atlas de 1854." In *Imaginando América Latina: historia y cultura visual siglos XIX–XXI*, edited by Sven Schuster and Oscar D. Hernández Quiñones, 173–201. Bogotá: Editorial Universidad del Rosario, 2017.

Rausch, Gisela Ariana. "Privatización, eficiencia e integración: la 'verdad' sobre la Hidrovía Paraguay–Paraná en la Argentina de los 90." *Íconos: Revista de Ciencias Sociales*, no. 69 (2021): 143–62. https://doi.org/10.17141/iconos.69.2021.4202

Reboratti, Carlos. "El Paraná: una pequeña geografía." In *Paraná Ra'anga: Un viaje filosófico*, edited by Graciela Silvestri, 44–48. Rosario, Argentina and Barcelona: Centro Cultural Parque de España (CCPE), Agencia Española de Cooperación Internacional y Desarrollo (AECID), Revista Altaïr S. A., 2011.

Restrepo, José Alejandro. *Musa paradisíaca: una video-instalación* [*exhibition catalogue*]. Bogotá: Instituto Colombiano de Cultura, 1997. https://icaa.mfah.org/s/en/item/854880

Rivera-Núñez, Tlacaelel, Lane Fargher, and Ronald Nigh. "Toward an Historical Agroecology: An Academic Approach in Which Time and Space Matter." *Agroecology and Sustainable Food Systems* 44, no. 8 (September 13, 2020): 975–1011. https://doi.org/10.1080/21683565.2020.1719450

Robbins, Paul, and Sarah A. Moore. "Ecological Anxiety Disorder: Diagnosing the Politics of the Anthropocene." *Cultural Geographies* 20, no. 1 (January 1, 2013): 3–19. https://doi.org/10.1177/1474474012469887

Robertson, Kellie. *Nature Speaks: Medieval Literature and Aristotelian Philosophy*. Philadelphia: University of Pennsylvania Press, 2017. https://doi.org/10.9783/9780812293678

Rodríguez, Abel. *Las plantas cultivadas por la gente de centro en la Amazonia colombiana*. Bogotá: Tropenbos Internacional Colombia, 2013.

Romo Torres, Claudio Andrés Salvador Francisco. *Bestiario mexicano*. Translated by Federico Taibi. Modena: Logosedizione, 2018.

Rosenzweig, Michael L. *Win-Win Ecology: How the Earth's Species Can Survive in the Midst of Human Enterprise*. New York: Oxford University Press, 2003.

Rossi, Michael. "Fabricating Authenticity: Modeling a Whale at the American Museum of Natural History, 1906–1974." *Isis* 101, no. 2 (2010): 338–61. https://doi.org/10.1086/653096

Saer, Juan José. *El río sin orillas: Tratado imaginario*. Buenos Aires: Planeta, 1991.

Sagredo Baeza, Rafael. "Ciencia, historia y arte como política. El Estado y la *Historia física y política de Chile* de Claudio Gay." In *Ciencia-Mundo: Orden republicano, arte y nación en América*, edited by Rafael Sagredo Baeza, 165–233. Santiago: Universitaria, Centro de Investigaciones Diego Barros Arana de la DIBAM, 2010.

———. "El Atlas de Claude Gay y la representación de Chile." *Cahiers des Amériques latines*, no. 43 (July 31, 2003): 123–42. https://doi.org/10.4000/cal.7309

Salgado, César Augusto. "Hybridity in New World Baroque Theory." *The Journal of American Folklore* 112, no. 445 (Summer 1999): 316–31.

Sarduy, Severo. "El barroco y el neobarroco." In *América Latina y su literatura*, edited by César Fernández Moreno, 167–84. Buenos Aires: Siglo XXI, 1972. https://openlibrary.org/books/OL5483269M/Ame%CC%81rica_Latina_en_su_literatura

———. "The Baroque and the Neobaroque." In *Baroque New Worlds: Representation, Transculturation, Counterconquest*, edited by Lois Parkinson Zamora and Monika Kaup, translated by Christopher Winks, 270–91. Durham and London: Duke University Press, 2010. https://doi.org/10.1215/9780822392521-015

Scheicher, Elisabeth. "The Collection of Archduke Ferdinand II at Schloss Ambras: Its Purpose, Composition and Evolution." In *The Origins of Museums: The Cabinet of Curiosities in Sixteenth- and Seventeenth-Century Europe*, edited by Oliver Impey and Arthur MacGregor, 37–50. London: House of Stratus, 2001.

Schiebinger, Londa. "Gender and Natural History." In *Cultures of Natural History*, edited by N. Jardine, J. A. Secord, and E. C. Spary, 163–77. Cambridge: Cambridge University Press, 1996.

Schmídel, Ulrich. *Viaje al río de la Plata, 1534–1554*. Alicante: Biblioteca Virtual Miguel de Cervantes, 2001. http://www.cervantesvirtual.com/obra-visor/viaje-al-rio-de-la-plata-1534-1554/html/

Silvestri, Graciela. "La historia de una idea." In *Paraná Ra'anga: Un viaje filosófico*, edited by Graciela Silvestri, 30–37. Rosario, Argentina and Barcelona: Centro Cultural Parque de España (CCPE), Agencia Española de Cooperación Internacional y Desarrollo (AECID), Revista Altaïr S. A., 2011.

———. *Las tierras desubicadas: Paisajes y culturas en la Sudamérica fluvial*. Paraná, Argentina: EDUNER [Universidad Nacional de Entre Ríos], 2021.

Silvestri, Graciela, Daniel García Helder, María Moreno, and Martín Prieto. "Diario de bitácora: El Paraná Medio." In *Paraná Ra'anga: Un viaje filosófico*, edited by Graciela Silvestri, 100–45. Rosario, Argentina and Barcelona: Centro Cultural Parque de España (CCPE), Agencia Española de Cooperación Internacional y Desarrollo (AECID), Revista Altaïr S. A., 2011.

———. "Diario de bitácora: Río Paraguay." In *Paraná Ra'anga: Un viaje filosófico*, edited by Graciela Silvestri, 146–66. Rosario, Argentina and Barcelona: Centro Cultural Parque de España (CCPE), Agencia Española de Cooperación Internacional y Desarrollo (AECID), Revista Altaïr S. A., 2011.

Simpson, Mark. "Powers of Liveness: Reading Hornaday's Camp-Fires." In *The Culture of Hunting*, edited by Jean L. Manore and Dale Miner, 56–86. Vancouver: UBC Press, 2006.

Smith, Raechell, and Mark Bessire. "Introduction." In *Cryptozoology: Out of Time Place Scale*, edited by Raechell Smith and Mark Bessire, 8–11. Lewiston, Maine; Zurich, Switzerland: Bates College Museum of Art and JRP Editions, 2006.

Soares, Daphne. "An Ancient Sensory Organ in Crocodilians." *Nature* 417 (2002): 241–42. https://doi.org/10.1038/417241a

Sontag, Susan. *On Photography*. New York: Penguin, 1977.

Soulé, Michael E. "What Is Conservation Biology?" *BioScience* 35, no. 11 (1985): 727–34. https://doi.org/10.2307/1310054

Stafford, Barbara Maria. *Artful Science: Enlightenment Entertainment and the Eclipse of Visual Education*. Cambridge, Mass.: The MIT Press, 1994.

Svampa, Maristella, and Enrique Viale. *El colapso ecológico ya llegó*. Buenos Aires: Siglo XXI, 2020.

Swyngedouw, Erik. "Depoliticized Environments: The End of Nature, Climate Change and the Post-Political Condition." *Royal Institute of Philosophy Supplement* 69 (2011): 253–74. https://doi.org/10.1017/S1358246111000300

The World Bank. "Southern Cone Inland Waterways Transportation Study. The Paraguay–Paraná Hidrovía: Its Role in the Regional Economy and Impact on Climate Change." Sustainable Development Department: Latin America and the Caribbean Region, March 2010. https://documents1.worldbank.org/curated/en/899101468091487396/pdf/549000ESW0WHIT1a0Report010NewFinal.pdf

Thomas, Keith. *Man and the Natural World: Changing Attitudes in England 1500–1800*. London: Allen Lane, 1983.

Thurner, Mark, and Jorge Cañizares-Esguerra, eds. *The Invention of Humboldt: On the Geopolitics of Knowledge*. Abingdon: Routledge, 2022.

Toriz, Rafael, and Édgar Cano. *Animalia*. Mexico City: Vanilla Planifolia, 2015.

Uribe Uribe, Lorenzo. "Los maestros pintores." In *Flora de la Real Expedición Botánica del Nuevo Reino de Granada*, 1:102–6. Madrid: Ediciones Cultura Hispánica, 1954. https://bibdigital.rjb.csic.es/viewer/15841

Varsavsky, Oscar. *Ciencia, política y cientificismo*. Buenos Aires: Capital Intelectual, 2010.

Villavicencio, Cristian. "Dimensiones paralelas." In *Dimensiones paralelas*, 49–51. Bilbao: Fundación Bilbaoarte Fundazioa, 2017.

Viveiros de Castro, Eduardo. *The Relative Native: Essays on Indigenous Conceptual Worlds*. Chicago: HAU, 2015.

Viveiros de Castro, Eduardo, and Déborah Danowski. "Humans and Terrans in the Gaia War." In *A World of Many Worlds*, edited by Marisol De la Cadena and Mario Blaser, 172–203. Durham and London: Duke University Press, 2018. https://doi.org/10.1215/9781478004318-007

Wantzen, Karl Matthias, Aziz Ballouche, Isabelle Longuet, Ibrahima Bao, Hamady Bocoum, Lassana Cissé, Malavika Chauhan, et al. "River Culture: An Eco-Social Approach to Mitigate the Biological and Cultural Diversity Crisis in Riverscapes." *Ecohydrology & Hydrobiology*, New Challenges and

Dimensions of Ecohydrology, Part II, 16, no. 1 (February 1, 2016): 7–18. https://doi.org/10.1016/j.ecohyd.2015.12.003

Wellen, Michael. "José Alejandro Restrepo: The Geography of a Video Installation." In *Contingent Beauty: Contemporary Art from Latin America*, edited by Mari Carmen Ramírez, 176–85. Houston: Museum of Fine Arts Houston, 2016.

Weston, Dagmar Motycka. "'Worlds in Miniature': Some Reflections on Scale and the Microcosmic Meaning of Cabinets of Curiosities." *Arq: Architectural Research Quarterly* 13, no. 1 (March 2009): 37–48. https://doi.org/10.1017/S135913550999008X

White, T. H., ed. *The Book of Beasts, Being a Translation from a Latin Bestiary of the Twelfth Century.* New York: Dover, 2020.

Whyte, Kyle. "Indigenous Climate Change Studies: Indigenizing Futures, Decolonizing the Anthropocene." *English Language Notes* 55, no. 1 (2017): 153–62. https://doi.org/10.1215/00138282-55.1-2.153

Williams, Raymond. *Culture and Materialism: Selected Essays.* London and New York: Verso, 2005.

Wonders, Karen. "Habitat Dioramas as Ecological Theatre." *European Review* 1, no. 3 (July 1993): 285–300. https://doi.org/10.1017/S1062798700000673

Wood, Marcus. *Black Milk: Imagining Slavery in the Visual Cultures of Brazil and America.* Oxford: Oxford University Press, 2013. https://doi.org/10.1093/acprof:oso/9780199274574.001.0001

Yelin, Julieta. *La letra salvaje: Ensayos sobre literatura y animalidad.* Rosario: Beatriz Viterbo Editora, 2015.

Yusoff, Kathryn. *A Billion Black Anthropocenes or None.* Kindle edition. Minneapolis: University of Minnesota Press, 2018. https://doi.org/10.5749/9781452962054

Zambrano, Jéssica. "Cristian Villavicencio subvierte lo objetivo." *El Telégrafo.* May 25, 2019, sec. Cultura. https://www.eltelegrafo.com.ec/noticias/cultura/10/cristian-villavicencio-objetivo

Zarrilli, Adrián. "Bosques y agricultura: Una mirada a los límites históricos de sustentabilidad de los bosques argentinos en un contexto de la explotación capitalista en el siglo XX." *Luna Azul* 26 (2008): 87–106. https://doi.org/10.17151/luaz.2008.26.6

Index

Acosta, José de 11, 40
Aedo, Tania 22
Africa, African 1, 102–104, 192, 211, 243
Agamben, Giorgio 27
agribusiness 108–110, 134
agroecology 108–110, 135, 244
Albertus Magnus 11
albums 2–4, 19, 137, 140, 147–149, 163–164, 172–175, 179–180
Aleijadinho 239
Aloi, Giovanni 202, 211, 228–229, 232
Alvarado, Fernando 87
Alzate y Ramírez, José Antonio de 133
Amazonian 18, 123, 131, 140
American Museum of Natural History (AMNH) 202, 211, 215, 234
Amerindian 41, 46, 243
Amoureux, Jack 144
Anchieta, Padre José de 5–6, 48–50, 54, 61, 230
Andermann, Jens 226–227
animals
  legendary or mythical 3, 9–10, 25–32, 34, 36–37, 39–47, 49–59, 82
  nonhuman 1, 10, 25–38, 40, 44–49, 52, 54–55, 59–61, 87, 95, 99, 116–117, 120–121, 124–125, 128, 130, 133, 141, 152, 154–155, 165–167, 176, 195, 202
  as specimens for display 67, 70–71, 73, 76–81, 86, 168–169
  as taxidermy objects 20, 198, 201–223, 225–234, 236, 238
Antequera, Hernando Cabarcas 56

Anthropocene 3, 12, 13, 14, 15, 16, 19, 60, 134, 144, 146, 153, 156, 157, 235, 237. *See also* anthropocentrism; post-anthropocentrism; *See also* temporality
anthropocentrism 21, 46–47, 59, 61, 131, 203
anthropometry 112–113, 138
anthropomorphism 29, 32–33, 59–60, 112–113, 115–116, 119–120, 131, 246
Archivo General de Indias 82, 177
Argentina, Argentine 17–20, 64–65, 67–68, 74, 81, 142–143, 146–150, 153–154, 156, 164–165, 177, 203, 209–210, 212, 234–235
Aristotle, Aristotelian 11, 25, 75
Armand'Ugon, Roberto Gardiol 224
Arreola, Juan José 16, 26–27, 29
Arteaga, Rodrigo 19–20, 22, 164, 167–172, 179, 200, 203, 213–218, 231, 235–236, 238, 246
Asunción 18, 142, 145
Atlantic ocean 5, 48, 145, 187
atlases 2–4, 19, 137, 163–164, 167–172, 179–180
Aztec 34, 36–37, 55

Badawi, Halim 23, 183
Baraya, Alberto 18, 22, 95–100, 102–105, 133, 138–141, 238, 244, 246
baroque. *See also* decolonial neobaroque
  aesthetics 75, 105, 238, 243
  co-option in Latin American art 21, 41, 237, 239–240, 242

folds 20, 105, 241
postmodern neobaroque 20, 238–242
Barthes, Roland 204
Baudelaire, Charles 92
Becerro, Antonio 202
Beck, Ulrich 13–14
Benedit, Luis Fernando 165–167
Benjamin, Walter 91
Berger, John 33
Bermúdez, Antonio 19, 23, 164, 182, 184, 200, 247
Bertuzzi, María Laura 159
Bessire, Mark 49, 56
bestiaries 2, 3–6, 9–11, 25–61
Bhabha, Homi 242
biocultural diversity 123–124, 135
biodiversity 14, 16, 18, 95–96, 112, 123, 125, 127–128, 155, 159, 179, 212–213, 226, 237, 244, 246–247
Bleichmar, Daniela 4–5, 94–95, 97, 105, 137
Boetzkes, Amanda 203, 205
Bogotá 22, 105–106, 123, 182
Boivin, Nicole L. 128–129
Bonnier, Gaston 169
Bonpland, Aimé 186, 196–197
Borges, Jorge Luis 16, 26–27, 29, 39, 52, 59
Bosteels, Bruno 2
botanical illustration 18, 93, 95–97, 99, 105–108, 112, 123–134. *See also* Floras; *See also* Herbaria
Bourke, Eoin 192
Bóveda, Ágatha 155–156, 158
Braidotti, Rosi 246
Brazil, Brazilian 16, 19–20, 22, 27, 35, 47–50, 52, 55, 57, 61, 96, 98, 104, 130, 140–141, 164, 172–173, 175, 179, 202–204, 208, 219, 227–228, 230–231, 233, 243
Buenos Aires 18, 23, 65, 67–68, 74, 142, 145, 177, 234–235
Bueno, Wilson 16, 27, 52, 55
Burmeister, Hermann 147–149

Bustos, Adriana 20, 22, 203, 209–213, 235–236, 247
cabinets of curiosities 2, 11, 17, 38, 63–92, 116
Calabrese, Omar 240
Caldas, Francisco José de 105–106, 133
Câmara Cascudo, Luís da 49–50
Cañizares-Esguerra, Jorge 4, 9, 94
Cano, Edgar 16, 22, 27–35, 37, 39, 61
capitalism 2–3, 12, 16–17, 19, 28, 33, 38, 44, 59, 64, 71–72, 75, 99–105, 132–134, 143–145, 157, 198, 202, 224, 229, 234, 243–245, 247
Cardoso, María Fernanda 18, 22, 95–96, 116–118, 120–122, 133–134, 238, 246
Carpentier, Alejo 239, 241
Carrasco González, Guadalupe 137
Casa Museo Francisco José de Caldas 106
Castro-Gómez, Santiago 6–7, 132, 187, 190
Centro de Arte y Naturaleza 22, 65, 67–68
chagra 126–129
Chen-Morris, Raz 76
Chiampi, Irlemar 240–241
Chichén Itzá 43
Chile, Chilean 16, 19–20, 27, 164, 167–169, 171, 202–203, 218
Chimborazo 19, 164, 182–184, 192, 195–197
Christian 26, 42, 49, 142
Christianization 192
Church, Frederic Edwin 180
Clarac, Comte de 130
Clark, Nigel 160
climate change. *See* environmental change; *See also* global warming
Coca, Claudia 19, 22, 164, 175–179, 200, 231, 238, 247
Coccia, Emanuele 122
co-essences in Mesoamerican ontologies 44–46
co-evolution 15–16, 18, 120, 122–123, 131, 133–134, 154, 238, 244

Cohen, Jeffrey Jerome 50, 52
Colombia, Colombian 6, 18–19, 23, 95–96, 98, 102, 105–106, 111–112, 123–124, 132, 140, 164–165, 181–183, 186, 193
colonialism 2, 3, 12, 14, 17, 37, 38, 44, 57, 64, 71–72, 91, 101, 102, 103, 104, 126, 134, 142, 143, 145, 156, 157, 160, 161, 164, 176, 179, 180, 190, 192–198, 200, 224, 229, 239, 241, 242, 243, 245. *See also* natural history
coloniality 41, 57, 104, 138, 182, 192, 200
Columbian 86–87, 156
Columbian Exchange 156
Columbus, Christopher 3, 54, 192–193
Comte, Auguste 1, 130, 223
conservation 13–15, 18, 21, 47, 72, 75, 95–96, 111, 126, 128, 133, 201–202, 212, 215, 224, 246
Corrêa, Walmor 5–6, 10–11, 16, 20, 22, 27–28, 47–55, 57–59, 61, 140–141, 173, 203, 227–236, 238, 243–244, 246
Cortázar, Julio 29, 38
Cortés, Hernán 37–38
cosmotechnics 17, 64, 89
Crary, Jonathan 86
Cratylus 29–30
Crosby, Alfred 156
cryptozoology 10, 16, 28, 47–59
Cuba, Cuban 39, 186
Cusco 138
Cusicanqui, Silvia Rivera 190

Danowski, Déborah 156
Darwin, Charles 111, 165–167, 180
Daston, Lorraine 10, 64, 70–71, 74–75, 81, 92, 97, 163
Davies, Surekha 90, 92
Davis, Wade 138, 140
De Assunção, Paulo 61
Debret, Jean-Baptiste 172–175
decolonial neobaroque 20–21, 237–243
decolonial theories and perspectives 2, 7–10, 15, 20, 23, 27, 57, 72, 86, 102–104, 134, 144, 164, 165, 180, 187, 190–199, 222, 238–243. *See also* environmental change
deep ecology 246
Deleuze, Gilles 20–21, 27, 105, 241
Dendle, Peter 10, 56
Denevan, William M. 129–130
Derrida, Jacques 27, 32–33
Dion, Mark 141, 222–223, 232
Dionysius 33
domestication of plants 108–111, 121–122, 133
D'Orbigny, Alcide 155
Dussel, Enrique 190, 240
Duttenhofer, Christian Friedrich Traugott 181
Dyer, Katie 116, 121–122

Echeverría, Bolívar 243
Ecuador, Ecuadorian 17, 19–20, 64, 77–79, 83, 87–89, 96, 164, 182–184, 186–187, 194, 198
Eden, Edenic 13–14, 213
El Indio Kondori 239
Elliott, David 166–167
Ender, Thomas 140–141, 173
Enenkel, Karl 11, 53
England, English 27, 35, 43, 210
Enlightenment. *See* natural history
environmental change 3, 12, 13, 18, 95, 129, 134, 141, 142, 144–146, 152–157. *See also* geoengineering solutions to environmental change
 apocalyptic visions of 3, 15–16, 19, 144, 156–157, 160, 237, 245
 decolonial perspectives on 3, 12, 15–16, 129–130, 142, 144, 157–162
 prior to colonialism 14, 128–130, 134, 161
environmental democracy 21, 237, 244–245
epistemicide 7, 187, 192, 197, 200
Escobar, Arturo 126, 130, 132
Escuela Politécnica Nacional 77, 79, 81
Espacio de Arte Contemporáneo (EAC) 219

Ette, Ottmar 185, 187, 196–197
extinction 15, 19, 36–37, 47, 123, 144, 146, 156–157, 209, 213, 224
extraction 3–5, 12–18, 104, 126, 137, 185–186, 188, 223, 225, 235, 241
extractivism 20, 22, 72, 99, 102–104, 134, 140, 164–165, 189, 193, 234, 247

feminism 8, 16, 116
floras and herbaria 2–4, 17, 93, 124–125, 135, 138–139, 171, 186–190, 238
Flusser, Vilém 84
Foucault, Michel 8, 40
Franciscan Order 6, 93
Freud, Sigmund 52

Galison, Peter 81, 92, 97, 163
Gal, Ofer 76
Gay, Claudio 167–168, 171
genetically modified crops 18, 95, 108–111
geoengineering solutions to environmental change 13, 21, 245
Gilpin, William 147, 150
global warming 12, 144
Glusman, Laura 22, 150, 152–154, 158–161, 247
Greenblatt, Stephen 54
Grünfeld, Thomas 230
Grupo Etcétera 234–235
Gruzinski, Serge 239, 243
Guattari, Felix 27
Guayaquil 87
Guerrero, Marguerita 26–27

Haeckel, Ernst 180
Haraway, Donna 8, 16, 202, 211–213, 215, 245
Hegel, Georg Wilhelm Friedrich 1–2
Heise, Ursula 14–15
Henderson, Caspar 60–61
herbals 93
herbaria. *See* floras and herbaria
Hernández, Francisco 54, 93, 106
Herodotus 11, 25

Hidrovía Paraguay–Paraná–Río de La Plata 145, 145–147, 146–147, 153, 156, 159
Hirst, Damien 203
Hispaniola 3
Homer 26
Hooke, Robert 90
Hornaday, William Temple 201
Hughes, Zoe 202
Hui, Yuk 17, 64, 89, 91–92
humanism 3, 27, 60, 115, 223, 241
Humboldt, Alexander von 1–2, 4, 19–20, 23, 140, 164, 180–200, 238
Humboldt Forum 23, 186, 189, 199
Hume, David 11
Hurtado, Diego 9
hybridization between species 28, 47, 49–55, 57, 81–82, 230–234

Iglesia de San Francisco 82
Impey, Oliver 91
Inca, Incan 138, 192, 194
indigenous cosmologies and philosophies of nature. *See* nature
indigenous knowledge. *See* nature
Ingapirca 194
Ingold, Tim 47, 131–132
institutional critique 222–223, 235
Isidore of Seville 25–26, 29–30

Jesuits 6, 48–49, 79, 230
John, Elton 43

Kafka, Franz 26
Kaup, Monika 239, 242–243
Koch, David H. 234
Koch, Joseph Anton 181
Kreimer, Pablo 9
Küchler, Sabine 209–213
Kueva, Fabiano 11, 20, 22–23, 140, 164, 182, 186–200, 238, 247

La Condamine, Charles Marie de 180
Lafuente, Antonio 4, 132–133
La Padula, Pablo 17, 20, 22, 64–66, 68–75, 90–92, 203, 218–227, 235–236, 238, 246–247

Latour, Bruno 99, 101, 168, 215
Leclerc, Georges-Louis 1
Leff, Enrique 12–13, 15, 21, 237, 244–246
León, Donjo 164, 175, 177, 179, 200
Lewis, C. S. 26
Lewis, Simon 157
Lima, José Lezama 239
Linnaean taxonomies 17–18, 77, 79, 93–97, 115–120, 122, 132
Lippit, Akira Mizuta 209

Macgregor, Arthur 91
Machu Picchu 99, 138
Maciel, Maria Esther 48, 52–55
Magdalena river 193
Malaspina, Alessandro 165
Maldonado, Camila Ramírez 166, 171–172
Malva, Daniel 20, 22, 203–209, 235–236, 238, 247
Marcaida López, José Ramón 5, 7, 91
Marey, Étienne-Jules 69
Marks, Laura 84–85
Martius, Carl Friedrich Philipp von 141
Maslin, Mark 157
Mauriès, Patrick 63, 66
Mayan 41, 43–44
Mendoza, Pedro de 18, 102, 142
Mergler, Agata 84–86
Mesoamerican 27, 29, 42, 44
Mexico City 22, 30, 32, 34, 37, 39, 186
Mexico, Mexican 12, 16, 22, 27, 29–30, 32, 34, 36–39, 41, 43, 93, 186, 202, 243
Mignolo, Walter 7, 242
Milton, John 26
Mizael, Vitor 202
Möbius, Karl 216
modernity
   alternative or multiple modernities 21, 44, 158, 237, 244
   economic and technological 13, 15, 17, 28, 43–44, 64, 86, 104, 156, 162, 175, 241, 244–245, 247
   Eurocentric and rationalist philosophies of 6–7, 16–17, 20–21, 27, 41–42, 55, 130, 175–176, 190, 196, 199–200, 215, 235, 237, 239–243, 247
monocultures and monocrop agriculture 10, 110, 126–127, 134, 218
Montevideo 219–221, 227
Moraña, Mabel 239–240
Morgan, Polly 203
Morris, Pat 76, 229
MTL Collective 235
Muinane 18, 123–124
Muller, Lizzie 116, 121–122
multisensory practices in art 8, 84–89, 200
Museo Nacional de Historia Natural (MNHN) 219, 222–223, 225
Mutis, José Celestino 17, 96, 98–99, 101–102, 132–133, 138, 140

Naess, Arne 246
Nahua 6
Nahuatl 93
National Geographic 164, 175–177, 179
Natterer, Johann 228
natural history
   influence of Classical texts on 7, 10–11
   in the colonial period 3–7, 22, 48–49, 54–56, 93
   in the Enlightenment 6, 7, 8, 9, 10, 17, 18, 21, 36, 38, 47, 54, 55, 57, 60, 61, 64, 73, 89–90, 94–96, 99–100, 104–105, 114–115, 210–211. See also Linnaean taxonomies
   primacy of the visual in 8, 17, 20, 76, 79–81, 86, 92
   role of artists in 5, 22–23, 23, 94–95, 137–138, 180
natural history collections and museums 17, 20, 39, 63–64, 66, 72–73, 75, 79, 87, 89–92, 116, 120, 179, 188–189, 194, 197–199, 201–232, 234–236, 247
natural history dioramas 2, 20, 168, 201–203, 209–227, 229–236, 238
nature. See also natural history
   commodification of 2, 7, 12, 17, 28, 64, 70, 75, 91, 101–102, 234

humanization of 21, 60, 119, 129, 246–247
indigenous cosmologies and philosophies of 3–4, 6, 14, 27, 42–47, 55, 130, 132
indigenous knowledge of 3–4, 6–7, 49, 54–55, 86, 87–89, 93, 96, 99, 111, 123–130, 132, 134, 187, 192, 198
reciprocity in 3, 16, 18, 27, 87, 95–96, 110, 113, 116, 120, 134, 246
relational ontology of 9, 35, 40, 126, 130–131
Romantic conceptions of 2, 14, 161, 195–196, 201
neobaroque 21. *See also* decolonial neobaroque
neocolonialism 44, 95, 126, 179
Nettle, Daniel 124
New World. *See also* colonialism; *See also* natural history in the colonial period
  European representations of the 1–7, 11, 19, 25, 28, 47–49, 52–54, 57, 59, 61, 81–82
Nonuya 18, 123–124

Ocampo, Silvina 16, 27
Olarte, Mauricio Nieto 4–5, 93–94
Ollantaytambo 138
Olmedo, Berenice 202
Orinoco Expedition 224
Österreichische Brasilien-Expedition 140
Oviedo y Valdés, Gonzalo Fernández de 11

Pacific ocean 102, 140
Padrón, Juan Nicolás 27, 39–41, 46, 61
Paraguay 18, 142, 145, 147, 154–155
Paraguay river 18, 145
Paraná Ra'anga expedition 18–19, 143, 145–147, 151, 155, 160–161
Paraná river 18–19, 141–143, 145–151, 153–155, 158–161, 247
Park, Katherine 10, 64, 70–71, 74–75
Paso del Quindío 140, 180–181
Patagonia 166

Patía river 106
Pavón Jiménez, José Antonio 138
performance art 19–20, 115, 138, 164, 172–175, 186–187, 200, 209–213
Peru, Peruvian 19, 96, 104, 138, 164, 176, 186
photography 22, 69, 84–86, 97–98, 106–107, 116–118, 121, 138, 147–151, 159, 188, 203–209, 227–228, 247
picturesque style of landscape painting 147–150
Pimentel, Juan 5, 11, 71–72, 137
plantations 12, 102–103, 132–133, 172, 218
plant sexuality 116–122
Plato 30
Pliny 7, 11, 25–26, 29
pluralism
  epistemological 6, 9, 21, 57, 243–245
  ontological 27, 40, 44–46, 131
pluriverse 130
political ecology in Latin America 13–14
Pollan, Michael 121–122, 133, 238
polyculture 96, 126–128, 134
positivism 79, 92, 198, 223, 226, 241
post-anthropocentrism 2, 20–21, 28, 31, 75, 116, 165, 167, 180, 203, 236, 238
postcolonialism 2, 179, 242
posthumanism 27
Potteries Museum and Art Gallery 213–214, 216
Pratt, Mary Louise 8, 99, 186, 193–194
Prieto, Martín 143
Putumayo river 140

Querandí 142
Quetzalcoatl 41, 46
Quijano, Aníbal 7, 42, 104, 242
Quiroga, Horacio 29
Quito 77–78, 82, 84, 186

racism 102–104, 112, 138, 164, 173, 192
Reboratti, Carlos 155–156
reconciliation ecology 127–128
Reddy, Varun 144
relational ontology. *See* nature

Renaissance era 11, 17, 48, 55, 93, 243
Restrepo, José Alejandro 1–2, 23, 140, 165, 180–182, 200
Rio de Janeiro 48, 231
Rio Grande do Sul 52, 228
Robertson, Kellie 60
Roca, José 22, 104
Rodríguez, Abel (Mogaje Guihu) 18, 22–23, 95–96, 123–128, 130–134, 238, 244, 247
Romaine, Suzanne 124
Romantic conception of nature. *See* nature
Romo, Claudio 5–6, 10–11, 16, 22, 27–28, 38–47, 55, 61, 238, 243–244, 246
Rosario 142, 145, 150
Rosenzweig, Michael 128
Rossi, Michael 230
Royal Botanical Expedition to New Granada 17, 96–97, 99, 132
rubber boom 104, 123
Rugendas, João Maurizio 173, 180
Ruiz López, Hipólito 138
Ruta del Comercio de Indias 176

Saer, Juan José 153
Saffray, Charles 180
Sagredo Baeza, Rafael 167–168
Sahagún, Fray Bernardino de 6, 36, 93
Salgado, César Augusto 242
Salta 210–211
Salvadoran 38
Sant'Ana, Tiago 11, 19, 22, 164, 172–175, 179, 200, 247
Santiago 6, 41, 132, 187, 190, 218
Santillán, Oscar 19–20, 22–23, 164, 182, 184–185, 200
Santos, Boaventura de Sousa 187, 192
São Paulo 48, 104, 141, 204, 208
Sarduy, Severo 105, 239–240
Sarmiento, Domingo Faustino 211
Scheicher, Elisabeth 91
Schmidl, Ulrich 142–143
Schultes, Richard Evans 138, 140
science. *See also* natural history

universalism in 2, 6, 8–9, 11, 55, 63, 77, 86, 89, 93–94, 97, 112, 114–115, 132–133, 140, 179, 182, 186–187, 190–192, 198
scientific expeditions to Latin America
of the colonial period 4–5, 17, 19, 48, 93–94, 96–102, 105, 132, 137–138, 163–165, 180–200
since Independence 155, 163–167, 172–173
twenty-first-century reworkings of 11, 18–19, 137–160, 186–199
seeds 95, 124, 161, 218. *See also* domestication of plants
local varieties of 18, 108–111, 141, 246–247
transgenic. *See* genetically modified crops
Seneca 32
Silvestri, Graciela 18, 143, 145, 147, 154, 161
Simpson, Mark 230
slavery 2, 102–104, 123, 157, 164, 172–175, 179, 189, 192
Smith, Raechell 49, 56, 128
Soares, Daphne 31
Sontag, Susan 204
Spivak, Gayatri Chakravorty 242
Stafford, Barbara 10
Stengers, Isabelle 8
storied world 131–132
Stuttgart 181
Svampa, Maristella 108, 110, 237, 245–246
Swyngedouw, Erik 13, 134

taxidermy 2, 20, 198, 201–236, 238
temporality 9, 12, 42, 124–128, 142–162, 171–172, 195, 200, 212, 217, 232, 242–243. *See also* environmental change
folds in 11–12, 18, 20, 144–145, 241
modern conceptions of 3, 9, 15, 19, 162, 175, 222
of the Anthropocene 15, 19, 142, 144–146, 156–157, 161
Tenochtitlán 37–38

Thibault, Jean-Thomas 184
Thomas, Keith 35
Toledo, Francisco de 52, 93
Toriz, Rafael 10, 16, 27–39, 52, 55, 61, 243–244, 246
transgenic seeds. *See* genetically modified crops
Tumaco 102–103
Tupi 6

Uruguay 219–221, 225

Valdenebro, Eulalia de 18, 22, 95–96, 105–116, 133–134, 244, 247
Varsavsky, Oscar 9
Venezuela 169, 186, 219
Viale, Enrique 108, 110, 237, 245–246
video art 77–81, 83–85, 87–88, 140, 150–154, 160–161, 181, 186, 190–198, 203, 209–213, 234, 247
Villavicencio, Cristian 17, 22, 64, 76–92, 166, 243, 246

Viveiros de Castro, Eduardo 6–7, 46, 131–132, 156, 187, 190

Wantzen, Karl 158–159
Wechsler, Diana B. 23
Weitsch, Friedrich Georg 196–197
Whyte, Kyle 156–157
Williams, Raymond 12
Wood, Marcus 173
World Bank 146
Wulf, Andrea 189
Wynter, Sylvia 132

Xavier, Héctor 26, 29

Yelin, Julieta 27
Yucatán 42
Yungas forest 210–212
Yusoff, Kathryn 144, 157

zoomorphism 33
Zuviría, Facundo de 22, 147, 150–151, 247

About the Team

Alessandra Tosi was the managing editor for this book.

Lucy Barnes performed the copy-editing and proofreading, and indexed the volume.

Mihaela Buna styled the manuscript and created the Alt-text.

Jeevanjot Kaur Nagpal designed the cover. The cover was produced in InDesign using the Fontin font.

Luca Baffa typeset the book in InDesign and produced the paperback and hardback editions. The text font is Tex Gyre Pagella; the heading font is Californian FB.

Cameron Craig produced the EPUB, PDF, HTML, and XML editions — the conversion was made with open-source software such as pandoc (https://pandoc.org/), created by John MacFarlane, and other tools freely available on our GitHub page (https://github.com/OpenBookPublishers).

This book has been anonymously peer-reviewed by experts in their field. We thank them for their invaluable help.

This book need not end here...

Share

All our books — including the one you have just read — are free to access online so that students, researchers and members of the public who can't afford a printed edition will have access to the same ideas. This title will be accessed online by hundreds of readers each month across the Globe: why not share the link so that someone you know is one of them?

This book and additional content is available at:

https://doi.org/10.11647/OBP.0339

Donate

Open Book Publishers is an award-winning, scholar-led, not-for-profit press making knowledge freely available one book at a time. We don't charge authors to publish with us: instead, our work is supported by our library members and by donations from people who believe that research shouldn't be locked behind paywalls.

Why not join them in freeing knowledge by supporting us:

https://www.openbookpublishers.com/support-us

Follow @OpenBookPublish

Read more at the Open Book Publishers BLOG

You may also be interested in:

Living Earth Community
Multiple Ways of Being and Knowing
Sam Mickey, Mary Evelyn Tucker and John Grim (eds)

https://doi.org/10.11647/OBP.0186

Ecocene Politics
Mihnea Tănăsescu

https://doi.org/10.11647/OBP.0274

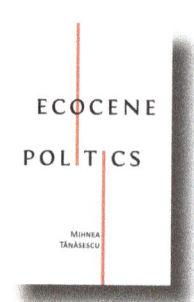

Global Warming in Local Discourses
How Communities around the World Make Sense of Climate Change
Michael Brüggemann and Simone Rödder (eds)

https://doi.org/10.11647/OBP.0212

www.ingramcontent.com/pod-product-compliance
Lightning Source LLC
Chambersburg PA
CBHW041731300426
44115CB00022B/2977